| DATE DUE | | | |
|---|---|---|---|
| | | | |
| | | | |
| | | | |
| | | | |
| | | | |
| | | | |
| | | | |
| | | | |
| | | | |
| | | | |
| | | | |
| | | | |

WEBSTER'S

*UNAFRAID*

DICTIONARY

# WEBSTER'S
# *UNAFRAID*
# DICTIONARY

———

Leonard Louis Levinson

COLLIER BOOKS · NEW YORK

COLLIER-MACMILLAN LTD · LONDON

Library of Congress Catalog Card Number: 67-10684

First Edition 1967

The Macmillan Company, New York

Collier-Macmillan Canada Ltd., Toronto, Ontario

Printed in the United States of America

This book is for my daughter

ROBIN DEGLI ESPINOSA

All definitions in this book are fictional
and any resemblance to words living or dead
is purely coincidental and not intended

## WEBSTER

One who weaves a web, warps a woof; a worker
manipulating the loom of language to fabricate
the whole cloth out of which lies are cut.


## UNAFRAID

Unaware of the true situation; ignorant of the
facts; less fearful; afraid of being called a
coward; paralyzed.


## DICTIONARY

A catalog of words with some of the popular
misunderstandings of their meanings; a
book with splendid vocabulary but poor plot;
Lingo Bingo; a volume in which it is impossible
to lose your place.

# Introduction

ALONG WITH everything else today, words are getting a terrible kicking around. In the attempt to achieve instant comprehension, mass communications have flattened words out so that shades of meaning are lost, categories and pigeonholes have replaced precise descriptions, punch and color have been abandoned. We have added some technical and pseudoscientific terms, but technicians and scientists tell us that these are imprecise and misleading.

Conversation is edging toward verbal shorthand. One-word excuses and explanations frequently suffice.

Arrive late for any appointment and all you have to say is: "Traffic!"

Refuse to eat any dish you dislike with: "Allergic!"

Turn down any physical activity: "Sacroiliac!"

The answer to any question dealing with mechanical science: "Electronics!"

On business deals or investments: "Tax-deductible!"

The magic word in medicine until recently was "psychosomatic." Now it's "sinus"!

And if someone asks you the reason you won't fly, the one-word answer is: "Coward!"

Then there are the euphemisms. I have heard of one married couple where the wife's "I love you" means "Will you please get out of the bathroom so I can come in"! A person no longer has cardiac trouble. It's a "heart condition," making it sound somewhat attractive, possibly a status symbol. And inebriates now have a "drinking problem." Which possibly means only having trouble paying for the stuff.

Advertising, with its ever-changing private lingo (*empathy, relate to, verbalize, image, creative*) will twist and adulterate any words it lays pen or tongue to for public consumption (free, meaning "if you buy something else"; instant, meaning "ten minutes of fast stirring"; optional, "it costs more"; giant economy size, meaning "spill what you save"; cellophane-wrapped, "you've got to tear it open with your teeth"; special price this week, "next week, cheaper"; processed cheese food, "stale cheddar, reworked with chemicals"; on sale at better stores, "try to find one"; styled in Italy, "made in New Jersey"; forever, "until something better comes along"; suggested retail price, "try haggling"; rich, full, satisfying flavor, "cancer"; music for your listening pleasure, "what else?"

Add the headline writers for the newspapers and news magazines, the television and radio news people who squeeze or expand the day's grim grist into their allotted time slots, and the politicos—who are the ones who should be restricted to time slots—and we have a universal tendency to use words to conceal or confuse thought, to take the juice and flavor out of speech and writing.

So this book includes a number of words with their original —and fresh—meanings as recorded by the father of the English dictionary, the great Dr. Sam'l Johnson. It also offers you some beautiful words of his time, since lost or abandoned, which wordsmiths of today would be wise to discover anew.

You will also find a number of items by the old master of the wry and cynical definition, Ambrose Bierce, who blazed the trail for all the heretical lexicographers who followed.

Wherever possible, definitions have been traced back to the originators and credit given. Where this could not be done, that prolific but shy writer, Anon., or his ubiquitous offspring, Anon., Jr., is credited. A great number of the contributions were never said or written in word-definition form but were edited, revised and sometimes reversed to make them fit our requirements and framework.

All of this was done by me and I am the author of all of the uncredited definitions, as well as the "Newords" and the "New Yorkese" definitions. Many of the last appeared originally in several issues of *McCall's*. Other regional words explained are "Charlestonese" and "Bostonese." A remarkable similarity exists between a number of words from these disparate localities.

I would welcome other regional definitions. In fact, any original ones sent to me in care of the publishers will be used with credit, if publishable, in future editions or future sequels.

When I finished the manuscript of *The Left Handed Dictionary* and wrote "The End," I added—in the tongue-in-cheek spirit of that book—"A signal to start a sequel."

It was not my intention to do so, but I was carried along on a momentum of definition-coining and gathering which did not stop after the book went to press. The habit persisted, one word led to another—and here we are.

That there is a lively interest in off-center, wry, opposite-but-true definitions has been demonstrated by the numerous times the LHD has been sent back to press. Now, with this volume, sporting the word "unafraid" in its title, I hope to call the attention of my readers to some true, pure meanings of words.

In conclusion, permit me to salute Miss Barbara Stark, who had the unenviable task (as she did for *The Left Handed Dictionary*) of alphabetizing (now, there's a word that's got to go) the thousands of index cards, deciphering my handwriting in the process, and typing this manuscript.

LEONARD LOUIS LEVINSON
New York City, February, 1966

WEBSTER'S

*UNAFRAID*

DICTIONARY

# A

**A.A.A.A.A.** A method for being first in a dictionary.
*Maxwell Shane\**

**abasement** A decent and customary mental attitude in the presence of wealth or power. Peculiarly appropriate in an employee when adressing an employer. *Ambrose Bierce*

**abatis** Rubbish in front of a fort, to prevent the rubbish outside from molesting the rubbish inside. *Ambrose Bierce*

**abbey-lubber** A slothful loiterer in a religious house.
*Dr. Sam'l Johnson*

**ablactate** To wean from the breast. O.F., to de-milk.
*Dr. Sam'l Johnson*

**abode** A wooden plank. *Charlestonese*

**abominable** Lousy in a high-class way.

**aborigines** Persons of little worth found cumbering the soil of a newly discovered country. They soon cease to cumber; they fertilize. *Ambrose Bierce*

**abortive** That which is born before the due time.
*Dr. Sam'l Johnson*

**aboveboard** In open sight; without artifice or trick. A figurative expression borrowed from gamesters, who, when they put their hands under the table, are changing their cards.
*Dr. Sam'l Johnson*

—It is the part also of an honest man to deal *aboveboard,* and without tricks. *L'Estrange*

**above-hay** Stand-up meal, as in: "We had furry people to above-hay dinner." *New Yorkese*

**abracadabra** A superstitious charm against agues.
*Dr. Sam'l Johnson*

**abrogate** To take advantage of the fine print in the contract.

**abrupt** Sudden, without ceremony, like the arrival of a cannon-shot and the departure of the soldier whose interests are most affected by it. *Ambrose Bierce*

**abscond** To "move in a mysterious way," commonly with the property of another. *Ambrose Bierce*

---

\* A sign that the definition was contributed to this dictionary.

1

**absence** That which either makes the heart grow fonder or the mind to forget.

—Those who are not present are always in the wrong. *Destouches*

ABSENTEEISM Hookey with no fear of the truant officer.

**absinthe** What really makes the heart grow fonder. *Addison Mizner*

**absolute** A night in which all cows are black. *G. W. F. Hegel*

**abstract art** The kind where you are not distracted by reality.

**abstract noun** One that cannot be heard, seen, touched or smelt. *Anon., Jr. (British Division)*

—It is the name of something which has no existence, as, goodness. *Anon., Jr. (British Division)*

**abusive** Deceitful—a sense little used, yet not improper. *Dr. Sam'l Johnson*

**accomplice** He who holds the ladder. *German proverb*

**accordionist** The only one who can successfully play both ends against the middle. *Salada Tea*

**accost** A price; e.g., "I promise accost of living wage increase to all Americans." *Bostonese*

**accuracy** To a newspaper what virtue is to a lady. *Joseph Pulitzer*

—But a newspaper can always print a retraction. *Adlai Stevenson*

**Achilles** A Greek who would have had it made if his mother had known about baptism.

—A hero who might have wound up a bum but for a press agent called Homer.

**acoustics** The mocking laughs which punctuate the nightmares of cultural architects. *Robert J. Landry*

—What you shoot pool with. *Zeke Canova*

ACOUSTICKS Medicine to help the hearing. *Quincy*

**acquaintance** A degree of friendship called slight when its object is poor or obscure and intimate when he is rich or famous. *Ambrose Bierce*

—A person whom we know well enough to borrow from, but not well enough to lend to. *Ambrose Bierce*

CASUAL ACQUAINTANCE Someone you know well enough to talk about, but not to. *Mannie Manheim*

**acquiescence** Saying "yes" in four syllables.

**acrimony** What a man gives his divorced wife. *Anon., Jr.*

**acting** The hardest job known to mankind. *Walter Mathau*

—An actor's responsibility is like a child's—there are only

two things he has to do: he has to show up on time and then he has to do what the little man tells him.

Elizabeth Ashley

—John Wayne demonstrating facial isometrics, based on newly discovered manuscripts of Calvin Coolidge.

Harvard Lampoon

ACTING TECHNIQUE    All there is to it is that the actors don't run into each other.      *Alfred Lunt*

**action**   The ultimate most holy form of theory.

Nikos Kazantzakis

**activity**   The essence of language.      *Dr. Jesperson*

**actor**   A show-oaf.

—A sculptor who carves on snow.      *Edwin Booth*

—An example of Nature abhorring a vacuum.

Morton Thompson

—A man whose head is too big for his toupee.

—The only person in the world who can fall in love with a full-length mirror.      *Vic Fredericks*

ACTORS    The only honest hypocrites.      *Hazlett*

—Refugees from life.      *Joan Littlewood*

—People you can identify by the glazed look that comes into their eyes when the conversation wanders away from themselves.      *Michael Wilding*

—People who never give their right age except in time of war.      *Paula Victor**

**actuary**   The man of the ages.

**ad infinitum**   Television commercials on "The Late Show."

**Adam**   The butt of the first ribbing.

—The only indispensable man.      *Tailspinner*

—The first great benefactor of the human race: he brought death into the world.      *Mark Twain*

ADAM AND EVE    The Pilgrim Fathers.      *Anon., Jr.*

ADAM'S ALE    $H_2$ ho-ho-ho!

ADAM'S APPLE    The projection of the thyroid cartilage of the larynx named after a supposed bit of forbidden fruit that stuck in the first man's throat when he was tempted by his wife.

**Adams, Henry**   A man who always moved about the earth with something of the shrinking gait of a professional violet crossing the ballroom floor.      *Alexander Woollcott*

**adapt**   To take more liberties with an original work of art than a drunken earl with a tavern wench.

Norbert Nadel, reviewing Oliver

**addle**   Originally applied to eggs, and signifying such as produce nothing, but grow rotten under the hen; thence transferred to brains that produce nothing.

*Dr. Sam'l Johnson*

**addle essence** The time between pluperty and mechewroddy. *Anon., Jr.*

**adherent** A follower who has not yet obtained all that he expects to get. *Ambrose Bierce*

**admiral** That part of a warship which does the talking while the figurehead does the thinking. *Ambrose Bierce*

**admiration** Our polite recognition of another's resemblance to ourselves. *Ambrose Bierce*

—The cream of human kindness.

**admonition** Gentle reproof, as with a meat-axe.

*Ambrose Bierce*

**adolescence** A time of rapid changes between the ages of twelve and seventeen, when a parent can get as much as twenty years older.

—That period in a child's life when his parents become more difficult. *Anon., Jr.*

—That wonderful time when you can work up an appetite by opening a refrigerator door. *Cy N. Peace*

—The time in a boy's life when he notices that a girl notices he is noticing her. *Today's Crosswords*

—The time between pigtails and cocktails. *Dan Bennett*

—That stage in life when a girl begins to powder and a boy begins to puff. *Changing Times*

**ADOLESCENT** A teen-ager who acts like a baby when you don't treat him like an adult. *Anon.*

—One who is well informed about anything he doesn't have to study. *Marcelene Cox*

**adore** To venerate expectantly. *Ambrose Bierce*

**adult education** What goes on in a household containing teen-age children. *Changing Times*

**adult western** One in which all of the Indians shot must be over twenty-one. *Jim Backus*

—One in which the lady who runs the gambling joint invariably shows the goodness and location of her heart.

*Pep Mealiffe*

**ADULT WESTERNS** Movies that drive me nuts. *Gene Autry*

**adulter** To commit adultery with another; a word not classical. *Dr. Sam'l Johnson*

**adultery** A new sport created by the marriage system.

*Holbrook Jackson*

—Democracy applied to love. *H. L. Mencken*

—The dullest of themes on the stage, and that from Francesca and Paolo down to the latest guilty couple of the school of Dumas fils, the romantic adulterers have all been intolerable bores. *Bernard Shaw*

—Watering the milk. *Sunday School card*

**adults** Individuals who are not wiser than children; they are simply more cunning.

*A. S. Neill, psychologist and educator*

**advertising** Perhaps the most wonderful development of the modern commercial age. *Richland (La.) Beacon-News*

—A ten billion dollar a year misunderstanding with the public. *Chester L. Posey, senior vice president and creative director, McCann-Erickson Advertising Agency*

—You have a hard time today to find an ad that isn't so busy being different it forgets to be an ad. Par for the course is an eye patch on one eye and a monocle on the other, topped by a beret and bordered by a bear, riding backward on a zebra, wearing tails with red shoes, and using a violin for a croquet mallet. When all around you are being too, too clever, then it's smart to be plain.

*Arnold Gingrich, publisher of Esquire*

—The science of arresting the human intelligence long enough to get money from it. *Stephen Leacock*

—A cult, a system of magic, practiced by magicians, witch doctors, sorcerers and shamans. *Bernard DeVoto*

—Is there a rule requiring that nothing be advertised over television unless it is miraculous, fabulous or at least marvelous? *Grit*

—Telling lies to attract shoplifters.

ADVERTISING AGENCY Eighty-five per cent confusion and fifteen per cent commission. *Fred Allen*

**advice** The smallest current coin. *Ambrose Bierce*

—The thing most blessed to give than to receive.

*Cy N. Peace*

—Information given by someone who can't use it to someone who won't. *Changing Times*

—What a person asks for when he wants you to agree with him. *Anon.*

GOOD ADVICE The worst kind of all. *Oscar Wilde*

**adviser** The deadliest word of our generation.

*American Mercury*

**affair** The distance from wink to mink.

—A game for two players in which each withholds what the other does not wish to take.    *Bill Manville*

**affiliation**  The act of taking a son.    *Chambers*

**afterclap**  Unexpected events happening after an affair is supposed to be at an end.    *Dr. Sam'l Johnson*

**afterdinner mint**  The kind you need after a meal in a New York restaurant . . . like the mint in Philadelphia or Denver.    *Changing Times*

**afterdinner speaker**  A man who talks in other people's sleep.    *Anon.*

**age**  A condition that has nothing to do with learning new ways to be stupid.    *J. C. Salak*

—There's no fool like an old fool. You just can't beat experience.    *D. O. Flynn*

—A student of twenty who has a bad memory is likely to rate a D in his course, but if a man over sixty-five forgets something, he may be suspected of senility.    *George Soule*

—The people who will always seem young are those who never reveal their rage.    *Wall Street Journal*

—As a man grows older and wiser, he talks less and says more.    *Wesleyan Methodist*

**agent**  A man who helps you get what's coming to him.

—A guy who bites the ham that feeds him.    *Paul and Helen Martin Denis**

**agog**  Heated with the notion of some enjoyment.    *Dr. Sam'l Johnson*

**ain't**  Sister of one of your parents.    *Charlestonese*

**air**  A nutritious substance supplied by a bountiful Providence for the fattening of the poor.    *Ambrose Bierce*

**air fright**  Groundless apprehension.

**air travel**  Seeing less and less of more and more.    *Raymond Haggard*

—Faster and faster.

—Hours of boredom interrupted by moments of stark terror.    *Shelly Berman*

**airplane**  A necessary bore.    *Clifton Fadiman*

**Alabama judge**  One who is about to declare the United States unconstitutional.    *Boston Globe*

**alabaster**  An illegitimate Mohammedan.    *Anon. oil man*

**Alaska**  An outlying state. We are glad to find a state that can out-lie us.    *Sen. Lyndon Johnson*

**Alcatraz**  A pen with a lifetime guarantee.    *The Eye Opener, 1963*

**alcohol**  What puts the wreck in recreation.          *Anon.*

**alcoholic**  One who magnifies his troubles by looking at them
through the bottom of a glass.

—One who has worked his way down from bottoms up.

—Someone you don't like who drinks as much as you do.
*Dylan Thomas*

**alcoholism**  A disease of the station wagon set and not con-
fined to Skid Row.        *Dr. C. Nelson Davis, psychiatrist*

**alderman**[1]  An ingenious criminal who covers his secret
thieving with a pretence of open marauding.
*Ambrose Bierce*

**aleconner**  An officer in the city of London, whose business
is to inspect the measures of publick houses. Four of them
are chosen or rechosen annually by the common-hall of the
city; and whatever might be their use formerly, their places
are now regarded only as sinecures for decayed citizens.
*Dr. Sam'l Johnson*

**alias**  A Latin word, signifying otherwise; often used in the
trials of criminals, whose danger has obliged them to change
their names; as, Simpson *alias* Smith, *alias* Baker; that is,
*otherwise* Smith, *otherwise* Baker.      *Dr. Sam'l Johnson*

**"Alice In Wonderland"**  An interminable fairy tale.
*Lewis Carroll*

**alien**  An American sovereign citizen in his probationary
state.                                    *Ambrose Bierce*

**alimony**  Industrial compensation in matrimony.

—Time balm.                          *Wall Street Journal*

—A splitting headache.

—A one-man war debt.                    *Herb Shriner*

—Disinterest, compounded annually.    *Walter McDonald*

—A reward collected by wives for staying away from their
husbands.

—Different from take-home pay; it's leave-home pay.
*Arthur Murray's press agent*

—Buying oats for a dead horse.        *Arthur "Bugs" Baer*

—Buying gas for another man's car.

—Paying on a subscription to a magazine that no longer is
being published.                        *Walter Slezak*

—One way to take the drudgery out of housework.    *Anon.*

—What makes an unhappily married woman happily unmarried.

[1] Today, read "councilman" or "assemblyman."

ALIMOANY   Alimony that hurts.

**all star cast**   Two stars plus some actors with good agents.
                                                              *Anon.*

**allergy**   Something a doctor says you have when he *does*
  know what it is—but doesn't know how to get rid of it.
                                                          *Al Bernie*

**alliance**   In international politics, the union of two thieves
  who have their hands so deeply inserted in each other's
  pocket that they cannot separately plunder a third.
                                                     *Ambrose Bierce*

**alms**   Upper limbs. Also, to bear alms.        *Bostonese*

**alone**   In bad company.                    *Ambrose Bierce*

**aloha**   Hawaiian for "hello" or "goodbye," depending on
  whether you're coming or going. (See HULA—a dance that
  says the same thing, silently.)

**alpenstock**   Swiss farm animals.          *Anon., Jr.*°

**altar**   A place where a bachelor loses control of himself. *Anon.*

**alteration**   Not always improvement, as the pigeon said when
  it got out of the net and into the pie.
                                         *Charles Haddon Spurgeon*

**amateur**   A person who is always willing to give you the
  benefit of his inexperience.

—A man who works hard at something else so he can paint
  in his spare time.

  PROFESSIONAL   A man whose wife works hard at some-
      thing else.                                      *Ben Shahn*

—A professional who has visible means of support.
                                                       *Jimmy Cannon*

  AMATEUR ATHLETE   One who does not accept checks.
                                                        *Roger Kahn*

  AMATEUR SHOW   A way for people with no talent to prove
      it.                                                  *Anon.*

**amazon**   A woman who's big at the mouth.      *Anon., Jr.*

**ambasadress**   In ludicrous language, a woman sent on a
  message.                                       *Dr. Sam'l Johnson*

**amber**   A yellow transparent substance of a gummous or
  bituminous consistence, but a resinous taste, and a smell
  like oil of turpentine; chiefly found in the Baltick sea, along
  the coasts of Prussia. Some naturalists refer it to the vegetable, others to the mineral, and some even to the animal
  kingdom.                                       *Dr. Sam'l Johnson*

**ambidexter**   A man who is equally ready to act on either
  side, in party disputes. This sense is ludicrous.
                                                 *Dr. Sam'l Johnson*

**ambidextrous**  Able to pick with equal skill a right-hand
pocket or a left.                              *Ambrose Bierce*

**ambiguity**  Having two wives living at the same time.
                                               *Anon., Jr.*

**ambition**  The last refuge of the failure.    *Oscar Wilde*
—An overmastering desire to be vilified by enemies while
living and made ridiculous by friends when dead.
                                               *Ambrose Bierce*
—What will get you to the top if the boss has no daughter.
                                               *Changing Times*

**ambush**  What age does to a man trying to recapture his
youth.                                          *Bruce Lefler*

**amendment**  A device of desperate legislators to make the
tail wag the dog.

**America**  The Land of Opportunity. That's why you hear so
much knocking.                                 *Changing Times*
—Still the land of opportunity, where a man can start out
digging ditches and wind up behind a desk—if he doesn't
mind the financial sacrifice.                  *Dick Rattazi*
—A hysterical, topsy-turvy country where people eat upside-
down cake, doors go around in circles and everybody has
an inside outhouse.                            *Radio Russia*
—Proof that immigration is the sincerest form of flattery.
                                               *Changing Times*
—A place that has a greater obsession with sex than Rome
ever had.                                      *Billy Graham*
—A land where in the middle of winter women buy spring
clothes for summer romances with fall guys.    *Quote*
—The country where you buy a lifetime supply of aspirin
for one dollar, and use it up in two weeks. *John Barrymore*
—The Air-Conditioned Nightmare.                *Henry Miller*
—A nation founded by four fathers.             *Anon., Jr.*
—A fine place to drive—if you don't want to stop.
                                               *Quoted by Earl Wilson*
—A land where everybody feels rich because they charge
each other so much.                            *Anon.*
—A land of untold wealth.        *Internal Revenue Service*
—Busy as we are polluting the air of our cities, fouling the
water in our rivers and burning our forests, we still are
patriotic enough to take time to sing about how we love
America, the beautiful.                        *Bill Vaughan*

AMERICA'S DOWNTRODDEN CLASS  People who don't have
remote controls for their color TV sets. *Terry McCormick*

AMERICAN  A citizen with more food to eat than a man of

any other country, and more diets to keep him from
eating it. *Quote*

—A creature who orders a new car three months before
it comes out and then buys his wife's Christmas present
on December 24. *Dan Bennett*

—One who, when he can finally afford a small car, buys
a large one. *Changing Times*

—A person who clings to this world's goods as if he were
certain never to die; and is so hasty in grasping at all
within his reach that one would suppose he was constantly afraid of not living long enough to enjoy them.
*Alexis de Tocqueville*

—One, an individualist; two, a partnership; three, a
monopoly. *Jerome Lawrence**

—One who refuses to take orders. *Maxwell Anderson*

AMERICAN CARS Vulgar and monotonous. They're like the
legendary brassy blonde. She's pretty dazzling for the
first five minutes, but then you're embarrassed to be seen
with her. *Henry Dreyfuss*

AMERICAN CONSTITUTION No constitution was written in
better English. *Winston Churchill*

AMERICAN ENTERPRISE The art of making toeless shoes a
fashion rather than a calamity. *Flame*

AMERICAN MYTH Part of it is that people who are handed
the skin of a dead sheep at graduation time think that
it will keep their minds alive forever. *John Mason Brown*

AMERICAN REVOLUTION A war that was caused by taxation
without relaxation. *Anon., Jr.*

AMERICAN WAY Going for broke on the installment plan.
*Dan Kidney*

AMERICANS People who look for a pill that will cure everything—and then send him to Congress.

—Prisoners of the Bell Telephone System, General Motors,
IBM, the American Medical Association, the airlines,
J. Walter Thompson, Sigmund Freud, the Internal
Revenue Service, the pollsters, the hucksters, the repair-
man, the discount store, their families, big business, big
government, suburbia, the PTA and sex. *Alan King*

—People who laugh at the gyrations of primitive African
witch doctors and spend $100,000,000 a year on fake
reducing systems.

—A group of people who can sell anything except themselves abroad. *Changing Times*

—Who, but Americans, can afford chairs that vibrate and cars that don't. *Philip Lindner*

—No good as jungle fighters. They first remove jungle— then fight. *Japanese prisoner*

—People who don't appreciate democracy because they don't know what it ain't. *Italian immigrant*

—People who insist on living in the present tense.
*Bob Goddard*

—People who act like Texans when they get to Europe.

EARLY AMERICAN  A furniture style that means paid for in cash. *Dorothy Sarnoff*

**amnesty**  The state's magnanimity to those offenders whom it would be too expensive to punish. *Ambrose Bierce*

**amusement**  The happiness of those that cannot think.
*Alexander Pope*

**analyst**  A man who takes forty-nine documents and from them produces a fiftieth. *Anon.*

**anatomy**  About the only thing today's child learns at his mother's knee. *Changing Times*

**anchovy**  A seasoned sardine.

**ancient**  A long time ago and maybe even before then.
*Anon., Jr.*

—The bearer of a flag, as was *Ancient Pistol*; whence in present use, ensign. *Dr. Sam'l Johnson*

**ancient mourner**  A polar bear at a funeral. *Anon., Jr.*

**anecdote**  Something yet unpublished. *Dr. Sam'l Johnson*

**anesthesia**  An aroma coma.

**angel**  A five-letter word meaning a heavenly body with a long, luminous tail. *Anon., Jr.*

**anger**  A bad counsellor. *Bernard Shaw*

—A momentary madness. *Horace*

**animal**  A living creature corporeal, distinct, on the one side, from pure spirit, on the other, from mere matter.
*Dr. Sam'l Johnson*

ANIMAL HUSBANDRY  The act of having more than one husband at the same time. *Anon., Jr.*

**anoint**  To grease a king or other great functionary already sufficiently slippery. *Ambrose Bierce*

**another**  The same. *Bill Manville*

**answer-jobber**  He that makes a trade of writing answers.
*Dr. Sam'l Johnson*

**answers**  What we have for other people's problems.
*Arthur Murray's press agent*

**Antarctica** The world's most fascinating icebox. *Ira Wolfert*

**antelope** A goat with curled or wreathed horns.
*Dr. Sam'l Johnson*

**anthology** A collection of flowers. *Dr. Sam'l Johnson*

**anthropology** The answer to who.

    ENGINEERING The answer to how.

    GEOGRAPHY The answer to where.

    HISTORY The answer to when.

    PHILOSOPHY The answer to why.

    RESEARCH The answer to what.

**anticlimax** A sentence in which the last part is lower than
the first. *Dr. Sam'l Johnson*

—A by-product of incest. *Anon., Jr.\**

**antidote** A medicine you take to prevent dotes.
*Overheard by Art Linkletter*

**antimony** Money inherited from your mother's sister.
*Anon., Jr.*

**antique** A dear old thing. *Jack Barett\**

—A fugitive from the junkyard with a price on its head.
*Kenneth J. Shively*

    ANTIQUES Everything over twenty-five years old.
*T. H. White*

—The meeting of old junk and new money.
*Stephen Leacock*

**antiquities** Rubbish old enough to be precious.

**antivivisectionist** One who strains at a guinea pig but swallows a baby. *H. L. Mencken*

**anyone's guess** A great name for a racehorse.

**aorta** A man who makes long speeches. *Anon., Jr.*

**apartment, studio** One where, if you are in the living room
and want to go into the bedroom, you stay where you are.
*Jose Cohn\**

**apiary** A bee flat.

—A place where they keep apes. *Anon., Jr.*

**aplomb** The assurance of a plumber.

**Apollinaire (Guillaume De Kostrowitsky)** A gypsy Villon.
*Marcel Arland*

**apologize** To lay the foundation for a future offence.
*Ambrose Bierce*

    APOLOGY Only egotism wrong side out.
*Oliver Wendell Holmes*

**apostate** A leech who, having penetrated the shell of a
turtle only to find that the creature has long been dead,

deems it expedient to form a new attachment to a fresh
turtle.                                    *Ambrose Bierce*

**apothecary** The physician's accomplice, undertaker's benefactor and grave worm's provider.          *Ambrose Bierce*

**apparition** A personal appearance by a ghost.

**appeal** In law, to put the dice into the box for another
throw.                                     *Ambrose Bierce*

**appeaser** One who feeds a crocodile, hoping it will eat him
last.                                      *Winston Churchill*

**appendix** Something found in the back of a book. Sometimes they get in people and have to be taken out.
                                           *Anon., Jr.*

**appetite** An instinct thoughtfully implanted by Providence
as a solution to the labor question.       *Ambrose Bierce*

**applause** The echo of a platitude.      *Ambrose Bierce*
—An actor should always bear in mind what clapping the
hands together does for a mosquito.

**apple** An excellent thing—until you have tried a peach.
                                           *George du Maurier*

**applecart** The human body.              *Bernard Shaw*

**April** From the Latin, *aperio,* "I open," referring to the
buds of spring and the bills of budding birds.
—The cruelest month.                       *T. S. Eliot*
—This is one of the few poetic utterances ever to be con-
firmed by the Internal Revenue Code.       *Changing Times*
—The time of the year when the taxpayer discovers what
a good loser he is.                        *O. A. Battista*
  APRIL 15   The day when many a patriotic American feels
  bled-white and blue.                     *Anna Herbert*
  —When not only fools and their money are soon parted.
                                           *Waldo G. Fechner*
  —The government's way of creating the rainy day we're
  always saving for.                       *Arkansas Baptist*
  APRIL FOOL   The March fool with another month added
  to his folly.                            *Ambrose Bierce*

**aqua mirabilis** The wonderful water, is prepared of cloves,
galangals, cubebs, mace, cardomums, nutmegs, ginger, and
spirit of wine, digested twenty-four hours, then distilled.
It is a good and agreeable cordial.        *Dr. Sam'l Johnson*

**Arab** An anti-Semetic Semite.

**archbishop** A Christian ecclesiastic of a rank superior to that
attained by Christ.                        *H. L. Mencken*

**archeologist** A scientist whose career lies in ruins. *John Amig*

—The best husband any woman can have; the older she gets, the more interested he is in her. *Agatha Christie*

**architect** One who drafts a plan of your house, and plans a draft of your money. *Ambrose Bierce*

ARCHITECTS Tomb builders. *Harold Rosenberg*

ARCHITECTURE Planned obsolescence.

—The art of making the superfluous necessary.

*Frederick Kiesler*

MODERN ARCHITECTURE A giant refrigerator with the ice trays half out. *Leo Mishkin\**

**are fuss** Where you work. Also, in sense of aspiring to high are fuss. *Bostonese*

**area code** A sinus coddidion.

**arenation** Is used by some physicians for a sort of dry bath, when the patient sits with his feet upon hot sand.

*Dr. Sam'l Johnson*

**argument** The worst sort of conversation. *Jonathan Swift*

**arising** Conflict between mind and mattress.

**aristocracy** Bad manners, organized. *Henry James*

ARISTOCRAT One who has gone to some pains in choosing his parents. *Figaro*

—A person who can trace his ancestry back three hundred years but can't tell you where his daughter was last night.

**arm** The hooked wing of the primordial bird and the pectoral fin of the fish. *Thomas Mann*

**armistice** Proof that truce is stronger than friction.

**armor** The kind of clothing worn by a man whose tailor is a blacksmith. *Ambrose Bierce*

**army food** Spoils of war.

**art** Concealing art. *Possibly Ovid*

—A lie that makes us realize the truth. *Pablo Picasso*

—A jealous thing that requires the whole and entire man.

*Michelangelo*

—The only teacher except torture. *Bernard Shaw*

—The magic mirror you make to reflect your invisible dreams in visible pictures. *Bernard Shaw*

—Life.

NEWS Death. *Tucci*

MODERN ART A positive evidence that things can't be as bad as they're painted. *M. Walthall Jackson*

—Oodles of doodles. *Lawrence Braun*

—Op goes the easel. *Peter Ermacora*

POP ART   Advertising art advertising itself as art that hates advertising.                    *Harold Rosenberg*

SPLATTER ART   The cultivated approach to insanity.
                                            *Boris Chaliapin*

ARTIST   One who cheats for the sake of beauty. *Max Jacob*

artful   When you've seen enough pictures at an exhibit.
                                            *Irvin S. Atkins**

artichoke   That vegetable of which one has more at the finish than at the start of a dinner.   *Lord Chesterfield*

artificial insemination   Copulation without representation.
                                            *Playboy*

Asheville   Nashville but for a typographical topographical error.

ashtray   A receptacle for hairpins, rubber bands, stamps, apple cores and all stuff like that there.   *Fibber McGee*

aside   A stage mutter.

asinine   Belonging to an ass.        *Dr. Sam'l Johnson*

aster   Having a lucky star; the opposite of disaster. *Newords*

astronaut   A truck driver with special problems.

—We have already begun to fly; several persons, here and there, have found the secret of fitting wings to themselves, of setting them in motion, so that they are held up in the air and are carried across streams. . . . The art of flying is only just being born; it will be perfected, and some day we will go as far as the moon.
        *Bernard le Bovier, Sieur de Fontenelle (1657–1757)*

ASTRONOUGHT   A person who affirms his terror of leaving terra firma.

astronomy   To look in the sky and see stars.

ASTROLOGY   To look up and see lions and virgins and other spooky creatures.                    *Anon., Jr.*

A. T. & T.   Always talking and talking.        *Anon., Jr.*

—The U.S. telephone monopoly, which, failing to automate its equipment efficiently, is attempting to automate its customers.

—A monopoly that has broadened its ownership so that it now has millions of accomplices.

atheism   A lack of religion which does not necessarily lead to moral corruption.                    *Pierre Bayle*

ATHEIST   One who has heard the expression "The brains God gave you."

—A man who can create his own holidays.

athletic scholarship   A football player's wages. *Jimmy Cannon*

**atom bomb** A leveling force which may prove that all men are cremated equal. *Kaye Phelps*

**atomic bra** One with a great deal of fallout.

**atomic energy** Energy with which to cook the world's goose. *In A Nutshell*

**attorney** It was anciently used for those who did any business for another; now only in law. *Dr. Sam'l Johnson*

**auction** A sales meeting where, if you're not careful, you'll get something for nodding. *Anon.*

AUCTIONEER A guy who always looks forbidding.

—The only one who should admire all schools of art.

*Oscar Wilde*

—The man who proclaims with a hammer that he has picked a pocket with his tongue. *Ambrose Bierce*

**audience** A corrupting influence on the theatre, demanding that most shows be all things to all seats. *Dore Schary*

FIRST-NIGHT AUDIENCE The unburied dead. *Orson Bean*

**augur** To bore into the future.

**August** The month when lots of people are back at work all ready to rest up from their vacations. *Changing Times*

—The month when the collapsible wading pool you bought in June does. *Ibid.*

**aurora australis** Northern Lights in the Southern Hemisphere.

**author** An instrument in the grip of Creative Evolution.

*Bernard Shaw*

—A fool who, not content with having bored those who have lived with him, insists on boring future generations.

*Baron de Montesquieu*

**auto** A misguided missile.

—A convenient place to sit out a traffic jam. *Ingrid Clement*

AUTO CLUB An organization which should always be up on its tows.

AUTO RACING Russian roulette with prizes. *Jimmy Cannon*

CLASSIC AUTO A car so old, it's paid for.

TRADE-UP A car that keeps you strapped without a seat belt.

AUTOMOBILE A machine with four wheels, a motor, and not quite enough seats, which enables people to get about with great rapidity and ease to places they never bothered going to before and where they'd just as soon not be now, because now that they're there, there is no place to park. *Elinor Goulding Smith*

—The trouble is that the car of tomorrow is being driven
on the highway of yesterday by the driver of today.

Rolfe, (Ia.) Arrow

**autobiography** A list of crimes, committed and suffered.

Bill Manville

—Fiction written by someone who knows the facts.     *Anon.*

—A book that usually reveals nothing bad about its writer
except his memory.                          *Franklin P. Jones*

**automation** Look, Ma, no hands.                          *Quote*

—A condition under which there will be more jobs for everyone because fewer people can do all the work.

**autopsy** Remains to be seen.

—Little Knell in *The Old Curiosity Shop*.

**autumn** A second spring, when every leaf's a flower.

Albert Camus

—That lovely season when September washes with dew the
dusty face of August.                       *Warwick Deeping*

**avast** Enough; cease. A word used among seamen.

Dr. Sam'l Johnson

**average** The best of the lousiest and the lousiest of the best.

Gary Gariepy

—A word that can be most confusing, particularly when used
by a statistician. If a man stands with his left foot on a hot
stove and his right foot in a freezer, the statistician would
say that, on the average, he's comfortable.

Dr. Walter W. Heller

**aviary** A cage big enough to give birds an illusion of freedom.

**avocat** (Fr.) Advocate, lawyer; also, avocado.

C. O. Sylvester Mawson, Dictionary of Foreign Terms


# B


**B** Among other things, B is a Roman numeral for 300; it is
also a symbol, in chemistry, for boron; in music, for the
seventh tone or note in the scale of C major, or the second
in the scale of A minor; in physics, for magnetic induction.
In education, it is a grade meaning second in quality.

Webster's New World Dictionary

**B.A.** Back ache. *Anon., Jr. (British Division)*

**baa** A mahogany-topped, brass-railed counter where drinks are served. *Bostonese*

**Babbitt** A businessman nimble in the calling of selling houses for more than people could afford to pay. *Sinclair Lewis*

**babery** Finery to please a babe or child. *Dr. Sam'l Johnson*

**baby** A sample of humanity entirely surrounded by yell.

—A person who eats twice as much as he weighs every year.

BABY-SITTER Someone you hire to clean out the icebox.

BABY-SITTER (EXPERT) One who can open the refrigerator without waking the baby. *Nick LaPole*

BABY-SITTERS What you call people whose children have grown up, gotten married and had children of their own. *Changing Times*

BABIES Angels whose wings grow shorter as their legs grown longer. *Mrs. Judy O'Reilly*

**Bacchus** A convenient deity invented by the ancients as an excuse for getting drunk. *Ambrose Bierce*

—A divine wino.

**Bach** A writer of music whose compositions were wonderful webs of exquisitely beautiful Gothic traceries in sound, quite beyond all ordinary human talent. *Bernard Shaw*

—A sublime sewing machine. *Colette*

**bachelor** A man with bathroom towels reading "His" and "To Whom It May Concern."

—A person who starts a wastebasket in the fireplace and vice versa. *Bruce Lefler*

—A fellow who knows where his next meal is coming from— a restaurant. *Al Cooper's press agent*

—A man who loves home-cooked meals—from different cooks. *Larry Matthews' press agent*

—A fellow who didn't have a car when he was young. *Early Oldsmobile saying*

—A permanent public temptation. *Oscar Wilde*

—Man who never Mrs. anybody. *Modern Maturity*

—A man who can take women or leave them—and prefers to do both. *Playboy*

—A guy who is foot-loose and fiancée free. *Ibid.*

—A man who is crazy to get married—and knows it. *Ibid.*

—A chap who believes it's much better to have loved and lost than to have to get up for the 2 A.M. feeding. *Anon.*

—A guy who doesn't have to explain how much of his take-home pay gets there.    *Changing Times*

—A guy who may not have all his buttons, but still has all his marbles.    *Harry Toffel*

—A man who has been lucky in love.

—A man who has no children, to speak of.    *Playboy*

—A fellow on a riverbank who has a better seat for a drowning than the boy out there in the water going under.
    *The Gang's All Here.*

—A man who thinks a weekend is something you rest up in.
    *Ken Kraft*

—A guy of single mind and double talk.  *Henna Arond Zacks*

—The one that two can live as cheap as.

—A man who believes only the brave deserve the fair but is still glad he's a coward.    *Frank J. Pepe*

—A man who has faults he doesn't know about yet.
    *Mannie Manheim*

—A guy who pokes fun at a woman for shopping all day and not buying anything.    *Russell Newbold*

—A rolling stone that gathers no boss.    *Anon.*

CONFIRMED BACHELOR  A guy who would rather change his girl than change her name.    *Cosmo Sardo*

—One who believes that what God has put asunder, no man should join together.    *Cy N. Peace*

BACHELOR GIRL  One who goes out with bachelors when no married men are available.    *Jimmy Cannon*

BACHELOR PARTY  An affair where a prospective bride-groom has the kind of wonderful time he could have every night if he weren't getting married.
    *Changing Times*

bachelors  Unlanded gentry.    *Ogden Nash*

back  That part of your friend which it is your privilege to contemplate in your adversity.    *Ambrose Bierce*

backache  Man's greatest labor saving device.    *Joe Ryan*

backgammon  The only athletic sport I ever mastered.
    *Douglas Jerrold*

back-seat driver  The only kind that never runs out of gas.

backward community  One you can go back to after ten years and still recognize.    *Changing Times*

backyard barbecues  Feasts that fill the neighborhood with the delicious odor of hamburgers marinated in bug spray.
    *Senator Soaper*

bacon  To save the *bacon,* is a phrase for preserving one's self from being hurt; borrowed from the care of housewives in the country, where they have seldom any other provision in the house than dried bacon; to secure it from the marching soldiers. *Dr. Sam'l Johnson*

**Bacon, Francis** The man who thought he wrote Shakespeare. *Anon., Jr. (British Division)*

**bacteria** The only culture many children are exposed to. *Bert Kruse*

**bad taste** Frequently a passion to decorate for the sake of decoration. *Alain*

**badinage** Jests with lace cuffs.

**bagnio** A house for bathing, sweating and otherwise cleansing the body. *Dr. Sam'l Johnson*

**bait** A preparation that renders the hook more palatable; the best kind is beauty. *Ambrose Bierce*

**baker** A dough nut.

**balderdash** Any thing jumbled together without judgment; rude mixture; a confused discourse.

TO BALDERDASH To mix or adulterate any liquor. *Dr. Sam'l Johnson*

**balks** A container, such as a match balks. *Charlestonese*
—A container such as the ballot balks. *Bostonese*

**ballet** The fairies' baseball. *Oscar Levant*
—Part of the popularity of ballet today is the fact that married men are able to watch a number of ladies who, for over two hours, never say a word! *Robin Goodfellow*

**balliards** A play at which a ball is driven by the end of a stick; now corruptly called *billiards*. *Dr. Sam'l Johnson*

**ball-point pen** A writing instrument of torture.

**baloney** The unvarnished lie laid on so thick you hate it. Blarney is flattery laid on so thin you love it. *Elizabeth Taylor*

**Balzac, Honoré De** A member of the opposition party called Life. *Balzac*
—A sort of word-machine. *Balzac*
—Prometheus. *André Maurois*

**bamboozle** (A cant word not used in pure or in grave writings.) To deceive; to impose upon; to confound. *Dr. Sam'l Johnson*

**ban** A place where you keep hay and horses. *Bostonese*

**banana** A dull, bland fruit which owes much of its popularity to its lack of seeds and the ease with which its skin is detached.

**bang**  A blow; a thump; a stroke; a low word.
*Dr. Sam'l Johnson*

I am a bachelor.—That's to say, they are fools
that marry; you'll hear me a *bang* for that.
Shakespeare, *Julius Caesar*

**bank**  An institution that urges you to save as much as possible of what you earn and urges you to borrow as much money as you can spend so you can spend more than you make.

—An institution which has a hard time getting all its vice presidents to attend a directors' meeting without giving the public the impression of a run on it.          *Anon.*

—More and more a money department store.

BANK ACCOUNT  Here today and drawn tomorrow.
*Hal Raymond*

BANK CHECK  An indication of money in motion.

BANKER  A man who spends his days from nine to six— nine hours of daylight and fresh air—in a stuffy little den counting another man's money.
*Adapted from Bernard Shaw*

**banquet**  A plate of cold chicken and peas entirely surrounded by warm charity appeals for dough.

—Something you come away from with somebody else's bad taste in your mouth.          *Morton Thompson**

**banting**  A system of weight-reduction advanced by a little sixty-seven-year old cabinet-maker after he had taken off 46 of his 202 pounds in a year.

**baptism**  A sacred rite of such efficacy that he who finds himself in heaven without having undergone it will be unhappy forever.          *Ambrose Bierce*

**barbarian**  Non-Greek.          *Greek version*

**barbecue**  Where the food is apt to be rare and the guests well done.          *Bruce Lefler*

BARBECUING.  A form of culinary exhibitionism. In modern America, the term is usually applied to the singeing of steaks over a too hot fire by a host who wears a chef's hat.
*Nicholas Roosevelt*

**barber**  Head gardener.          *Anon.*

**barber-monger**  A word of reproach in Shakespeare, which seems to signify a fop, a man decked out by his barber.
*Dr. Sam'l Johnson*

**bargain**  These days anything you can buy for only twice what it's worth.          *Anon.*

—Anything your wife buys and can't explain any other way.
*Changing Times*

—Something you cannot use at a price you cannot resist.

—Something so reasonably priced that they won't take it back when you find out what's wrong with it. *Anon.*

—A deal in which each party thinks he is cheating the other.

BARGAIN BASEMENT A department store's attempt to cheapen its image.

barometer An ingenious instrument which indicates what kind of weather we are having. *Ambrose Bierce*

barrel-bellied Having a large belly. *Dr. Sam'l Johnson*

barrister A thing which is put up in the street to keep the crowds back. *Anon., Jr. (British Division)*

bartender's guide A stirring account.

baseball A child's game played by a few dozen illiterates.
*F. Scott Fitzgerald*

—A ridiculously simple game. *Albert Einstein*

BASEBALL ANNOUNCER A baritone who sells beer.
*Jimmy Cannon*

BASEBALL MANAGER The guy who is fired for the owner's mistakes. *Jimmy Cannon*

basketball coach A fellow who tries to convince tall students they shouldn't go out for track and field. *Jimmy Cannon*

basketball referee Hamlet with a whistle.
*Jimmy Cannon, again*

bass A beverage made from a fish of that name.
*Anon., Jr. (British Division)*

bass stone The capital of Massachusetts. *Bostonese*

bass viol A violin with elephantiasis.

bastardy The increase of population on an aimless and nameless basis.

baste To keep in stitches.

bath mat Something you seek while you drip.

bathing beauty A girl worth wading for. *Anon.*

—A sand witch.

bathing suit The difference between not very much and nothing at all. *Anon.*

battering ram A two-hundred pound calling card.

battle A method of untying with the teeth a political knot that would not yield to the tongue. *Ambrose Bierce*

—Where a whole lot of white men kill a few Indians.

MASSACRE Where a whole lot of Indians kill a few white men. *Anon., pioneer*

**bawdy**   Having to do with the body.
—Consisting of arms, legs and torso.                *Bostonese*
**B.C.**   Before calories.
**beal**   The sad news at the end of the mill.   *New Yorkese*
**bean wetted?**   Are you being waited on?   *New Yorkese*
**bear**   Improved in health; excellent; superior in quality.
   "Are you feeling bear now?"                  *New Yorkese*
**bear-garden**   A word used in familiar or low phrase for *rude*
   or *turbulent;* as, a *bear-garden* fellow; that is, a man rude
   enough to be a proper frequenter of the bear-garden. *Bear-
   garden sport* is used for gross inelegant entertainment.
                                          *Dr. Sam'l Johnson*
**beard**   What does not make the philosopher. *Italian proverb*
**bearward**   A keeper of bears.        *Dr. Sam'l Johnson*
—The bear is led after one manner, the multitude after another; the *bearward* leads but one brute, and the mountebank leads a thousand.                      *L'Estrange*
**beatnik**   A poor man imitating a member of the jet set.
—A figure who is rapidly going the way of the American
   buffalo, to which he bears a strong resemblance.
                                          *Burton Hillis*
   BEATNICK   Santa Claus the day after Christmas. *Playboy*
**beau**   (*Beau,* Fr. It is sounded like *bo,* and has often the
   French plural *beaux.*) A man of dress; a man whose great
   care is to deck his person.            *Dr. Sam'l Johnson*
   BEAU BRUMMEL   A clothes stallion.
**beauty**   What a girl would rather have than brains, because
   the average male can see better than he can think.
—A fading flower.                           *Isaiah 28:1*
   BEAUTY PARLOR   A place where men are rare and women
      are well-done.                       *Changing Times*
—An institution intended for the improvement of women.
**bed**   Love's theatre.                          *Balzac*
—The perfect climate. But why do so many people die there?
—A flying mammal. Example: "You got beds in your palfrey."
                                          *New Yorkese*
—Not good; e.g., "She's a bed girl."          *New Yorkese*
   COMFORTABLE BED   The best night spot. *Arnold H. Glasow*
   WOODEN BED   Better than a golden coffin. *Russian proverb*
**bedpresser**   A heavy, lazy fellow.    *Dr. Sam'l Johnson*
   This sanguine coward, this *bedpresser,* this
   horseback-breaker, this huge hill of flesh.
                          Shakespeare, *Henry IV, Part One*

**bedrock** The day before pay-day. *Wall Street Journal*

**bedroom** The place where most household accidents occur.
*Playboy*

**bedswerver** One that is false to the bed; one that ranges or swerves from one bed to another. *Dr. Sam'l Johnson*

**bee** A hum-bug.

**befriend** To make an ingrate. *Ambrose Bierce*

**beggar** One who has relied on the assistance of his friends.
*Ambrose Bierce*

BEGGING The only profession in which a gentleman can address a beautiful woman without an introduction.
*Anon. beggar*

**beginning** The last thing one knows to do when writing a book. *Pascal*

**belated** Benighted; out of doors late at night.
*Dr. Sam'l Johnson*

**belch** To throw out from the stomach; to eject from any hollow place. It is a word implying coarseness; hatefulness; or horrour. *Dr. Sam'l Johnson*

**belgard** A soft glance; a kind regard; an old word, now wholly disused. *Dr. Sam'l Johnson*

**belibone** A woman excelling both in beauty and goodness. A word now out of use. *Dr. Sam'l Johnson*

**belief** People will believe anything that amuses them, gratifies them, or promises them some sort of profit.
*Bernard Shaw*

—A matter of taste. *Bernard Shaw*

**belladonna** In Italian a beautiful lady; in English a deadly poison. A striking example of the essential identity of the two tongues. *Ambrose Bierce*

**Belloc, Hilaire** An author who wrote: "When I am dead, I hope it may be said: 'His sins were scarlet, but his books were read.'"

**belly dancers** Girls who stand around twiddling their tums.
BELLY DANCING One of the few professions where a beginner starts in the middle. *Shalimar*

**bellyfeel** Blind, enthusiastic acceptance.
*George Orwell's "Newspeak," 1984*

**bellygod** A glutton; one who makes a god of his belly.
*Dr. Sam'l Johnson*

**belly-timber** Food; materials to support the belly.
*Dr. Sam'l Johnson*

**belswagger** A cant word for a whoremaster.
*Dr. Sam'l Johnson*

You are a charitable *belswagger,* my wife
cried out fire, and you called out for engines.
>                               John Dryden, *Spanish Friar*

**belt**   The oldest form of social security.

**benefactor**   One who makes heavy purchases of ingratitude,
without, however, materially affecting the price, which is
still within the means of all.          *Ambrose Bierce*

—One who makes two smiles grow where one grew before.
>                               *Chauncey Depew*

**benevolence**   A natural instinct of the human mind; when
A sees B in distress, his conscience always urges him to
entreat C to help him.          *Sydney Smith*

**benison**   Thanks for the venison.

**Bennett, Arnold**   A traitor during the American revolution.
>                               *Anon., Jr.*

**Bernstein, Leonard**   An educator who has been disclosing
musical secrets which have been well-known for years.
>                               *Oscar Levant*

—A performer who could fly if he used two batons.

**bet**   A place where bathing takes place. Not to be confused
with bat, a place where reclining takes place.
>                               *New Yorkese*

**betrayed**   Having lent your pot to someone who uses it to
cook your goose in.

**betty**   (Probably a cant word, without etymology.) An instrument to break open doors.          *Dr. Sam'l Johnson*

**Beverly Hills**   A pool's paradise.

**Bierce, Ambrose**   Born in a log cabin, Bierce defied Horatio
Alger's law and didn't become President. *Clifton Fadiman*

**bifocals**   Glasses you use to read books by during the television commercials.

**bigamist**   One who has loved not wisely but two well.

  BIGAMY   One way of avoiding the painful publicity of
divorce and the expense of alimony.          *Oliver Herford*

—A crime with a horrible penalty; two mothers-in-law.

**bigot**   One who is obstinately and zealously attached to an
opinion that you do not entertain.          *Ambrose Bierce*

—A person with a concrete mind—set, mixed up and hard-
ened.          *Paul and Helen Martin Denis**

  BIGOTRY   Being certain of something you know nothing
about.          *Changing Times*

**bikini**   A baiting suit.

—A Freudian slip.          *Llewellyn Miller**

—A garment that begins somewhere below the navel and proceeds rapidly to the point of astonishment.

*Lewis Gillenson**

—A sack for a tomato. *Bertha Shore*

**Bilingsgate** (A cant word, borrowed from *Bilingsgate* in London, a place where there is always a croud of low people, and frequent brawls and foul language.) Ribaldry; foul language. *Dr. Sam'l Johnson*

BILLINGSGATE The invective of an opponent.

*Ambrose Bierce*

**bill poster** An outdoor paperhanger.

**billion dollars** A man gave his wife a million dollars and told her to go out and spend $1,000 a day. She did and came back in three years to tell him the money was all gone and she wanted more. So he gave her a billion dollars with the same instructions, and she didn't come back for 3,000 years. *George Champion, board chairman, Chase Manhattan Bank*

**billow** Form of accounting or printed noticed: "Waiter, let me see the billow fare." *New Yorkese*

**bills** One of the things in life bigger than money. *Anon.*

**bins** There are navy, lima, green and kidney. *New Yorkese*

**biography** About chaps.

GEOGRAPHY About maps. *E. C. Bentley*

—Shutting a man up in a book.

—One of the new terrors of death. *John Arbuthnot*

**bipartisan issue** One that has been fought to a draw.

*Changing Times*

**birchbark** What very few people can hear. *Anon., Jr.*

**bird** A feathered nester.

—Boids is on the wing, I hoid.
    But doze woids is absoid,
    'Cause wings is on the boid.

**bird sanctuary** The White House.

*Eugene (Oreg.), Register-Guard*

BIRD-WATCHING A hawk's racket. *Jimmy Cannon*

**birth** The first and direst of all disasters. *Ambrose Bierce*

—But a sleep and a forgetting. *William Wordsworth*

BIRTH CONTROL A policy it will be very difficult to enforce.

**birthday candles** Making light of your age.

**bisque** A thick soup made out of bisquits. *Anon., Jr.*

**Bisquit Tortoni** The man who discovered radio. *Anon., Jr.*

**bit**  As much meat as is put into the mouth at once.
*Dr. Sam'l Johnson*

**bitch**  Land and sand bordering the water.    *New Yorkese*

**"Black Beauty"**  A kind of "Uncle Tom's Cabin" of the horse kingdom.    *Clifton Fadiman*

**black clouds**  Clouds formed by the evaporation of dirty water.    *Anon., Jr. (British Division)*

**black eyes**  Something you get when you look for a pair of socks.

**blackguard**  A man whose qualities, prepared for display like a box of berries in a market—the fine ones on top— have been opened on the wrong side. An inverted gentleman.    *Ambrose Bierce*

**blackmail**  A shush fund.

**blacksmith**  One who strikes the iron while it is hot for a living.

**blackwhite**  A loyal willingness to say that black is white when discipline demands it.

George Orwell's "Newspeak," 1984

**blanket insurance**  Recompense for those who smoke in bed.

**blessing**  Every misery I miss.    *Izaak Walton*

**Bligh, Capt. William**  A great explorer and navigator who was the victim of some very poor labor relations.

**blockade**  Picketing with submarines.

**blonde**  A cross between a brunette and a drugstore.
*Southern Planter*

PLATINUM BLONDE  A common ore.    *Anon.*

**blotter**  The soul of any police station.    *The New Yorker*

**Blue Cross**  New York's Number One Get Well Card.
*New York Blue Cross*

**bluebeard**  A husband with the neatest solution for the alimony problem.

**blunderer**  A man who starts a meat market during Lent.
*James Montgomery Bailey*

**boa constrictor**  A snake that squeezes.

**boaster**  One who tries to push himself forward by patting himself on the back.

**boat**  A wood-lined hole in the water into which you pour money.    *Reported by Robert P. Sutton**

**body**  The chief function of the body is to carry the brain around.    *Thomas A. Edison*

BODYGUARD  A heavy laborer who gets paid by the weak.

BODY-SNATCHER  A robber of grave-worms. One who supplies the young physicians with that which the old physicians have supplied the undertaker. *Ambrose Bierce*

**bogtrotter** One that lives in a boggy country.

*Dr. Sam'l Johnson*

**bold** Without covering hair. *New Yorkese*

**bologna** A sausage known in Bologna as mortadella.

**bomb tests** Contamination without representation.

*Mort Sahl*

**Bond, James** The unfortunate British agent whose efforts always seem to result in thud and blunder.

**bondsman** A fool who, having property of his own, undertakes to become responsible for that entrusted by another to a third.

—Philippe of Orleans wishing to appoint one of his favorites, a dissolute nobleman, to a high office, asked him what security he would be able to give. "I need no bondsmen," he replied, "for I can give you my word of honor." "And pray what may be the value of that?" inquired the amused Regent. "Monsieur, it is worth its weight in gold."

*Ambrose Bierce*

**bone** Blessed event; e.g., "I was bone a Charlestonian" (a *very* blessed event in the minds of all Charlestonians).

*Charlestonese*

TO MAKE NO BONES To make no scruple; a metaphor taken from a dog, who readily swallows meat that has no bones.

*Dr. Sam'l Johnson*

**bonus player** A young baseball player with a greedy father.

*Jimmy Cannon*

**booby** (A word of no certain etymology; Henshaw thinks it a corruption of *bull-beef,* ridiculously; Skinner imagines it to be derived from *bobo,* foolish, Span. Junius finds *bowhard* to be an old Scottish word for a *coward,* a *contemptible fellow;* from which he naturally deduces *booby,* but the original of *bowbard* is not known.) A dull, heavy, stupid fellow; a lubber. *Dr. Sam'l Johnson*

**book** What they make a movie out of for television.

—Private property, until a visitor is intrigued with the title.

BOOK BORROWERS Those mutilators of collections, spoilers of the symmetry of shelves, and creators of odd volumes.

*Charles Lamb*

BOOKSTACKED A girl with a desirable shelf of volumes.

*Newords*

**boom** An economic boomerang.

BOOM TOWN  Any place discovered by Daniel Boom.
*Anon., Jr.*

**boomerang**  What seems to follow every boom.
—The perfect gift for the woman who returns everything.
—Something you throw and an angry guy with a bump on
his head brings it back to you.                    *Bob Lewis*
**borachio**  A drunkard.                    *Dr. Sam'l Johnson*
—How you stink of wine! D'ye think my niece will ever
endure such a *borachio!* you're an absolute *borachio*.
William Congreve, *Way of the World*

**Bordeaux**  Take Versailles and add Antwerp to it and you
have Bordeaux.                              *Victor Hugo*
**bore**  A guy who has to hold your lapel to hold your attention.                                      *Jackie Kannon*
—A person who deprives you of solitude without providing
you with company.          *Gian Vincenzo Lavina*
—The secret of being a bore is to tell everything. *Voltaire*
—A fellow talker who can change the subject to his topic of
conversation faster than you can change it back to yours.
*Changing Times*

—A visitor who can stay longer in an hour than others do
in a week.
—The best way to be boring is to leave nothing out. *Voltaire*
**BOREDOM**  The price of virtue.
—The sound of tireless voices is the price we pay for the
right to hear the music of our own opinions. *Adlai Stevenson*
**boss**  Spelled backwards, a double s.o.b.
**Boston**  A festering mud puddle.
*Ex-Gov. Ellis Arnall of Georgia*

—A city suffering from what has been called "Grandfather
on the Brain."                          *Cleveland Amory*
—Where the fire exits in the concert halls are to be used in
case of Brahms.                          *Anon. musician*
—Possessed of all the hilarious overtones of Liverpool on a
Sunday evening in March.                    *Lucius Beebe*
—A place in the corner, not on the main line to anywhere
in particular.                        *The Proper Bostonians*
**BOSTON IRISH**  The poor downtrodden majority.
*The Proper Bostonians*

**BOSTON SOCIETY**  Self-conscious and senseless; a society
which seemed to have to pass through a long period of
cold storage. I have summered it and wintered it, tried
it drunk and tried it sober; and, drunk or sober, there's

nothing in it—save Boston. *Charles Francis Adams II*
—Quite uncivilized—but refined beyond the point of civilization. *T. S. Eliot*

**BOSTONIAN** One who suffers from hardening of the hearteries.

**botch** An adscititious, adventitious part clumsily added. If both those words are not notorious *botches*, I am much deceived; though the French translator thinks otherways. *Dryden's dedication, Aeneid*

**botcher** A mender of old cloaths; the same to a taylor as a cobbler to a shoemaker. *Dr. Sam'l Johnson*

**bottle-nosed** Having a nose created in the image of its maker. *Ambrose Bierce*

**botulism** The pig's revenge.

**bought 'em** Opposite of taup; e.g., "Hunted from taup to bought 'em." *Bostonese*

**bounty** The liberality of one who has much, in permitting one who has nothing to get all that he can. *Ambrose Bierce*

**bowels** A, E, I, O, U, and sometimes W and Y. *Anon., Jr. (British Division)*

**Bowery bum** Someone who tried too hard to become a Man of Distinction. *New York minister*

**bowling** Marbles for big boys.

**BOWLING ALLEY** A tavern with a rumpus room. *Jimmy Cannon*

**boy** The person who is going to carry on what you have started. *Anon.*

**SMALL BOY** A restless noise with dirt on it. *Anon.*

**braggadocio** The patter of little feats.

**braggart** One who blows his horn so loud, he hasn't any wind left for climbing.

**bragly** Finely, so as it may be bragged. *Dr. Sam'l Johnson*

**brakes** In cars, there are two kinds: lucky ones and unlucky ones. I'm not sure about the difference, but my daddy has lucky ones and my mother has the other kind. *Anon., Jr.*

**brandy** A cordial composed of one part thunder-and-lightning, one part remorse, two parts bloody murder, one part death-hell-and-the-grave and four parts clarified Satan. Dose, a headful all the time. Brandy is said by Dr. Johnson to be the drink of heroes. Only a hero will venture to drink it. *Ambrose Bierce*

**brat** With mit and muss-did, makes a sang-wish. *New Yorkese*

—A child who acts like your own but belongs to a neighbor.
*Florence Marley*

**bread** The best advice to the hungry.    *Russian proverb*

**break-even point** The moment when you stop trying to balance the budget and begin trying to budget the balance.

**breakfast nook** Real Estatese for "We took the door off this closet."    *William V. Shannon*

**breakvow** He that practices the breach of vows.
*Dr. Sam'l Johnson*

**breast** A milk depot.

—The most attractive container yet devised for dairy products.

**breathing** A form of life insurance.

**bride** A woman with a fine prospect of happiness behind her.    *Ambrose Bierce*

—A girl who has discovered that where there's smoke, there's toast.    *Changing Times*

—A bridesmaid who made good.

—A made maid.    *Bill Manville*

BRIDEGROOM A player who is being penalized for holding.

—A wolf whose whistle got stuck.    *Dan Bennett*

**bridge** A game which has taught women the art of concentration and also how to get their husbands' supper in ten minutes.    *Changing Times*

—Because of its tendency to encourage prolonged smoking and its deadly immobility, is probably the most dangerous game played in England now.    *English doctor*

BRIDGE PLAYER One who calls a spade two spades.
*Changing Times*

**Britain** A lump of coal entirely surrounded by fish.
*Nye Bevan*

**Briton** That eater of unclean foods, never sufficiently washed in his person or his garments.
East Indian in *On The Rocks*, by Bernard Shaw

**Britten, Benjamin** A composer whose music frequently has all the joie de vivre of an impacted wisdom tooth.

**Broadway** What a glorious garden of wonders the lights of Broadway would be to anyone lucky enough to be unable to read.    *G. K. Chesterton*

—A string of orange-juice stands and movie houses—all going out of business.

BROADWAY PHONY A guy who gets cavities in his false teeth.    *Nicky Blair*

BROADWAY WOLF   One who has three Rockettes in orbit at the same time.

**broker**   One who deals in old household goods.
*Dr. Sam'l Johnson*

—A procurer. A pimp.   *Elizabethan meaning*

**Broun, Heywood Hale**   A Little-League Renaissance man.
*Heywood Hale Broun*

**brute**   See *Husband*.   *Ambrose Bierce*

**bucks**   A container or enclosure such as a titter bucks.
*New Yorkese*

**budge**   To stir; to move off the place; a low word.
*Dr. Sam'l Johnson*

**budget**   A plan for pay-as-you-go if you don't go anywhere.
*Les and Liz Carpenter*

—Merely a mathematical confirmation of your suspicions.
*F. G. Kernan or A. Latimer*

—The outgo outcome of the income.

—A device to tell you where your money should have gone.
*Anon.*

—A system of reminding yourself that you can't afford the kind of living you've grown accustomed to.
*Changing Times*

—A formula for determining that you need a raise.   *Ibid.*

**bull**   On Wall Street, an optimist. In Spain, in the ring, an animal that is always sacrificed.

**bulldozer**   A device to make molehills out of mountains.

**bully**   (Skinner derives this word from *burly*, as a corruption in the pronunciation; which is very probably right; or from *bulky*, or *bull-eyed;* which are less probable. May it not come from bull, the pope's letter, implying the insolence of those who came invested with authority from the papal court?) A noisy, blustering, quarrelling fellow: it is generally taken for a man that has only the appearance of courage.   *Dr. Sam'l Johnson*

**bumble**   To act like the beadle of the same name in *Oliver Twist.*

**bumpkin**   (This word is of uncertain etymology: Henshaw derives it from *pumpkin*, a kind of worthless gourd, or melon. This seems harsh. *Bump* is used amongst us for a knob, or lump; may not *bumpkin* be much the same with *clodpate, loggerhead, block* and *blockhead.*) An awkward heavy rustick; a country lout.   *Dr. Sam'l Johnson*

**bunk**   Hell's Kitchen for "bump."   *New Yorkese*

BUNKHOUSE  A politician's headquarters.  *Lyda Fairbanks*
burr  A dairy product, such as burr-milk.  *New Yorkese*
busiless  At leisure, without business; unemployed.
                                              *Dr. Sam'l Johnson*
business  The concentration on the major problem of secur-
  ing the consumer's dollar before the other fellow gets it.
                                              *Stuart Chase*
—The playthings of our elders.  *St. Augustine*
—A combination of war and sport.  *André Maurois*
—Other people's money.  *Alexandre Dumas, fils*
—When you learn to call a bill an invoice, and stir your
  coffee with your pen.  *Judith Beach\**
  BUSINESS SUCCESS  The art of making a good bit of your
    income appear as an expense.  *Changing Times*
  SMALL BUSINESS  One that never has been investigated by
    a Congressional committee.  *Dan Kidney*
  —One which can't afford a Washington office.
                                              *Thurman Arnold*
  BUSINESSMAN'S LUNCH  Something to hold down a couple
    of martinis.
  BUSINESS RECESSION  The time when people get their
    clothes out of mothablls instead of department stores.
                                              *Dan Bennett*
bustle  A covered waggin'.  *Jack Herbert*
—Haste or waste below the waist.
—An annex in the rear with decorative intent.
—A cushion for the sitting room.
—A deceitful seatful.
—Headquarters for the hindquarters.
—A false front in the rear.
—A fender on a bender.
—A false bottom attached to the rear of the trunk.
—A fashion accessory at present behind the times.
busy  Confused.  *Herbert V. Prochnow*
butter  To be discommoded, as in "Snow butter a tall."
                                              *New Yorkese*
butterfly  A beautiful insect, so named because it first ap-
  pears at the beginning of the season for butter.
                                              *Dr. Sam'l Johnson*
buzz  What don't a cage make.  *New Yorkese*

# C

**cab bit**  A prom nit Bah-stun family.  *Bostonese*

**cabbage**  (A cant word among taylors.) To steal in cutting clothes.  *Dr. Sam'l Johnson*

**caboose**  An Indian baby.  *Anon., Jr.*

**Cabots**  A Boston family that has never been remarkable for personal distinction, but rather for shrewd business sense, family solidarity and ability to marry money.  *Fortune*

—This verdict is harsh; in any case, what money Cabots did not marry, they made.  *Cleveland Amory*

**cacophony**  Phony cackling.

**cactus**  A truculent succulent.  *Karl L. Metzenberg*

—Defense plant.  *Jack Herbert*

**cad**  A fellow who refuses to help his date with the breakfast dishes.

**cadger**  A huckster; one who brings butter, eggs, and poultry, from the country to market.  *Dr. Sam'l Johnson*

**Caesar, Julius**  A Roman general renowned for his great strength. He threw a bridge across the Rhine.

*Anon., Jr. (British Division)*

**caff**  The English ice cream joint.

**cajole**  To flatter; to sooth; to coax; a low word.

*Dr. Sam'l Johnson*

**Cal Tech**  A mental reservation.

**calamity**  A more than commonly plain and unmistakable reminder that the affairs of this life are not of our own ordering. Calamities are of two kinds; misfortune to ourselves and good fortune to others.  *Ambrose Bierce*

**calculated risk**  Politicalese for "We have every hope and assurance that the plan will be successful, but if it doesn't work, we knew all the time it wouldn't and said so."

*James Thurber*

**calendar**  A gift for the man who has everything, to remind him when the payments are due.

**California**  A state that has a way of making its boosters look like prophets.  *Carey McWilliams*

—Where you marry in haste and repent insolvent.

*Dodie McKenzie*

—A great place to visit, but I would hate to leave there.
*Anon., Jr.*
—Nowhere else in the world is there more to enthrall a child.
*Elizabeth Nichols*

**calves** Slices meat. *Bostonese*

**camerade** One that lodges in the same chamber; a bosom companion. By corruption we now use comrade.
*Dr. Sam'l Johnson*

**cam-owner** A Japanese nigh-gun. *New Yorkese*

**camp** Anything outrageous or odd . . . not seen in anger or joy or lust but in fun. *George Frazier—a vogueword*
—Something you don't make fun of—you make fun out of it.
*Christopher Isherwood*
—A quality that makes you exclaim, "Somebody has to be kidding! . . . Why this is so terrible that it's terrific."
*George Frazier*
   REAL CAMP A portrait of Tony Curtis done in chicken feathers. *George Frazier*
   CAMPING Going for baroque.

**Canada** A country bounded on the north by gold, on the west by the East, on the east by history and on the south by friends. *Frances Shelley Wees*
—A triumph of politics over geography and economics—and sometimes it seems over common sense. *Robert T. Elson*

**Canaletto** A painter of small canals. *Anon., Jr.* *

**candidate** A Roman who wore a *toga candida*—white toga —when seeking public office, so that he could be splattered with the mud of calumny by his rivals.
—A person who is taking a kind of voluntary mud bath.
*Anon.*
—A mother before and a stepmother after election.
*Illustrated Weekly of India*

**candlewaster** That which consumes candles; a spendthrift.
*Dr. Sam'l Johnson*

**candy** The late president, Jawn Fitzgerald Candy.
*Bostonese*

**cannibal** A gastronome of the old school who preserves the simple tastes and adheres to the natural diet of the pre-pork period. *Ambrose Bierce*
—A white-hunter.

**cannon** The final argument of kings. *Louis XIV*

**cap it** A rug; e.g., "We spread a red cap it for vot-uhs of all races, creeds and culluhs." *Bostonese*

**Cape Kennedy** Disneyland East. *Mort Sahl*

**cape-happy** A disease likely to afflict actors in classical repertory.

**capital** The seat of misgovernment.

**capital punishment** A penalty regarding the justice and expediency of which many worthy persons—including all the assassins—entertain grave misgivings. *Ambrose Bierce*

**capitalism** Not an orgy of human villainy, but a Utopia that has dazzled and misled very amiable and public spirited men. The upholders of capitalism are dreamers and visionaries who, instead of doing good with evil intentions like Mephistopheles, do evil with the best of intentions. *Bernard Shaw*

—An economic system that leaves men of extraordinary and beneficial talent poor whilst making nonentities and greedy money hunters absurdly rich. *Bernard Shaw*

—The difference between capitalism and communism is that in Russia they shoot farmers for not raising enough wheat and here we pay them.

—The father of communism. *Nikita Khrushchev*

—The exploitation of man by man.
   SOCIALISM The exact opposite. *Anon.*

**capsule** Something that used to travel inside a man.

**Capuchin Father** A beatnik priest. *Anon., Jr.*

**caramba** (Spanish) An exclamation denoting admiration or annoyance. *Dictionary of Foreign Terms*

**card sharp** A corrector of bad fortune. *Old definition*

**career girl** A female who prefers plots and plans to pots and pans. *Anon.*

—One who can watch a group of children playing in the mud without thinking of a washing machine. *Dan Bennett*

**cargo** Goods sent by ship. Goods that go in a car are a shipment. *Anon.*

**carpet** Floor covering bought by the yard and used by the foot. *Anon.*

**carriage** Sometimes a proud bearing is only the result of a stiff neck. *Eberhard Seybold*

**carrying-on** An occupational disease of actors, actresses, dancers and singers. *Liza Redfield*

**cartel** A gang of businesses.

**cartoon** A device used by newspapers to suggest what the editor dare not say. *Changing Times*

**Casablanca** A Pittsburgh with palm trees. *Robert Ruark*

**Casanova**   Not a sex maniac; he just had an insatiable curiosity about how women acted in bed.

**Cassandra**   A misfortuneteller.

**castle in the air**   A home where you are the architect.

    CASTLES IN THE AIR   An important branch of building in which governments cannot indulge.     *Bernard Shaw*

**castrate**   To take away the obscene parts of a writing.
                                           *Dr. Sam'l Johnson*

**Castro, Fidel**   All preaches and scream.      *M. A. Sens*

    CASTROPHOBIA   A disease that closes in on Cubans.

**casualness**   In raising children, the rarest of virtues.
                                       *Phyllis McGinley*

**cat**   A miniature tiger kept in a home to remind children to wash their faces.

—A pet who sleeps away
A goodly portion of the day
So he can prowl around and fight
When we would like to sleep at night.    *Richard Wheeler*

—A woman who licks herself with her tongue.

**catalogue**   A dialogue by four people.      *Anon., Jr.*

**catamountain**   A fierce animal, resembling a cat.
                                       *Dr. Sam'l Johnson*

**catastrophe**   The change or revolution which produces the conclusion or final event of a dramatick piece.
                                       *Dr. Sam'l Johnson*

**catcal**   A squeaking instrument, used in the playhouse to condemn plays.      *Dr. Sam'l Johnson*

**caterpillers**   Fuzz and squash.      *Anon., Jr.*

**cater-cousin**   A corruption of *quatre-cousin*, from the ridiculousness of calling cousin or relation to so remote a degree.
                                       *Dr. Sam'l Johnson*

**Catskills**   A range of mountains where you can suffer snow blindness from the cottage cheese.    *Muriel Rafalsky**

**catsup**   A kind of pickle, made from mushrooms.
                                       *Dr. Sam'l Johnson*

**caucus**   A sort of big parrot that has been taught to swear.
                                       *Anon., Jr.*

**caught age**   A simple residence; such as the Candy caught age at Hyannis Port.      *Bostonese*

**cauliflower**   God's forsaken vegetable.    *Judith Beach**

**caulked**   Capped and ready to shoot; e.g., "Our government must not go off half-caulked."      *Bostonese*

**caution** When you are afraid; cowardice is when the other fellow is afraid. *Anon.*

—The only thing anyone learns from experience.
*Robert Morley*

**caviar** An expensive bread spread.

—A year's work for a sturgeon. *Ernie Byfield*

**celibacy** A disease of the brain. *Anon., Jr.*

**CELIBATE** One who cleans out cellars. *Anon., Jr.*

**cemetery** An isolated suburban spot where mourners trade lies. *Ambrose Bierce*

—The place where you'll find a lasting peace.
*Russian proverb*

**cenotaph** A tombstone in memory of someone buried somewhere else at some other time.

**censor** One who takes a census. *Original Latin meaning*

—A horticulturist who would attempt to weed the Garden of Eden.

—A man who knows more than he thinks you ought to.
*York Trade Compositor*

—An official who can see three meanings in a joke that only has two. *Martin Ragaway*

—I'm going to introduce a resolution to have the Postmaster General stop reading dirty books and just deliver the mail.
*Sen. Gale McGee*

**BOOK CENSORSHIP** It seems to me we were all better off when the Postal Department used to deliver the mail and left it to a Higher Authority to deliver us from evil.
*Herbert L. Block*

**centaur** One of a race of persons who followed the primitive economic maxim, "Every man his own horse."
*Ambrose Bierce*

—Member of the Senate. *Bostonese*

**Cerberus** The watchdog of Hades, whose duty it was to guard the entrance—against whom or what does not clearly appear; everybody, sooner or later, had to go there, and nobody wanted to carry off the entrance.
*Ambrose Bierce*

**ceremony** The smoke of friendship. *Chinese proverb*

**chafing dish** A girl who has been stood up on a date.
*Playboy*

—A girl in a tight leotard. *Ibid.*

**chair** A shout of approval, e.g., "Let me hair you chair and haulher for The Citadel." *Charlestonese*

ELECTRIC CHAIR  An example of period furniture. It ends
a sentence.                          *Anon. schoolboy*

**chairman**  Like the minor official at a bullfight whose main
function is to open and close the gates to let the bull in
and out.                              *Nan Hampton*

**chamois**  A mountain goat used to polish cars.

**champagne**  Only grapes served in liquid form.
                                      *Jayne Mansfield*

**les champs élysées**  The final resting place of the blessed.
                                      *Greek mythology*

**chance**  The pseudonym of God when He did not want to
sign.                                 *Anatole France*

**change**  What makes the world go round. Not love—love
only keeps it populated.              *Charles H. Brower*

**channels**  The fellow who has his desk between two ex-
pediters.                             *Governmentalese*

**chaos**  The oldest of the Greek gods.
—The empty, formless infinite, especially before the Creation.
                                      *Primary sense*

**chaperone**  One who never made the team but is still in
there intercepting passes.            *Playboy*

CHAPERONING  A spectator spoil-sport.    *Stan Delplane*

**chaplain**  A man who works to beat hell.
                                      *Norfolk Naval Base*

**character**  Merely habit long continued.    *Plutarch*
—What you are in the dark.            *Dwight L. Moody*

**charge**  The final word in women's fashions.   *E. K. Banfill*

CHARGE ACCOUNT  What a woman uses to keep her husband from becoming too independent.   *Dan Bennett*

**charity**  The sister of pity.          *Russian proverb*
—A thing that begins at home—and usually stays there.
                                      *Elbert Hubbard*

PROFESSIONAL CHARITY  The milk of human blindness.
                                      *Tom Masson*

**charm**  A glow within a woman that casts a most becoming
light on others.                      *John Mason Brown*
—The quality in others that makes us more satisfied with
ourselves.                            *Henri-Frederic Amiel*
—The ability to make somebody else think both of you are
pretty wonderful.

                    Arlene Frances, quoted by Earl Wilson,
                    Hall Syndicate, in *The Reader's Digest*

**charm-main**  A Chinese dish served with rice. *New Yorkese*

**chastity** The sleep of passion. *Michel de Ghelderode*
—A word to be avoided—it's too damned suggestive.
*Anon. newspaper editor*

**cheat** Have you partaken of food? "I'm hungry; cheat yet?"
*New Yorkese*

CHEATING More honorable than stealing. *German proverb*

**Chekhov, Anton** A genius who escaped from a privy.
*Chekhov*

**cheese** Milk plus microbes.
—Falsely believed to be the favorite food of mice. The mouse, scientists have found, will content himself with cheese for want of something better, but his real passion is for gumdrops. *Vivienne Marquis and Patricia Haskell*

**cherchez la femme** A French phrase meaning "a chicken in every plot." *S. S. Biddle*

**cherish** To keep warm. *Early meaning*

**chess** A game for which Life is too short. *Byron*
—An activity that blights more lives than drugs or alcohol because it is respectable. . . . If the chess bums in America could be reclaimed and rehabilitated, it would have a lasting effect on our economy. *Alfred Bester*

**Chicago** A pompous Milwaukee.

**chicane** The art of protracting a contest by petty objection and artifice. *Dr. Sam'l Johnson*

**chicken** A term for a young girl. *Dr. Sam'l Johnson*
—Then, Chloe, still go on to prate
Of thirty-six and thirty-eight;
Pursue your trade of scandal-picking.
Your hints, that Stella is no *chicken*. *Jonathan Swift*
—An egg plant.

**child** If a growing object is both fresh and spoiled at the same time, the chances are it is a child.
*Morris Goldfischer*
—Formerly an economic asset for a farmer, but now that he has a tractor, two cars and two television sets, a new status symbol.
—One of the most unmistakable effects of a child's presence in the household is the fact that the worthy parents turn into complete idiots. Without the child, they might have been mere imbeciles. *Georges Courteline*
—An appetite surrounded by noise. *Changing Times*
—An accident in the Tunnel of Love.

PROBLEM CHILD One who puts two and two together and gets curious. *Franklin P. Jones*

CHILDHOOD The age when a baby stops wearing its food and starts eating it.

—The age when a baby stops wearing its food and starts not eating it.

—Substituting for mother's milk a diet richer in minerals. *Bernard Shaw*

—That happy period when nightmares occur only during sleep. *Changing Times*

—The brief interval between infancy, when they say "a whole penny," and adolescence, when they say "only five dollars." *Ibid.*

—The period of human life intermediate between the idiocy of infancy and the folly of youth—two removes from the sin of manhood and three from the remorse of age. *Ambrose Bierce*

—That wonderful time when all you need to do to lose weight is bathe. *Kim McGinnis*

CHILDREN Beings who scream, kick you and throw up on buses, while riding free.

—The hardest people to convince that they've reached retirement time. *Arnold H. Glasow*

—The behavior of some children suggests that their parents embarked on the sea of matrimony without a paddle. *Anon.*

—Coupons on the bonds of matrimony. *Frances Keller**

—The death of marriage. *C. Green*

—Small people who are not permitted to act as their parents did at that age. *Josephus Henry*

—In backward countries, a method of growing your own old-age pension; in progressive countries, a method of growing old quickly. "If you must hold yourself up to your children as an object lesson, hold yourself up as a warning and not as an example." *Bernard Shaw*

—All geniuses until the age of ten. *Aldous Huxley*

chili sauce Catsup with seeds.

chinchilla The skin a girl loves to touch.

chip A cud-chewing mammal or timid, indecisive person. *New Yorkese*

chipper Less. As in: "Surrey, we got nuttin' chipper." *New Yorkese*

chiropodist A specialist who is always down at the heel.

—One man who is always eager to start off on the wrong foot. *F. G. Kernan*

**chiropractors** Work-weary plumbers and retired piano movers. *H. L. Mencken*

**chivalry** A man's inclination to defend a woman against every man but himself. *One Stripe McGork*

—An age when men were kind to their horses. *Elaine Kendall*

—A trait that may not be dead but certainly isn't riding on busses or subways these days.

—The act of a man who gives his seat to a lady in a public convenience. *Anon., Jr.*

**chocolate** A flavor that tastes just the opposite of vanilla. *Anon., Jr.*

**chophouse** A mean house of entertainment, where provision ready dressed is sold. *Dr. Sam'l Johnson*

**Christian** One who believes that the New Testament is a divinely inspired book admirably suited to the spiritual needs of his neighbor. *Ambrose Bierce*

—One who follows the teachings of Christ insofar as they are not inconsistent with a life of sin. *Ambrose Bierce*

**Christmas** When you buy your friends all those books you wish someone would give you.

—And read them before you wrap them.

—After a man unwraps the Christmas presents he gets from his family, he begins to realize how the Woolworth fortune grew. *Anna Herbert*

**Christmas Eve** The shortest night of the year, from sundown to son-up. *Burton Hillis*

CHRISTMAS EVE SHOPPERS People fit to be Yuletied. *Llewellyn Miller\**

OLD-FASHIONED CHRISTMAS One when whisky came in ordinary bottles. *Dan Kidney*

**chummy** Fascinating. "He's a regular Prince Chummy." *New Yorkese*

**chums cool** A place where they make girls more chummy. *New Yorkese*

**church** A hospital for sinners, not a museum for saints. *Abigail Van Buren*

—The gin-shop in which men stupefy themselves against the weight of the world's woes. *Karl Marx*

—Empty front pews in the average church indicate that the congregation is afraid of what it may hear and desires to be as close as possible to a convenient exit. *Douglas Meador*

—A pack of common men calling themselves clergymen and priests, and trying to persuade us that they are demigods by wearing ugly black clothes. . . . They pretend to see events with glass eyes, and to hear the music of the spheres with asses' ears.       *Bernard Shaw*

CHURCHES Places where people will continue to go to sleep as long as only 3 per cent are air-conditioned.

CHURCHGOERS People spending six days sowing wild oats, so they can go to church on Sunday and pray for a crop failure.       *Fred Allen*

cigarette lighter A flame-producing device in which the spirit is willing but the flash is weak.

cigarette smoking Tobacco Road that runs into a dead end.       *Nathan Nielsen*

cimeter A sort of sword used by the Turks; short, heavy; and recurvated, or bent backward. This word is sometimes erroneously spelt *scimitar*, and *scymeter*.       *Dr. Sam'l Johnson*

ciplinarian One who teaches disorder.       *Newords*

circus A place where horses, ponies and elephants are permitted to see men, women and children acting the fool.       *Ambrose Bierce*

city life Millions of people being lonesome together.       *Henry David Thoreau*

civil marriages Ceremonies performed by court clerks and police magistrates mumbling unintelligibly out of a mysterious book, perhaps only a stolen Gideon Bible. Marriages after midnight cost double and if the bridegroom has the fumes of wine in his head he is apt to lose his watch as well as his liberty.       *H. L. Mencken*

civic pride When you toss an empty cigarette pack on your neighbor's lawn instead of in the street.       *Bert Kruse*

civic-mindedness Continuing to vote for new schoolhouses after your kids have grown up.       *Wall Street Journal*

Civil War A conflict which cost more than ten billion dollars. For less than half, the freedom of all the four million slaves could have been purchased.       *Charles and Mary Beard*

civilization A system under which a man pays a dollar to park his car so he won't be fined five while spending a dime for a nickel cup of coffee.

—Improvement in the world's condition which soars ahead at about the same speed as Sunday traffic.

—The victory of persuasion over force.       *Palmer Wright*

—The art of shewing worthless attentions and paying insincere compliments in a kindly charming way. *Bernard Shaw*
—The triumph of the cultivation of a flat onion to fit the demands of the hamburger trade.
—An imposture; we are a crowd of savages on whom a code of makeshift regulations is forced by penalties for breaking them. *Bernard Shaw*
—A coat of paint that washes away when the rain falls.
*Auguste Rodin*
—The substitution of a traffic jam for a forest preserve.
*Changing Times*
—A joke on us. It's a scheme devised by women to make men do the work. It creates a great many more needs than the means to supply them. Civilization is an income tax blank, an atom bomb and a worried look. *Arnold H. Glasow*
—Heaps of agonizing human maggots, struggling with one another for scraps of food. *John Ruskin*
—A stage in progress that can be measured by the degree of helplessness when the electricity goes off. *Dan Bennett*
—A matter of domesticating sex.

**civilized country** One where a person must go to a backward area in order to breath pure, clean air.
*Chicago Sun-Times*
**clairvoyancy** The ability to forecast rain even if your corns don't hurt.
**clarinet** An instrument of torture operated by a person with cotton in his ears. There are two instruments that are worse than a clarinet—two clarinets. *Ambrose Bierce*
**clarity** The politeness of the man of letters. *Jules Renard*
**classic** A great book they give you free to join a club that charges a lot for cheap books.
CLASSICAL RECORDS Good wax for your ears. *Anon.*
**clavical** A medical condition commonly known as having a collarbone. *Anon., Jr.*
**clear conscience** The best tranquilizer. *Dinah Shore*
**cleavage** The quickest distance between two points.
*Robert M. Levinson**

**Cleopatra** A sand witch.
—An adult eastern. *Joseph Mankiewicz*
**clergy** Mostly dull dogs; but with a little disguise and ritual they will pass as holy men with the ignorant. *Bernard Shaw*
CLERGYMAN An interpreter of religion who does not be-

lieve that the Bible means what it says: he is always convinced that it says what he means.    *Bernard Shaw*
—One who feels himself called upon to live without working, at the expense of rascals who work to live.

*Voltaire*

—A ticket speculator outside the gates of heaven.

*H. L. Mencken*

—A guy who marries for money.                    *Anon.*

**Cleveland**  Two Hobokens back to back.    *Joan Holman\**

**climate**  Something caused by the emotion of the earth around the sun.                          *Anon., Jr.*

**clinics**  Cellulose substitute for handkerchiefs. "Kachoo! Hand me a piece clinics, please."          *New Yorkese*

**clock**  A machine of great moral value to man, allaying his concern for the future by reminding him what a lot of time remains to him.

A busy man complained one day:
"I get no time!" "What's that you say?"
Cried out his friend, a lazy quiz;
"You have, sir, all the time there is.
There's plenty, too, and don't you doubt it—
We're never for an hour without it."    *Ambrose Bierce*

—A fatuous machine which supposedly organizes eternity into measurable quantities.              *Bill Manville*

—Something they have in an office, so you can tell how late you wish you weren't in the morning, what time to go out for lunch and coffee breaks before, and come back after, and how long you must wait before you can start stopping work by stalling until.              *Office Economist*

**clog**  A cog gone wrong.

**clotheshorse**  A lady, who when she puts on her clothes, looks like a horse.                        *Anon., Jr.*

**clothestrophobia**  The curse of preferring life in the raw.

**clothing**  The material that covers a multitude of sins.

**cloudburst**  A rainstorm that overdid itself.

**coal**  Decayed vegetarians.    *Anon., Jr. (British Division)*
—A portable climate.              *Ralph Waldo Emerson*

**coal-slur**  Chopped raw cabbage with dressing.

*New Yorkese*

**cocker spaniard**  A make of dog.              *Anon., Jr.*

**cockney**  A native of London, by way of contempt. Any effeminate, ignorant, low, mean, despicable citizen.

*Dr. Sam'l Johnson*

**cocktails** Drinks that have all the disagreeability without the utility of a disinfectant. *Sir Shane Leslie*

COCKTAIL GLASSES Hic cups. *Jacob M. Braude*

COCKTAIL PARTY A social occasion where sandwiches and absent friends are cut into little pieces.

—A gathering at which drinks mix people.
*Guardian Chemical pamphlet*

—A gathering where mixed drunks imbibe mixed drinks.
*Martha Kay*

—A function where you meet people who drink so much you can't remember their names. *Cosmo Sardo*

—Where you meet old friends you never knew before.
*Mac Benoff*

—Where they give you a canapé and a napkin and it doesn't matter which one you put in your mouth—both taste the same. *Lucius Beebe*

—A battleground where a wife must meet, face to face and simultaneously, her worst enemies; babes and booze.
*Emily Hahn and Eric Hatch*

—Where all are had by a good time. *Judith Beach*

—The use of alcohol to drug guests into unintelligent babbling; an admission that the hostess isn't mature enough, and isn't sure enough of herself, to entertain guests by such intellectual tools as good music and intelligent conversation.
*Dr. Andrew C. Ivy, former head of University of Illinois department of clinical science*

**c.o.d.** Call on Daddy. *Anon., Jr.*

**coffee break** The only fifteen minutes in the morning when the help stops doing nothing. *Theodore Rubin*

—Any time you can get a cup for a nickel.
*Francis O. Walsh*

**coffee nerves** Tension induced by the continual increase in the price of a cup of coffee.

**coffee plantation** An establishment where the staff takes work breaks. *Tommy Leonetti*

**coin** The sinews of war. *Rabelais*

**cold** How it feels to act in the nude. *Carroll Baker*

—I remember once I was on location in a snowbound mountain resort. It was so cold I almost got married.
*Shelley Winters*

COLD TABLET Nowadays about the only thing a guy can save for a rainy day. *Rosina Pagan*

**cold war** Actually, a cold peace.
—Throwing snowballs. *Anon., Jr. (Art Linkletter Dept.)*

**Coleridge** A retired mariner who took to verse.
*Anon., Jr. (British Division)*

**collective bargaining** A man discussing clothes with his wife and teen-age daughters. *Changing Times*

**college** A place where we pass from adolescence to adultery.
*Professor R. Barry*

—A four-year period in which a young man is going to flounder around trying to find himself in any case, so he might as well spend it in school trying to learn something.
*Prof. Esteys, principal, Hamburg, N.Y., High School*

—I find that the three major administrative problems on a campus are sex for the students, athletics for the alumni and parking for the faculty.
*Clark Kerr, University of California*

COLLEGE CREWMEN Scholar-scullers.

COLLEGE HOMECOMINGS Events that make a man wonder why his fellow alumni have aged so much. *Eben Stebbin*

COLLEGE ROWING A sport in which a man may achieve obscurity at his peak. *Jimmy Cannon*

COLLEGE YEARS The only vacation a boy gets between his mother and his wife. *Anon.*

**collision** The result of a tie.

**Colosseum** Rome's rotten tooth.
*Len Deighton, from the air*

**columnists** The daily substitute for immortality.
*Ernest Hemingway*

**comedian** A man who does not think it is funny but hopes you will. *Morton Thompson**

COMEDY Like a cigar; if good, everybody wants a box; if bad, no amount of puffing will make it draw.
*H. J. Byron*

—A dramatick representation of the lighter faults of mankind. *Dr. Sam'l Johnson*

—The most difficult acting to do because your option comes up after each joke. *Dick Shawn*

**comfort** A state of mind produced by contemplation of a neighbor's uneasiness. *Ambrose Bierce*

**commencement address** A speech almost no one listens to except perhaps a few parents engaged in one last effort to get something for their money.
*Dr. William E. Moran, president, Colorado State University, during a commencement address*

**commendation** The tribute that we pay to achievements that resemble, but do not equal, our own. *Ambrose Bierce*

**commerce** A kind of transaction in which A plunders from B the goods of C, and for compensation B picks the pocket of D of money belonging to E. *Ambrose Bierce*

**commercial aviation** Not flying Bunny Clubs, but just another means of transportation.
*Rep. William D. Hathaway (D.–Maine)*

**commercial traveler** One who goes to the refrigerator during the sponsor's message. *Suzanne Douglass*

**committee** A group of the unfit appointed by the unwilling to do the unnecessary. *Carl C. Byers*

—A meeting of people to homogenize their thinking.
*Anon., Jr.*

—A group consisting of one person who does the work and the balance who pat him on the back, except for one, who brings in the minority report. *Changing Times*

—And the chairman, who takes all the credit.

COMMITTEE WORK Like a soft chair—easy to get into but hard to get out of. *Kenneth J. Shively*

**Common Market** A merger of nations and nationalisms into a supermarket of a super state. *Joseph Barry*

**common sense** Not letting your opinions sway your judgment. *Changing Times*

**commoner** A prostitute. *Dr. Sam'l Johnson*

**communication** The art of concealing what you think.

PHATIC COMMUNICATION Speech which fills a social function of reducing silence without growing out of a producing thought. *S. I. Hayakawa*

—The fine art of grunting.

**communique** A press release from a general's publicity man.

**communism** One reason Americans won't go Communist is that when they hear the shout "Workers Arise," they think it's time for the coffee break. *Jack Wassweman*

COMMUNIST One who has yearnings for equal division of unequal earnings. *Ebenezer Elliot*

COMMUNISTS Fanatical believers in a god made in their own distorted image. *Dr. Harold Cooke Phillips*

**community** A large number of people striving to avoid being hit by an automobile. *Anon.*

**commuter** One who goes to the city every day to make enough money to sleep in the suburbs. *Changing Times*

—Like a hamster on a treadmill, he is embarked on an endless ramble.                                    *Caskie Stinnett*

COMMUTERS  Most of the men running for offices.
                                    *Llewellyn Mitstifer*

**Como, Perry**  The only man I know who falls asleep in the middle of a nap.                                    *Jack E. Leonard*

**compensation**  If you are losing a little on top, cheer up, you are probably gaining it in the middle.

**complaining**  The thing to try when all else fails.

**compliment**  An act, or expression of civility, usually understood to include some hypocrisy, and to mean less than it declares.                                    *Dr. Sam'l Johnson*

—A little touch of love surrounded by great imagination.
                                    *Emile Faquet*

**compose**  To remember a tune that nobody else has thought of.                                    *Robert Schumann*

**composer**  The waif of music.        *Nineteenth-century view*

**compromise**  Such an adjustment of conflicting interests as gives each adversary the satisfaction of thinking he has got what he ought not to have, and is deprived of nothing except what was justly his due.        *Ambrose Bierce*

**compulsion**  The eloquence of power.        *Ambrose Bierce*

**con woman**  One who uses the males to defraud.

**conceit**  One's opinion of oneself.

—A form of I-strain.                                    *Anon.*

—That which causes more conversation than wit.
                                    *La Rochefoucauld*

—What makes a woman think that her face is her fortune when it's only her beautician's.        *Midge Bowlin*

**conceitration**  Being all wrapped up in one's self but still making a pretty small package.                                    *Newords*

**concentration**  The ability to do your child's homework while he is watching television.        *Terry McCormick*

**concert**  What a queen has if she cannot marry another king.
                                    *Anon., Jr.*

**conchologist**  The operator of a shell game.

**concoct**  To digest by the stomach, so as to turn food to nutriment.                                    *Dr. Sam'l Johnson*

**concubine**  When several businesses merge.        *Anon., Jr.*

**condite**  To pickle; to preserve by salts or aromaticks.
                                    *Dr. Sam'l Johnson*

**condole**  To show that bereavement is a smaller evil than sympathy.                                    *Ambrose Bierce*

**conductor** A musical leader who cuts arabesques in the air with his baton—and sometimes, himself.

**conference** A meeting at which people talk about things they ought to be doing. *Arthur Murray's press agent*

ATHLETIC CONFERENCE A federation of colleges with athletic directors who never become stool pigeons unless they have a bad season. *Jimmy Cannon*

**confession** May be good for the soul but it's bad for the reputation. *Thomas R. Dewar*

—Good for the soul—but bad for the heel. *Agnes Guilfoyle*

CONFESSION AUTHOR One who writes his wrongs.

**confiscate** From two Latin words meaning "put into the public treasury."

**conformism** The collective wisdom of individual ignorance. *Thomas Carlyle*

CONFORMITY Being a collection of mirrors reflecting what everyone else wants you to be. *Anon.*

—When perfectly healthy bodies stagger around under the weight of dead minds. *Gerald Johnson*

**confusion** One woman plus one left turn.

EXCITEMENT Two women plus one secret.

BEDLAM Three women plus one bargain.

CHAOS Four women plus one luncheon check.
*The Earl of Wilson*

CONFUSIONISM In our generation the most popular religion. *Christian Business Men's League Bulletin*

**congratulation** The civility of envy. *Ambrose Bierce*

**Congress** Reader, suppose you were an idiot; and suppose you were a member of Congress; but I repeat myself.
*Mark Twain*

CONGRESSIONAL RECORD The L.P. that brings us the wind on Capitol Hill.

CONGRESSMAN An orator who can continue running off at the mouth long after his brain has run out of gas.

CONGRESSIONAL INVESTIGATION An inquiry made for the benefit of photographers. *Will Rogers*

CONGRESSIONAL INVESTIGATION COMMITTEE A group that travels far, works little and produces big headlines.
*Arthur T. Hadley*

**Connally, Tom** A Senator in the grand style—the only member of the Senate who could wear a Roman toga without looking like a fat man in a nightgown.
St. Louis *Post-Dispatch*

**connivance** The act of winking; not in use.

**connoisseur**   A specialist who knows everything about something and nothing about anything else.

—An old wine-bibber having been smashed in a railway collision, some wine was poured upon his lips to revive him. "Pauillac, 1873," he murmured and died. *Ambrose Bierce*

CONNOSEWER   A member of the French underground.

*Anon., Jr.*

**conscience**   A small, still voice that makes minority reports.

*Franklin P. Jones*

—The small inner voice that tells you the Internal Revenue Service might check your return.   *Changing Times*

—A playback of the small voice that told you not to do it in the first place.   *Walt Streightiff*

—As good as a thousand witnesses.   *Italian proverb*

—It doesn't kick up any fuss until after you've had your fun.

*Alan Schwab*

—That impediment which so often rudely interrupts while money is talking.   Cincinnati *Enquirer*

—What tells you that instinct is wrong.   *Judge*

—Something that no's what's wrong.   *Edith Ogutsch*

—Part of the equipment of the normal man and it never fails in its work.   *Bernard Shaw*

—A thinking man's filter.   *The Liguorian*

CLEAR CONSCIENCE   A good pillow.   *French proverb*

GUILTY CONSCIENCE   The mother of invention.

*Carolyn Wells*

**conservationists**   Voices crying out for the wilderness. *Time*

**conservative**   A statesman who is enamored of existing evils, as distinguished from the liberal, who wishes to replace them with others.   *Ambrose Bierce*

—One who wants to keep what the liberals of a generation ago fought for.   *Changing Times*

—A liberal with grandchildren.   *Leo L. Rockwell*

—One who entertains a new thought as if it were an unwelcome relative.

—A man who just sits and thinks, mostly sits.

*Woodrow Wilson*

—A person full of love of the past and regret for the future.

—A man with an income.

CONSERVATIVES   People whose minds become unbalanced just because the budget is.

**conserve**   A sweetmeat made of the inspissated juices of fruit, boiled with sugar 'till they will harden and candy.

*Dr. Sam'l Johnson*

**consistency** The last refuge of the unimaginative.
*Oscar Wilde*

—A verbal criterion which cannot be applied to the phenomena of life. *Aldous Huxley*

**consolation** The knowledge that a better man is more unfortunate than yourself. *Ambrose Bierce*

**constipate** To croud together into a narrow room; to thicken; to condense. *Dr. Sam'l Johnson*

**consul** In American politics, a person who having failed to secure an office from the people is given one by the Administration on condition that he leave the country.
*Ambrose Bierce*

**consult** To seek another's approval of a course already decided on. *Ambrose Bierce*

**consummation** Death; end of life. *Dr. Sam'l Johnson*

**contact** Unable to perform; i.e., "I contact on that until off-ta the election." *Bostonese*

CONTACT MAN All con and no tact. *Ernest Truex*

**contentment** The result of a poor memory and no imagination. *Grit*

—A warm sty for eaters and sleepers. *Eugene O'Neill*

—Success with pleasure.

**continence** Mind over what matters. *Playboy*

**continental shelf** Where the ocean stores its excess water.
*Anon., Jr. (Art Linkletter Dept.)*

**contortionist** A lady who recites pieces. *Anon., Jr.*

**contract** A legal agreement in which the big type gives it to you and the little type takes it away.
*Look, Ma, I'm Dancin'*

**contrary** To oppose; to thwart; to contradict.
*Dr. Sam'l Johnson*

—When I came to court I was advised not to *contrary* the king. *Latimer*

**contrition** The act of grinding; or rubbing to powder.

—Penitence; sorrow for sin: in the strict sense, the sorrow which arises from the desire to please God, distinguished from *attrition,* or imperfect repentance produced by dread of hell. *Dr. Sam'l Johnson*

**controversy** A battle in which spittle or ink replaces the injurious cannonball and the inconsiderate bayonet.
*Ambrose Bierce*

**convenient** A mistress. *Old English slang*

CONVENIENT TO BUS LINE  Real estate term meaning: "No garage." *William V. Shannon*

**convent**  A place of retirement for women who wish for leisure to meditate upon the vice of idleness.
*Ambrose Bierce*

**convention**  A girdle which society wears with indifference and frequent discomfort. *Douglas Meador*

POLITICAL CONVENTION  A chess tournament disguised as a circus. *Alistair Cooke*

CONVENTION KEYNOTE ADDRESS  A combination of oratory, grand opera and hog calling. *Mark Sullivan*

RIGGED CONVENTION  One with the other man's delegates in control. An Open Convention is when your delegates are in control. *James A. Farley*

**conventionality**  A system that saves people so much time and thought and trouble and social friction of one sort or another that it leaves them much more leisure for freedom than unconventionality does. *Bernard Shaw*

**conversation**  A fair for the display of the minor mental commodities, each exhibitor being too intent upon the arrangement of his own wares to observe those of his neighbor. *Ambrose Bierce*

—A form of communication in which some men never stop to think and many women never think to stop. *Anon.*

—When three women stand on the corner talking. Gossip is when one of them leaves. *Herb Shriner*

—An art in which a man has all mankind for competitors. *Ralph Waldo Emerson*

—Talk that should be fired in short bursts; anybody who talks steadily for more than a minute is in danger of boring somebody. *Harlan Miller*

—The least reliable form of communication, next to reading the newspapers.

**convert**  A Republican who becomes a Democrat.

TRAITOR  A Democrat who becomes a Republican.
*Quoted by Adlai Stevenson*

CONVERTED CANNIBAL  One who, on Friday, only eats fishermen. *Emily Lotney*

**conviction**  The opinion you have. Prejudice is another's conviction.

—A prejudice you can explain without getting mad.

CONVICTIONS  What an employee has after he knows what the boss thinks. *Anon.*

**cook** One who takes everything with a grain of salt.

—When she cooked a dinner it was a prelude to an autopsy.

COOK BOOK A convenience that an old-fashioned house-keeper uses for filing her own recipes. *Ken Kraft*

BRITISH COOK A foolish woman who should be turned, for her iniquities, into a pillar of salt, which she never knows how to use. *Oscar Wilde*

COOKING A pleasure; the only trouble is, it's so daily.
*Anon. cook*

AMERICAN COOKING The art of taking food out of containers and putting it on plates.

FRENCH COOKING A cuisine that has been ruined by American tourists blowing kisses to the headwaiter after abominable meals. *Robert Morley*

SAVORY COOKING The best way to lead a man around by his nose. *Arnold H. Glasow*

**coolie** A quickie in the snow. *Chinese proverb*

**cooperation** A situation where the girl coos while the guy operates.

**copple-stones** Lumps and fragments of stone or marble, broke from the adjacent cliffs, rounded by being bowled and tumbled to and again by the action of the water.
*Woodward*

**core** A place where you get suit; also where you play tan-is.
*New Yorkese*

**corinth** A small fruit commonly called currant.
*Dr. Sam'l Johnson*

**coroner** A beggar on hearse-back. *Dorothy Gulman\**

**corp** A dead business. *Anon., Jr.*

**corporal** A man who occupies the lowest rung of the military ladder.

Fiercely the battle raged and, sad to tell,

Our corporal heroically fell!

Fame from her height looked down upon the brawl

And said: "He hadn't very far to fall." *Ambrose Bierce*

**corporation** An artificial person that can do everything but make love. *The Left Handed Dictionary*

—An artificial person that could do everything including making love—if it could make a buck doing it.

**corpse** A human been. *Kay Goodman*

**correctioner** One that has been in the house of correction; a jayl-bird. This seems to be the meaning in Shakespeare.
*Dr. Sam'l Johnson*

—I will have you soundly swinged for this, you blue-bottle rogue! you filthy famished *correctioner*.

Shakespeare, *Henry IV*

**corsair** A politician of the seas.      *Ambrose Bierce*

**cortege** What you buy for your girl when you take her to a dance.      *Anon., Jr.*

**cost of living** Always a problem. With inflation you worry about the cost, and with deflation you worry about the living.      *Anon.*

—When I first started working I used to dream of the day when I might be earning the salary I'm starving on now.      *Anon.*

**cough** A convulsion of the lungs, vellicated by some sharp serosity. It is pronounced *coff*.      *Dr. Sam'l Johnson*

**country** A kind of healthy grave.      *Sydney Smith*

**couple-begger** One that makes it his business to marry beggers to each other.      *Dr. Sam'l Johnson*

**courage** A special kind of knowledge; the knowledge of how to fear what is to be feared and how not to fear what is not to be feared.      *David Ben-Gurion*

—Fear that has said its prayers.      *Anon.*

—A strong desire to live taking the form of readiness to die.      *G. K. Chesterton*

—Doing alone what one could do in the presence of others.      *La Rochefoucauld*

—Walking naked through a cannibal village.
  FOOLHARDINESS Doing the same thing with a sprig of parsley behind your ear.      *N.Y. Bus Riders Digest*

**Courrèges** A woman in his clothes is an apricot that has a mental life.      *Violette Leduc*

**court fool** The plaintiff.      *Ambrose Bierce*

**courtesan** A woman with method in her badness.
  COURTEZAN Generally a better class whore. *Eric Partridge*
—A kind woman.      *Italian derivative*

**courtesy** A form of consideration for others practiced by civilized people when they have time.      *Changing Times*

**courtship** A period in limbo when two people behave themselves as they never have before and never will again.

—The process of seeking a girl's hand until she has you under her thumb.      *Mickey Rooney*

—The Royal Boat where the king does it.      *Anon., Jr.*

**cow** An animal very like a bull, but a bull hurts more.      *Anon., Jr.*

**coward** Landlord to a ghost. *Lloyd Douglas*

COWARDICE Of the various protections against temptation, this is the surest. *Mark Twain*

—What we call our own caution when displayed by others.

**coxcomical** Foppish; conceited; a low word unworthy of use. *Dr. Sam'l Johnson*

**crab** It is used by way of contempt for any sour or degenerate fruit; as a crab *cherry*, a crab *plum*. *Dr. Sam'l Johnson*

**crackrope** A fellow that deserves hanging. *Dr. Sam'l Johnson*

**craft** A fool's substitute for brains. *Ambrose Bierce*

**crank** A person well informed on a subject in which you are not interested. *Changing Times*

**cream** The flower of milk. *Dr. Sam'l Johnson*

**credit** A person who can't pay, gets another person who can't pay, to guarantee that he can pay. *Charles Dickens*

CREDIT CARD A system enabling one to play now and glower later. No money down today if you'll settle up in a month.

—How did the pioneers get from the Atlantic to California without a credit card? *Arnold H. Glasow*

**creet** Being a blabbermouth. *Newords*

**crepe** "Beulah, peel me a crepe." *New Yorkese*

**crime** A deed committed by a dishonest person who has been caught at it and is unable to hire a good lawyer. *Max Wilk*

—Kissing your own wife in public. *Current Roman law*

**crimestop** Faculty of stopping short at the threshold of a dangerous thought. *George Orwell's "Newspeak," 1984*

**crisis** A detail previously overlooked. *Thomas H. Chevako**

**critic** A man who never pushed a noun against a verb except to blow up something. *Inherit the Wind*

—A person who boasts himself hard to please because nobody tries to please him. *Ambrose Bierce*

—A man is a critic when he cannot be an artist, just as a man becomes a stool pigeon when he cannot be a soldier. *Flaubert*

—A tone-deaf piano tuner.

—He o'er the works of Shakespeare
   A hundred hours spent;
And found a million meanings
   That Shakespeare never meant. *Tom Pease*

CRITICS Sentinels in the grand army of letters, stationed at the corners of newspapers and reviews, to challenge every new author. *Longfellow*

—Because English majors can scarcely sign their own names at the end of a course of English instruction, many become serious critics. *Kurt Vonnegut, Jr.*

—Like dentists, are a good deal occupied in hurting sensitive people in sensitive places; and as they have to do it in an entertaining manner, which no doubt gives them an air of enjoying it, they produce an impression of sadism. *Bernard Shaw*

DRAMA CRITIC A person who surprises the playwright by informing him what he meant. *Wilson Mizner*

GOOD CRITIC One who tells the story of his mind's adventures among the masterpieces. *Anatole France*

CRITICISM Don't be afraid of criticism. Anyone who can fill out a laundry slip thinks of himself as a writer. Those who can't fill out a laundry slip think of themselves as critics. *George Seaton*

—Taboo or not to boo.

—The disapproval of people for having faults different from ours. *Anon.*

—A commodity of which you are never short.
*Winston Churchill*

—The art d'object.

—Easy. Art, difficult. *Destouches*

DRAMATIC CRITICISM The venom from contented rattlesnakes. *Percy Hammond*

—Pieces of Hate. *Heywood Broun*

CRITICIZE To knock without entering.

crooning A modern form of singing derived from sub-animal or vegetable sources. *Anon., Jr. (British Division)*

crop-dusting Making everything even dustier than it had been. *Anon., Jr.*

croquet player A horseshoe pitcher with money.
*Jimmy Cannon*

cruelty One of the primitive pleasures of mankind.
*Bernard Shaw*

crunch Vox popcorn.

Crusaders Cross people. *Anon., Jr.*

crystal ball Round TV.
*Anon., Jr., quoted by Robert Sylvester*

Cubans The chief export of Cuba. *Anon., Jr.*

cube A square no matter how you look at it. *W. F. Engel*

cuckoo A bird which appears in the spring; and is said to suck the eggs of other birds, and lay her own to be hatched in their place, from which practice, it was usual to alarm a husband at the approach of an adulterer by calling cuckoo, which, by mistake, was in time applied to the husband. This bird is remarkable for the uniformity of his note, from which his name in most tongues seems to have been formed. *Dr. Sam'l Johnson*

**cuddle** (A low word, I believe, without etymology.) To lye close; to squat. *Dr. Sam'l Johnson*

—To coagulate or congeal; e.g., "It cuddled my blood."
*New Yorkese*

**cudgel** The best argument. *Spanish proverb*

**cull** To summon. "Many are culled, but few are chosen."
*New Yorkese*

**culture** An implement professors wield to turn out more professors, who will then turn out more professors.
*Albert Camus or Simone Weil*

—One thing—and varnish is another. *Ralph Waldo Emerson*

—The habit of being pleased with the best and knowing why.
*Henry van Dyke*

—According to many people, stuffing modern houses full of antique furniture. *Pablo Picasso*

—The passion for sweetness and light. *Dean Swift*

—To cultivate; to manure; to till. *Dr. Sam'l Johnson*

**cummerbund** A girdle substituting for a vest.

—A belly-band for adults.

**curiosity** The mother of fables. *Giovanni di Lampadusa*

—An objectionable quality of the female mind. The desire to know whether or not a woman is cursed with curiosity is one of the most active and insatiable passions of the masculine soul. *Ambrose Bierce*

**curmudgeon** (It is a vitious manner of pronouncing *coeur mechant*, Fr., an unknown correspondent.) An avaritious churlish fellow; a miser, a niggard; a churl; a griper.
*Dr. Sam'l Johnson*

**curve** The longest way between two points.
*Anon., Jr. (British Division)*

**cuss** A path. "The cuss of true love never runs smooth."
*New Yorkese*

**cynic** One who puts all human actions into two classes: openly bad and secretly bad. *Henry Ward Beecher*

—The human owl, vigilant in darkness, and blind to light, mousing for vermin, and never seeing noble game.
*Henry Ward Beecher*

—One who thinks the world never changes, only short changes. *Wall Street Journal*

—A man who looks at the world with a monocle in his mind's eye. *Carolyn Wells*

—A blackguard whose faulty vision sees things as they are, and not as they ought to be. *Ambrose Bierce*

—A man who found out when he was about ten that there wasn't any Santa Claus, and is still upset.
*James Gould Cozzens*

CYNICISM  Often the shamefaced product of inexperience.
*A. J. Liebling*

**cynigrin**  A happy pessimist. *Newords*

# D

**daddy**  The kin a girl loves to touch.

**dairying**  You raise more feed to make more milk so you can have more money to buy more land so you can have more cows and raise more feed, to, etc.
*Food Marketing in New England*

DAIRYMAN  The operator of a manufacturing plant, who, considering the price of manure, could keep one hundred cows and give the milk away.

**Dallas**  The Athens of the Alfalfa Fields. *Anon.*

**dam**  The objective case of they, as: "Where'd you get dam great big ice?" *New Yorkese*

**Dan**  A nook or room of relaxation as in "The lion went in his dan." *New Yorkese*

**dance**  To leap about to the sound of tittering music, preferably with arms about your neighbor's wife or daughter.
*Ambrose Bierce*

ECCENTRIC DANCER  One who dances with her clothes on.
*Stripper Tempest Storm*

PERFECT DANCER  The one who dances to the tips of her fingers and the top of her head. *Bernard Shaw*

DANCING  An art. *Headlam*

ART  Praise. *Ruskin*

—"Praise is surely not out of place in a church. We sing there: why should we not dance?" *Bernard Shaw*

—The poetry of the foot. *Dryden*

—The embracin' bit.

**dandelion** Another thing, which, if given an inch, will take a yard. *Edith A. Van Sant*

**dandruff** Personal fallout.

**dapper** Little and active; lively without bulk. It is usually spoken in contempt. *Dr. Sam'l Johnson*

**D.A.R.** A mutual admiration society for the promotion of pink teas and ancestor worship.
*Former D.A.R. president quoted by G. I. Rees*
—An organization created in 1890 to recreate the social distinctions their ancestors had fled and defend the shibboleths their ancestors had attacked. *Henry Steele Commager*

**dark horse** The candidate who keeps his availability well curried and groomed. *Bob Stannard*

**darling** The popular form of address used in speaking to a person of the opposite sex whose name you cannot at the moment recall. *Oliver Herford*

**data** A female child. *Bostonese*

**dawn** One of the ten most beautiful words in the English language, along with hush, lullaby, murmuring, tranquil, mist, luminous, chimes, melody—and golden.
*Wilfred J. Funk*

**daybed** A bed used for idleness and luxury in the daytime. *Dr. Sam'l Johnson*

**daylight saving** Letting the day stay up late. *Mary Charge*
—A system invented by an old Indian who cut off his blanket at one end and sewed it onto the other to make it longer. *Clarke A. Sanford*

**dead end street** That means nobody can run over ya unless he lives on this street. *Dennis the Menace*

**deadline** Where something dies. And you know what. Well, life is compromise. *Christopher Morley*

**deadpan** To have your face in neutral. *Dorothy Waldo Phillips*

**death** That ugly, snub-nosed one.
*Tchaikovsky, the day before he died*
—The drear candlesnuffer. *Julie de Lespinasse*
—The old whore. *Ernest Hemingway*
—The only woman who never leaves you. *Pablo Picasso*
—The last word in matadors. *R. Osborn*
—The cure of all diseases. *Thomas Browne*
—The debt you pay nature. *From the Latin*
—The final argument for all but the survivors. *Paul Tabori*°
—Going in search of a great perhaps. *Rabelais*

—The wages of sin.

—To stop sinning suddenly. *Elbert Hubbard*

—The only thing we're sure won't get worse every time the legislature meets.

—Nature's way of getting you to slow down. *Caskie Stinnett*

—Complete maturity.

—All men are cremated equal.

DEATH SENTENCE   We are not condemning someone to death, which we don't know about; we are condemning them to spend the last hours of their lives as unpleasantly as possible, which is something quite different.

*Peter Ustinov*

**debauchee**   One who has so earnestly pursued pleasure that he has had the misfortune to overtake it. *Ambrose Bierce*

**debt**   An ingenious substitute for the chain and whip of the slave-driver. *Ambrose Bierce*

—The only commodity on which a man does not have to pay taxes. *H. L. Mencken*

—An obligation you try to pay with money you never have. *Paul and Helen Martin Denis\**

—Running into debt isn't such a bad thing. It's running into your creditors that's so embarrassing. *Puck*

**debutante**   A gal whose life is one mad whirl of activity . . . day in and night out. *Changing Times*

**Decalogue**   A series of commandments, ten in number—just enough to permit an intelligent selection for observance, but not enough to embarrass the choice. Following is the revised edition of the Decalogue, calculated for this meridian.

> Thou shalt no God but me adore:
> 'Twere too expensive to have more.
>
> No images nor idols make
> For Robert Ingersoll[1] to break.
>
> Take not God's name in vain; select
> A time when it will have effect.
>
> Work not on Sabbath days at all,
> But go to see the teams play ball.
>
> Honor thy parents. That creates,
> For life insurance, lower rates.

[1] American agnostic, 1833–99.

Kill not, abet not those who kill;
Thou shalt not pay thy butcher's bill.

Kiss not thy neighbor's wife, unless
Thine own thy neighbor doth caress.

Don't steal; thou'lt never thus compete
Successfully in business. Cheat.

Bear not false witness—that is low—
But "hear 'tis rumored so and so."

Covet thou naught that thou hast not
By hook or crook, or somehow, got. *Ambrose Bierce*

**deceased** The future tense of diseased. *Anon., Jr.*
**December** The end of a failure.
*Bill Manville* (See JANUARY)
—The time when people come in different sizes—none of
which you know. *David Savage*
**decision** What a man makes when he can't get anybody to
serve on a committee. *Fletcher Knebel*
**décolletage** A neckline low enough to make a baby cry.
*Morey Amsterdam*
—Pearls on the half-shell.
**Dee, Sandra, and Darrin, Bobby** The Lunt and Fontanne
of San Fernando Valley. *Leo Mishkin*
**deed** Past tense of do. "Macbeth deed the bloody did."
*New Yorkese*
**defame** To lie about another. To tell the truth about another. *Ambrose Bierce*
**defeat** An orphan (Victory has a hundred fathers).
*John F. Kennedy, after the Bay of Pigs*
**definition** A description that inadequately represents a much
more complicated situation.
*Marie Claire Davis and/or Doris Bennett*
**deflating** Letting the hot air out of a stuffed shirt.
**De Gaulle, Charles** A sort of Henry Wallace—if Wallace
had gone to West Point. *Changing Times, 1948*
—Louis the 19th.
**déjeuner** The breakfast of an American who has been in
Paris. *Ambrose Bierce*
**deli** A store that serves preserved meats and fish via fresh
waiters. *New Yorkese*
**deliberation** The act of examining one's bread to determine
which side it is buttered on. *Ambrose Bierce*

**Delphi** Located in the center of Greece, was considered the navel of the universe—by the Greeks, that is.

**deluge** A notable first experiment in baptism which washed away the sins (and sinners) of the world. *Ambrose Bierce*

**de luxe** The model that costs no more than the standard one—you just pay a little longer. *Anon.*

—With a pickle. *The Automat*

**dementia praecox** A precocious little demon.
*Richard Armour*

**demijohn** A French powder room.

**democracy** A form of religion; the worship of jackals by jackasses. *H. L. Mencken*

—A condition where people believe that other people are as good as they are. *Stuart Chase*

—The recurrent suspicion that more than half the people are right more than half the time. *E. B. White*

—A place where we have complete control over how we pay our taxes—cash, check or money order. *Imp*

—A political system which gives every man the right to be his own oppressor. *James Russell Lowell*

—A device that insures that we shall be governed no better than we deserve. *Bernard Shaw*

—The worst form of government except for all the other systems that have never been tried. *Winston Churchill*

—A place where a man can get a recount. *Morris L. Ernst*

**Democrats** If you'll take off their feathers, you'll find just a bunch of sophomores trying to work their way through the electoral college. *Rep. Page Belcher*

**Denmark** The home of Danish blue cheese.

**Dennis** Dentist. *New Yorkese*

—A doctor of teeth.

—A magician who, putting metal into your mouth, pulls coins out of your pocket. *Ambrose Bierce*

**departing visitor** One who thinks that when he stands up, he's gone.

**department store** A commercial enterprise designed to traffic on a woman's desires. *Émile Zola*

**deportment** Being put out of the country. *Anon., Jr.*

**descendants** Those people who presently reside in the future tense. *Anon., Jr.*

**desecrate** To divert from the purpose to which any thing is consecrated. *Dr. Sam'l Johnson*

**deuce** Two: a word used in games. The Devil. See "deuse."
*Dr. Sam'l Johnson*

**deuse** (More properly than *deuce*, Junius, from *Dusius*, th name of a certain species of evil spirits.) The devil: ludicrous word. *Dr. Sam'l Johnso*

**devil** The father of lies, but he neglected to patent the ide and the business now suffers from competition.

*Josh Billin*

DEVIL'S ADVOCATE A prosecuting attorney retained to se that a potential saint is holy inadequate.

**dew** Air that looks wet.

**diabetes** The malfunction of the organ that keeps sug from being a bitter pill.

**dialogues** Monologues cut in two. *Arthur "Bugs" Ba*

**diamonds** Stepping stones from success.

—A burglar's best friend. *Mrs. Susan Wildin*

**diapers** The humble banners of fertility. *Bruce Hutchinso*

**diary** Anybody's home journal.

—Penned-up emotions. Oskaloosa (Ia.) *Hera*

—A daily record of that part of one's life which he can rela to himself without blushing. *Ambrose Bier*

**dickens** A kind of adverbial exclamation, importing, as seems, much the same with the *devil;* but I know n whence derived. *Dr. Sam'l Johnso*

**dictator** A stenographer's boss. *R. W. Dawso*

**dictionary** A mortuary of words. *Bill Manho*

—A malevolent literary device for cramping the growth of language and making it hard and inelastic. This dictionar however, is a most useful work.

Ambrose Bierce, *The Devil's Dictiona*

—The only place where success comes before work.

*Man's Sho*

**did** A lick-hell dog-you-mint. *New Yorke*

**diddle** (Colloquial) To move rapidly up and down or bac ward and forward. (akin to dodder).

*American College Dictiona*

**Dido** Queen of Carthage, who was offered all the land be encompassed by a cow's hide and then cut it into stri to get the greatest spread of real estate. Today cutting u didoes has a less profitable connotation.

**die** The singular of "dice." We seldom hear the word, b cause there is a prohibitory proverb, "Never say die." long intervals, however, someone says: "The die is cast which is not true, for it is cut. *Ambrose Bier*

—One of a pair of die-cut dice which can be cast, but if done on an Army blanket, beware!

**diet** No matter what kind you are on, you can usually eat as much as you want of anything you don't like.
*Walter Slezak*

—Fast talk. *Jack Herbert*

—What you keep putting off while you keep putting on.
*Herb Sherry*

—Something to take the starch out of you. *Anon.*

DIETING The new national pastime.

—Breaking the pound barrier. *Richard Whalley*

**the difficult** That which can be done immediately.

THE IMPOSSIBLE That which takes a little longer.
*George Santayana*

**digestion** The great secret of life. *Sydney Smith*

**dignity** What you lose with. *Senator Soaper*

—One thing that cannot be preserved in alcohol.
*Graem and Sarah Lorimer*

**diligence** An old-fashioned vehicle of success.

**dime** A dollar with the taxes taken out. *Anon.*

—The price of a wrong number. *Cynic's Cyclopaedia*

**din** Contraction of "did not"; e.g., "The noise din have her ther-mom-mit-her." *New Yorkese*

**ding** To bluster; to bounce; to huff. A low word.
*Dr. Sam'l Johnson*

DING DONG BATTLE A rousing fight described by a reporter who doesn't have a Thesaurus. *Jimmy Cannon*

**dinosaur** A docile colossal fossil. *Anon.*

**dip** Extending for a considerable length inward, backward or downward. "Dip in my heart, dear." *New Yorkese*

**diplomacy** The art of treating a noisy neighbor as if he was going to appear for you as witness in a traffic case against a film star. *Morton Thompson\**

—The art of handling a porcupine without disturbing the quills. *Anon.*

—The art of doing and saying the nastiest things in the nicest way. *Isaac Goldberg*

—The art of removing something that belongs to a guy who thanks you for taking it away.

DIPLOMAT One who can tell a man he's open-minded when he means he has a hole in the head. *F. G. Kernan*

—One who can keep his shirt on while getting something off his chest. *Anon.*

—A man who can juggle a hot potato until it becomes cold issue.                    *Dr. Wilfred Platze*

—Anyone who thinks twice before saying nothing.
                                        *Alex Dreie*

—A person who uses his head without anyone suspectin it.                                *Dan Revell*

—A person who can be disarming even though his countr isn't.                        *Mrs. Deane Binde*

—An official who can make his country's greed seem lik altruism.                    *Herbert V. Prochno*

—A government employee who is taught never to be caugh with his striped pants down.

—In the U.N. his social life can be defined in three words— protocol, alcohol and Geritol.        *Adlai Stevenso*

**director** A stuffed polo shirt with a pair of cutting roor shears in its back.            *Morton Thompson*

DIRECTOR (STAGE) A midwife with opinions.
                                    *John Mason Brow*

**disarmament** Scrapping without fighting.

—Like a party. Nobody wants to arrive until everyone els is there.                    *Changing Time*

—What the next war is to be fought over.        *Ano*

**discotheque** A jukebox that forgot to say "when!"

—A place where dancers exercise just about everything ex cept discretion.                        *WQX*

**discretion** The difference between keeping your chin u and sticking your neck out.

—Knowing the difference between pulling your weight an throwing it around.

—Stepping outside before you are invited there.

**discussion** A method of confirming others in their error
                                    *Ambrose Bierc*

**dishwasher** An appliance which has become popular be cause most husbands would rather buy than be one.
                                        *Harold Coffi*

**disillusionment** Discovering that the man who writes th bank advertising is not the one who makes the loans.
                                    *Changing Time*

**disk jockey** A spinster with a record.    *Maxwell Shane*

**Disney, Walt** The master of the nightmare.
                        Henry Miller, *The Air-Conditioned Nightmar*

—The Gustave Doré of the world of Henry Ford & Co., In
                                        *Ibi*

DISNEYLAND   A simonized Coney Island. *Kevin Wallace*
—The greatest people trap ever built by a mouse.
*Changing Times*

**disobedience**   The silver lining to the cloud of servitude.
*Ambrose Bierce*

**dissemble**   To put a clean shirt upon the character. *Let us dissemble*.   *Ambrose Bierce*

**distance**   The only thing that the rich are willing for the poor to call theirs and keep.   *Ambrose Bierce*

**distiller**   One who makes and sells pernicious and inflammatory spirits.   *Dr. Sam'l Johnson*

**distract**   To pull different ways at once. *Dr. Sam'l Johnson*

**distress**   A disease incurred by exposure to the prosperity of a friend.   *Ambrose Bierce*

**distrust**   An ax at the tree of love.   *Russian proverb*

**diver, deep-sea**   A man for hire to go lower.

**divorce**   Flying out of the little hate-nest.
—What many a woman has to do to get the money she married a man for.
—Divorces are made in heaven.   *Oscar Wilde*
—Divorce dates from just about the same time as marriage; I think that marriage is a few weeks older.   *Voltaire*

DIVORCE SUIT   A damage action after which the wife gets half and her lawyer the rest.

HOLLYWOOD DIVORCE   Where the wife asks for custody of the money.

**Dixieland musician**   One with an ear of corn.

**doctor**   The best kind is the one you run for and can't find.
*Denis Diderot*

DOCTOR OF DIVINITY   The only doctor who can cure a young couple who are lovesick.   *Imogene Fey*

**dog**   The only popular talebearer.
—A kind of additional or subsidiary Deity designed to catch the overflow and surplus of the world's worship. This Divine Being in some of his smaller and silkier incarnations, takes, in the affection of Woman, the place to which there is no human male aspirant. The Dog is a survival—an anachronism. He toils not, neither does he spin, yet Solomon in all his glory never lay upon a doormat all day long, sunsoaked and fly-fed and fat, while his master worked for the means wherewith to purchase an idle wag of the Solomonic tail, seasoned with a look of tolerant recognition.
*Ambrose Bierce*

—Well, this man we heard about just the other day was motoring along at a reasonable pace, when all of a sudden a dog appeared directly in his path. Swerving sharply to avoid a collision, our motorist ran his car off the highway. It overturned and he was thrown out the front door, rather bruised and battered. What really gets us down, however, is the attitude of the dog. Not the least abashed, it walked calmly over and bit the motorist on his protruding posterior. *Quote*

**DOGMATIC** Acting as stubborn as a dog.

**doily** A species of woollen stuff, so called, I suppose, from the name of the first maker. *Dr. Sam'l Johnson*

**doll** Standard monetary unit; e.g., "That'll cost you fifty-fi' dolls." *New Yorkese*

**Don Juan** A town in the West Indies. *Anon., Jr.*

**don't** Advice to persons about to marry. *Punch*

**donkey** A critter wit four down standers, two outriggers and a thing to brush de flies away wit. *Bermuda native*

**Donohue's Law** Anything worth doing is worth doing for money. *Joseph C. Donohue\**

**don't** Advice to persons about to marry. *Punch*

**doom** Performing, occurring, as in: "Hi, what's doom?" *New Yorkese*

**dope** A man who picks up a cute blonde's handkerchief and turns it in to the lost-and-found desk. *D. O. Flynn*

**dormitory** A burial place. *Dr. Sam'l Johnson*

**dot** The thing we are talking about, as "Where did you get dot poker-dot tie?" *New Yorkese*

**double entendre** Something which can only be understood one way. *Gene Raskin\**

**double jeopardy** A woman teaching another woman how to drive.

**double martinis** Sips that passion the night. *Sonny Eliot*

**doublethink** Power of holding two contradictory beliefs simultaneously, and accepting both. *George Orwell's "Newspeak," 1984*

**doubt** A tribute paid to hope. *Lautréamont*

**dowager** A woman who has grown too big for her brooches.

**down** One way for a newspaperman to look at a politician *Frank H. Simonds*

**draft board** The world's largest travel agency. *Electricity on the Farm*

**draft card** Your social insecurity number. *Fletcher Knebel*

**dragoon**   A soldier who combines dash and steadiness in so
equal measure that he makes his advances on foot and his
retreats on horseback.                          *Ambrose Bierce*

**drama**   No mere setting up of the camera to nature: it is
the presentation in parable of the conflict between Man's
will and his environment: in a word, of problem.
                                                 *Bernard Shaw*

DRAMATIST   One who adapts plays from the French.
                                                 *Ambrose Bierce*

**drape**   To jeer, or satyrize. It is used in this sense by the
innovator Temple, whom nobody has imitated.
                                             *Dr. Sam'l Johnson*

**draw**   Part of a bureau. Also, as in top-draw secret.
                                                     *Bostonese*

DRAWING   Putting a line around what you think. *Anon., Jr.*

**drawl**   To utter any thing in a slow driveling way.
                                             *Dr. Sam'l Johnson*

**dream**   The pauper's movie.
—To think by moonlight.                          *Jules Renard*

DREAMS   The children of an idle brain.
                        Mercutio in *Romeo and Juliet*, by Shakespeare

DREAMING   A wonderful way to avoid work.

**drink**   A violently abused word reflecting the prejudice and
often the ignorance of the prohibitionist. It is impossible
to say with conviction why so innocent, general and simple
a word should have acquired a specialized and often sin-
ister meaning. Consider the sentence: "Drink this drink of
ginger beer and thus avoid getting drunk by drinking
drink." The fact that this has meaning is a sad reflection
upon the influence of a certain type of citizen upon the
fate of words.                              Oscar O. Mendelsohn,
                        *The Dictionary of Drink and Drinking*

—2 pints equal 1 quart; 1 quart equals 1 argument; 1 argument equals 1 fight; 1 fight equals 2 cops; 2 cops equal
1 arrest; 1 arrest equals 1 judge; 1 judge equals 30 days.
                        *Seventh Day Adventist Bible Conference*

DRINKING   What certainly won't solve your problem, but
it'll give you some interesting new ones.      *Tony Pettito*
—The guest who has to be drugged with alcohol to make
him interesting is hardly worth inviting in the first place.
          *Dr. Roy L. Smith, Indiana Temperance League*
—Never drink on an empty wallet.
—While gruesome exploitation and the horror of unem-

ployment drive people into the arms of alcohol in capitalistic countries, the Soviet citizens like to drink because of their overflowing joy of life and the desire to celebrate the great success of socialism.

*Radio Moscow speaker*

**PROBLEM DRINKER** One who never buys. *Jackie Kannon*

**drip** A person you can always hear but rarely can turn off.

**drive-in movie** Wall-to-wall car-petting. *Playboy*

**DRIVE-IN MOVIE OWNER** A person who lives on love.

*Franklin P. Jones*

**driving** An activity which is supposed to be a pleasure. But it is a peculiar form of pleasure. In many respects a car fulfills the same function as that drug which the upright Dr. Jekyll took to transform himself into the diabolical Mr. Hyde. A man will wait in line for hours to buy World Series tickets, but bristles with impatience at every red light. He doffs his hat whenever he meets a woman he knows, but narrowly misses running over a housewife who does not cross the street fast enough for him. He keeps a sharp eye on his family's vocabulary, but swears like a trooper at any driver who gets in his way. *Reálites*

—Always try to drive so that your license will expire before you do. *Puck*

**drop-dead coat** A coat so that when my jealous neighbor sees it, she should drop dead.

*Journal of the American Medical Association*

**dropout** Quiz skid. *Frank Rose*

**drought** When the Baptists sprinkle, the Methodists use a damp cloth and the Presbyterians issue rain checks. *Anon.*

—A period during which you can get the dresser drawers open. Allendale (S.C.) *County Citizen*

**drug** Any wholesome vegetable good for taking once in a while, but not for regular food.

*Anon., Jr. (British Division)*

**WONDER DRUGS**

We're well supplied with many kinds
In bottle, tube and jar:
They've been so long upon the shelf
We wonder what they are! *S. Omar Barker*

**DRUGSTORE** A telephone booth with lunchcounter attached.

**DRUGGIST** A man who is paid for counting pills.

**drumstick** Oh, chicken-on-the-cob. *June Files*

**drunk** The future of drink. *Anon., Jr.*

DRUNKNICK   An emotional midget who climbs into a bottle to feel like a giant.

*James V. Scully, American Temperance Society*

duck   To bow low; to cringe. In Scottish *duyk*, or *juyk*, to make obeisance, is still used.          *Dr. Sam'l Johnson*

—A tin pipe that brings in air.          *New Yorkese*

duckspeak   To quack like a duck; implies praise if opinions quacked are orthodox ones.

*George Orwell's "Newspeak," 1984*

DUCKY   The wife of a duke.          *Anon., Jr.*

duel   A formal ceremony preliminary to the reconciliation of two enemies. Great skill is necessary to its satisfactory observance; if awkwardly performed the most unexpected and deplorable consequences sometimes ensue. A long time ago a man lost his life in a duel.          *Ambrose Bierce*

duffer   A golfer who addresses his ball before and after swinging.

Duke of Windsor   Ex-Rex.

dull   A toy or mannequin; e.g., "You're a real baby dull."

*New Yorkese*

—Not exhilarating; not delightful; as, to make dictionaries is dull work.          *Dr. Sam'l Johnson*

Dumas, Alexandre, père   An author who made French history like an opera by Meyerbeer for me.          *Bernard Shaw*

dunking   Bad taste that tastes good.

*Franklin Pierce Adams*

durst   What a glass war quenches.          *New Yorkese*

duty   That which sternly impels us in the direction of profit, along the line of desire.          *Ambrose Bierce*

—A task we anticipate with distaste, perform with reluctance and brag about forever afterward.          *Anon.*

dying   The way people lose their lifes.          *Anon., Jr.*

dyspeptic   A man that can eat his cake and have it too.

*Austin O'Malley*

# E

**eame** Uncle; a word still used in the wilder parts of Staffordshire. *Dr. Sam'l Johnson*

**early spring** A forward March. *Anon.*

**earth** A moon of the sun. *Leonardo*

—A parking lot.

—A place where if the population continues to multiply at present rates for the next two thousand years, the people on it would weigh more than the planet itself.
*Kentucky School Journal*

—The ball the East and West are halving.

—Only a ball-bearing in the hub of the universe.
*Christopher Morley*

EARTHQUAKE A motion to adjourn.

—A big movement in real estate. *Californian*

**East Berlin** Where every child dreams of becoming an adult Western. St. Paul *Pioneer Press*

**easy credit** A convenience costing America about four billion in hard cash annually.

**easy street** A thoroughfare littered with a lot of nervous wrecks. *Changing Times*

**eat** To perform successively (and successfully) the functions of mastication, humectation, and deglutition.
"I was in the drawing-room, enjoying my dinner," said Brillat-Savarin, beginning an anecdote. "What!" interrupted Rochebriant; "eating dinner in a drawing-room?" "I must beg you to observe, monsieur," explained the great gastronome, "that I did not say I was eating my dinner, but enjoying it. I had dined an hour before." *Ambrose Bierce*

EATING The hand-to-mouth struggle to exist.

**ebriety** Drunkenness; intoxication by strong liquors.
*Dr. Sam'l Johnson*

—Bitter almonds, as an antidote against *ebriety*, hath commonly failed. Browne, *Vulgar Errours*

**eccentric** Off-center.

—A rich man you can't call a nut.

ECCENTRICITY Often a kind of innocent pride, and the

72

man of genius and the aristocrat are frequently regarded as eccentrics because genius and aristocrat are entirely unafraid of and uninfluenced by the opinions and vagaries of the crowd.                                        *Edith Sitwell*

—A method of distinction so cheap that fools employ it to accentuate their incapacity.                          *Ambrose Bierce*

**echo**  To hit high C and have it hit back.

—The only thing that can cheat some women out of the last word.

**economics**  The way things would work out, if we let them.

—Stating the obvious in terms of the incomprehensible.
                                                          *Anon.*

—The dismal science.                               *Thomas Carlyle*

  ECONOMISTS  Blind men feeling their way around in a nudist colony.                                        *Anon.*

—People who know more about money than the man who has it.                                      *Sen. Frank J. Lausche*

  ECONOMY  Anything your wife wants to buy. *Fred Neher*

—The secret is to live as cheaply the first few days after payday as you lived the last few days before.
                                                  Arkansas *Baptist*

—The wealth of the poor and the wisdom of the rich.
                                            *Alexandre Dumas, père*

  ECONOMY SIZE  Under the American system, big in soap flakes and small in cars. *Anon., Jr. (Art Linkletter Dept.)*

**edify**  To build.                            *Dr. Sam'l Johnson*

**education**  That method whereby man is imbued with a sense of duty and with a total command of his capabilities, when, holding both as vivid trusts, he becomes, through service and through sweat, a happiness to himself and a benediction to his brothers.

              *Dr. Ivor Griffith, president, Philadelphia*
                   *College of Pharmacy and Science*

—The process of transforming an impulsive, self-centered little animal into a civilized adult who can think with the symbols of language and can thereby develop the ability to subordinate his animal impulses, habits, and immediate ends to long-range personal and social ends.
                                            *Eugene H. Sloane*

—Man's going forward from cocksure ignorance to thoughtful uncertainty.                              *Kenneth G. Johnson*

—A succession of eye-openers each involving the repudiation of some previously held belief.                *Bernard Shaw*

—Where to be penny-wise is people-foolish.

*Adlai Stevenson*

—A delayed-action bomb, assembled in the classrooms for explosion at a later date. *Clifton Fadiman*

—What you must acquire without any interference from your schooling. *Mark Twain*

—That which discloses to the wise and disguises from the foolish their lack of understanding. *Ambrose Bierce*

—What remains when we have forgotten all that we have been taught. *Marquis of Halifax*

—Nothing but the methodical creation of the habit of thinking. *Ernest Dimnet*

—You can't teach people anything they don't want to know.

*Bernard Shaw*

—The first step to something better. *Wendell Phillips*

—Largely a matter of choosing one's company and listening.

*Anon.*

—The ability to describe fully a bathing beauty without using your hands. San Francisco *Chronicle*

—A race against catastrophe. *H. G. Wells*

EDUCATED MAN One who can give directions without taking his hands out of his pockets. *Changing Times*

effect The second of two phenomena which always occur together in the same order. The first, called a Cause, is said to generate the other—which is no more sensible than it would be for one who has never seen a dog except in pursuit of a rabbit to declare the rabbit the cause of the dog. *Ambrose Bierce*

eggnog A sneaky ice cream soda. *Maxine Marx\**

eggplant An apoplectic squash.

EGGPLANTS Where baby chicks think they come from.

*Anon., Jr.*

egotism A drug which enables some people to live with themselves. *Anon.*

—The art of seeing qualities in yourself which others can't see. *Bruce Magazine*

—Nature's compensation for mediocrity. *L. A. Safian*

EGOTIST A person of low taste, more interested in himself than in me. *Ambrose Bierce*

—A guy who never says a bad word about anyone, because he is always talking about himself.

*Arthur Murray's press agent*

—A person who would be more attractive if his I's were not so close together.

—One who gets carried away by the sound of his own
mouth.                                    *Shelley Winters*

—One who thinks that if he had not been born, people
would wonder why.                         *Changing Times*

—A person who doesn't go around talking about other
people.

**Einstein, Albert**  The only violinist I ever saw who really
looked like a violinist.                   *Bernard Shaw*

**Eisenhower**  The man to vote for—he kept us out of space.
*Mort Sahl*

**election year**  When the outs want to help the people out of
all the trouble the ins got us into.

—When some politicians get free speech mixed up with
loose talk.                                *Dan Bennett*

**elector**  One who enjoys the sacred privilege of voting for
the man of another man's choice.          *Ambrose Bierce*

**electorate**  Voters who, in an election year, pick a President
and then for four years pick on him.      *Adlai Stevenson*

**electric chair**  An example of period furniture. It ends a
sentence.                                 *Anon. schoolboy*

**electrician**  A guy who's always wiring home for money.

**electricity**  Bottled light, only fit for corpses. *Pierre Renoir*

—The power that causes all natural phenomena not known
to be caused by something else. Electricity seems destined
to play a most important part in the arts and industries.
The question of its economical application to some purposes is still unsettled, but experiment has already proved
that it will propel a street car better than a gas jet and
give more light than a horse.         *Ambrose Bierce, 1881*

**electrocardiograph**  Ticker tape.          *Lil O. Olsen*

**elephant**  An animal occurring in one of three colors, depending on whether you are on safari, a church committee
or a week-end party.                          *Anon.*

—A mouse that was constructed according to government
specifications.                               *Anon.*

PINK ELEPHANT  A beast of bourbon.   *MacGowan Miller*\*

**elevator**  A little room where you get in, so the upstairs can
come down.                                    *Anon., Jr.*

**Elijah**  The original hot-rod driver.

**Ellen Noah**  Mrs. F. D. R.                   *Bostonese*

**elocution**  A hideous affectation, accent, false emphases, un-
meaning pauses, aggravating slowness, ill-conditioned gravity, and perverse resolution to "get it from the chest" and
make it sound as if you got it from the cellar. *Bernard Shaw*

**eloquence** What you think you have after five martinis.
*Monte Proser**

**emasculation** Chewing gum in a high-toned manner.
*Anon., Jr.*

**embalm** To cheat vegetation by locking up the gases upon which it feeds. By embalming their dead and thereby deranging the natural balance between animal and vegetable life, the Egyptians made their once fertile and populous country barren and incapable of supporting more than a meagre crew. The modern metallic burial casket is a step in the same direction, and many a dead man who ought now to be ornamenting his neighbor's lawn as a tree, or enriching his table as a bunch of radishes, is doomed to a long inutility. We shall get him after a while if we are spared, but in the meantime, the violet and rose are languishing. *Ambrose Bierce*

**eminence** Frequently a matter of outliving more capable people.

**emotion** A prostrating disease caused by a determination of the heart to the head. It is sometimes accompanied by a copious discharge of hydrated chloride of sodium from the eyes. *Ambrose Bierce*

**empathy** Akin to sympathy, but whereas sympathy says, "I feel as you do," empathy says, "I know how you feel." In other words, empathy enables us to use our heads more than our hearts, and allows us to appreciate another person's feelings without becoming emotionally involved with him. *R. W. Armstrong*

**emphasis** It is always necessary to overstate a case startlingly to make people sit up and listen to it, and to frighten them into action on it. I do this myself habitually and deliberately. *Bernard Shaw*

**enemy** One who is seeking the end of me.

—Love your enemies. At least they don't try to borrow money from you.

**energy cell** A tiny electrical battery that costs so much it must be called something else.

**engagement ring** A test band. *Ray Haws*

**engineer, practical** One who perpetuates the errors of his predecessors. *J. M. Rankin*

**England** A queer, attractive, contradictory phenomenon. A strange land ten minutes by air from the continent of Europe. *Tony Mayer*

—The only country where it takes ten men in formal clothes to serve you melted mud.          *Rep. James Tumulty*

ENGLISH   A language not accessible even to Englishmen.
                                          *Bernard Shaw*

—People who defend themselves.          *Voltaire*

—People who amuse themselves sadly. *The Duc de Sully*

—A hardy race that considers plain boiled turnips to be food.          *The Garrulous Gourmet*

ENGLISHMAN   One whose head contains many facts and few ideas.          *Hippolyte Taine*

—One, an odd chap; two, a cricket match; three, The Empire.          *Jerome Lawrence**

—One who thinks he is moral when he is only uncomfortable.          *Bernard Shaw*

ENGLISHMEN   People who, when they are behaving badly, pretend they are mad.          *John Quincy Adams*

engrosser   He that purchases large quantities of any commodity, in order to sell it at a high price. *Dr. Sam'l Johnson*

enjoyment   A minor form of happiness.          *Thomas Mann*

enormous   The difference between a little money and no money.          *Hello, Dolly!*

enough   The difference between democracy and communism.

entertainment   Any kind of amusement whose inroads stop short of death by dejection.          *Ambrose Bierce*

—It is easy to entertain most people. All you have to do is listen.          *Changing Times*

enthusiasm   What the other guy lacks for your project.

—A distemper of youth, curable by small doses of repentance in connection with outward applications of experience.
                                          *Ambrose Bierce*

—Filled with God.          *Ancient derivation*

envelope   The coffin of a document; the scabbard of a bill; the husk of a remittance; the bedgown of a love-letter.
                                          *Ambrose Bierce*

epicure   One who gets nothing better than the cream of everything but cheerfully makes the best of it.
                                          *Oliver Herford*

—A poet who writes epics.          *Anon., Jr.*

epigram   A short, sharp saying in prose or verse, frequently characterized by acidity or acerbity and sometimes by wisdom. Following are some notable epigrams:

   We know better the needs of ourselves than of others. To serve onself is economy of administration.

In each human heart are a tiger, a pig, an ass and a nightingale.

Diversity of character is due to their unequal acidity.

There are three sexes; males, females and girls.

Beauty in women and distinction in men are alike in this; they seem to the unthinking a kind of credibility.

Women in love are less ashamed than men. They have less to be ashamed of.

While your friend holds you affectionately by both your hands, you are safe, for you can watch both his.
*Ambrose Bierce*

—A grain of truth in the twinkling of an eye.
*Louis A. Safian*

**Episcopalians** Simply Roman Catholics who vote the straight Republican ticket. *Judge James Garfield Stewart*

**epitaph** A monumental lie. *Arnold H. Glasow*

—An inscription on a tomb, showing that virtues acquired by death have a retroactive effect. *Ambrose Bierce*

—Reading the epitaphs, our only salvation lies in resurrecting the dead and burying the living. *Paul Eldridge*

—A horse with the head of a man.
*Anon., Jr. (British Division)*

**equestrienne** A saddlebag. *Anon.*

**erosion** When the ground suffers from dry scalp. *Anon., Jr.*

**esoteric** Very particularly abstruse and consummately occult. The ancient philosophies were of two kinds—exoteric, those that the philosophers themselves could partly understand, and esoteric, those that nobody could understand. It is the latter that have most profoundly affected modern thought and found greatest acceptance in our time.
*Ambrose Bierce, 1881*

**Esperanto** A journalistic gibberish with plurals in "oj."
*G. K. Chesterton*

—One language no one speaks like a native.

**essensual** What a dictionary is. *Anon., Jr. (British Division)*

**esq.** What you write at the end of a man's name when you forget to put "Mr." at the beginning. *Anon., Jr.*

**Esquimaux** God's frozen people.

**estrich** (Commonly written *ostrich*.) The largest of birds.
*Dr. Sam'l Johnson*

**eternal** Frequent. *George Mikes*

ETERNITY A clock which says "tick" in one century, and
    "tock" in the next.                    *George A. Buttrick*
—A clock without hands.                        *Anon., Jr.*
—A heap of time.                            *Negro spiritual*
ethics Pity.                            *Albert Schweitzer*
ethnick Heathen; pagan; not Jewish; not Christian.
                                    *Dr. Sam'l Johnson*
ethnology The science that treats of the various tribes of
    Man, as robbers, thieves, swindlers, dunces, lunatics, idiots
    and ethnologists.                    *Ambrose Bierce*
etiquette The art of knowing the right way of doing the
    wrong thing.                            *Anon.*
—Red tape in society.
—The noise you make when you sneeze.
                        *Anon., Jr. (British Division)*
eulogy—Praise of a person who has either the advantages
    of wealth and power or the consideration to be dead.
                                    *Ambrose Bierce*
eunuch A conscientious objector in the war between the
    sexes.
euphoria Feeling so good, you are over the weather.
Evangelist A bearer of good tidings, particularly (in a re-
    ligious sense) such as assure us of our own salvation and
    the damnation of our neighbors.        *Ambrose Bierce*
—One who brings the gossip.                    *Anon., Jr.*
Eve The first person who ate herself out of house and home.
                                    *Jack Herbert*
everyman His own ancestor and his own heir. He devises
    his own future and he inherits his own past. *H. F. Hedge*
—An impossibility until he is born.    *Ralph Waldo Emerson*
evitable Avoidable; that may be escaped or shunned.
                                    *Dr. Sam'l Johnson*
evolution A clever trick performed by Darwin, who made
    a monkey of Adam.                    *Robert Jones*
—The pursuit of omnipotence and omniscience. It is the path
    of godhead. A man differs from a microbe only in being
    further on the path.                    *Bernard Shaw*
exaggeration Merely corroborative detail intended to give
    verisimilitude to an otherwise bald or unconvincing narra-
    tive.                    *W. S. Gilbert, The Mikado*
excavate To hollow; to cut into hollows. *Dr. Sam'l Johnson*
exception A thing which takes the liberty to differ from
    other things of its class, as an honest man, a truthful

woman, etc. "The exception proves the rule" is an expression constantly on the lips of the ignorant, who parrot it from one another with never a thought of its absurdity. In the Latin, *"Exceptio probat regulam"* means that the exception tests the rule, puts it to the proof, not confirms it. The malefactor who drew the meaning from this excellent dictum and substituted a contrary one of his own exerted an evil power which appears to be immortal.

*Ambrose Bierce*

**excise** A hateful tax levied upon commodities, and adjudged not by the common judges of property, but wretches hired by those to whom excise is paid. *Dr. Sam'l Johnson*

**excoriate** To take off the hide. *Original Latin meaning*

**execution** When a president kills anyone.

ASSASSINATION When anyone kills a president.

*Bernard Shaw*

**executive** Someone who knows something about everything.

TECHNICIAN Someone who knows everything about some-things.

SWITCHBOARD OPERATOR Someone who knows everything.

*Harold Coffin*

—One who can hit the bull's-eye without shooting the bull.

*Changing Times*

—One who never puts off until tomorrow what he can get someone else to do today. *Ibid.*

—A man who can take two hours for lunch without hindering production. *Anon.*

—A person who follows his work schedule to a tee.

*Chet Michaels*

—A man who brings his secretary along to fill out his job application.

—A man who talks to visitors while the employees get their work done.

—The man who puts murderers to death. *Anon., Jr.*

EXECUTIVE SUITE A sugar daddy. *Playboy*

BORN EXECUTIVE A fellow whose father is the head of the movie studio. *Tom Jenk*

GOOD EXECUTIVE One who never does anything that he can get anybody else to do for him. *Fred C. Kelly*

—A man who believes in sharing the credit with the guy who did the work. *Changing Times*

MODERN EXECUTIVE One who wears out two pairs of pants for every pair of shoes. *Ibid.*

REAL EXECUTIVE  A guy who gets his secretary to do the
   crossword puzzles for him.                    *Jimmy Dean*
SUCCESSFUL EXECUTIVE  Today a man who has an infinite
   capacity for taking planes.                *Changing Times*
—One who can delegate all the responsibility, shift all the
   blame and appropriate all the credit. *Robin Goodfellow*
xile  One who serves his country by residing abroad, yet is
not an ambassador. An English sea captain being asked
if he had read "The Exile of Erin," replied: "No, sir, but
I should like to anchor on it." Years afterwards, when
he had been hanged as a pirate, after a career of un-
paralleled atrocities, the following memorandum was found
in the ship's log that he had kept at the time of his reply:
Aug. 3d, 1842. Made a joke on the ex-Isle of Erin. Coldly
received. War with the whole world!      *Ambrose Bierce*
xistence

   A transient, horrible fantastic dream,
   Wherein is nothing yet all do seem:
   From which we're wakened by a friendly nudge
   Of our bedfellow Death, and cry: "O fudge!"

                                          *Ambrose Bierce*

xpedience  Hitting your wife over the head with your
   mother-in-law.
xpense account  Your wife's story of her trip downtown.
xperience  What you get when you are trying to find some-
   thing else.                                *Changing Times*
—The universal mother of sciences.               *Cervantes*
—The universal father of silence.
—The daughter of time.                       *Russian proverb*
—Knowledge of the effects which follow acts.
                                               *Max Heindel*
—As soon as people are old enough to know better, they
   don't know anything at all.                 *Oscar Wilde*
—By the time a man learns to watch his step, he isn't going
   anywhere.                                    *Max Benoff*
—Knowledge acquired when it's too late.       *Cosmo Sardo*
—The wisdom that enables us to recognize as an undesirable
   old acquaintance the folly that we have already embraced.
—To one who, journeying through night and fog,
   Is mired neck-deep in an unwholesome bog,
   Experience, like the rising of the dawn,
   Reveals the path that he should not have gone.
                                          *Ambrose Bierce*

—What permits you to make the same mistake again without getting caught.                    *Franklin P. Jones*

—What keeps a man who makes the same mistake twice from admitting it the third time around.    *Terry McCormick*

—A school where a man learns what a big fool he has been.
                                                *Josh Billings*

—A good school, but not very strong on vacations.
                                                *Changing Times*

—What makes you wonder how it got a reputation for being the best teacher.                    *Franklin P. Jones*

—A hard teacher. She gives the test first and the lesson afterward.                                        *Spuditems*

—What teaches us that men never learn from experience.
                                                *Bernard Shaw*

—Unwanted knowledge.

**EXPERIENCED MARRIED MAN**  One who can tell when his wife comes to the end of one argument and begins another.                                      *Dan Bennett*

**expert**  One who knows more and more about less and less.
                                        *Nicholas Murray Butler*

—From "ex," a has-been, and "spurt," a drip under pressure.

**EFFICIENCY EXPERT**  A man who spends all day getting out of an hour's work.                          *Dan Bennett*

—A guy who heats the knives to cut down the butter bill.

—A man who says his prayers once a year—and the rest of the year says "Ditto."                        *Anon.*

**EFFICIENCY EXPERTS**
At least those I've known
Can cope with my troubles
But not with their own.                            *Puck*

**FARM EXPERT**  One who knows enough to tell others how to farm but is too smart to try it himself. *Henry C. Byce*

**TURF EXPERT**  A newspaperman who hasn't run out of co signers.                                      *Jimmy Cannon*

**explorer**  A dreamer who goes to the limit of his dreams.
                                    *Paul-Emile Victor, explorer*

—A hobo with an excuse.                            *J. P. McEvoy*

**extinct**  What an animal is, if it doesn't have instinct.
                                                *Anon., Jr*

**extrasensory**  More perceptive of buried misdeeds than you wife is.

**extravagant**  Living beyond your dreams.

**eye**  The light of the body.                    *Matthew, 6:2*

**eyes**  The windows of the body's prison.    *Leonardo*
—Those silent tongues of love.    *Cervantes*

**eyeservant**  A servant that works only while watched.
    *Dr. Sam'l Johnson*

**eye dear**  A thought, and something the opposition is deficient in; e.g., "Our patty is the patty of new eye dears."    *Bostonese*

**eye oar**  An important midwestern state whose people need relief from the fam prawblim.    *Bostonese*

**eyes-grim**  A cold dessert.    *New Yorkese*

# F

**F**  A medieval Roman numeral for forty; in genetics, it is the symbol for filial generation; in chemistry, for fluorine; in mathematics, for function; in physics, for farad. In education, it is a grade meaning failure.
    *Webster's New World Dictionary*

**Fabianism**  The belief that capitalism would come round to socialism, if coaxed.

**fable**  An Aesop story.

**facetious**  An adjective with all of the vowels in alphabetical order.

**facts**  The brute beasts of the intellectual domain.
    *Oliver Wendell Holmes*

**failing**  One of the greatest arts in the world. We must teach the highly educated person . . . how to fail intelligently.
    *Charles F. Kettering*

**fairy tale**  A glamorous lie.
—An interesting lie.
—A well-told lie.
—A well-established lie.
—A playable lie.

**faith**  Belief without evidence in what is told by one who speaks without knowledge, of things without parallel.
    *Ambrose Bierce*
—Believing something you know ain't so.    *Anon.*
—Not worrying.    *John Dewey*

**alderal**  (also falderol, folderol). Meaningless syllables form-

ing the refrain of various old songs—the forerunner o
rock 'n' roll.

**fall** The season when your wife buys new winter clothe
so she'll have something to wear when she goes shoppin
for spring outfits. *Harold Coffi*

**fallout** Atomic dandruff.

**falsies** Twin bluffs. *Leo W. Steine*

—Hidden persuaders. *Playbo*

—Something that conniving women use to pad their expanses
*Shelby Friedma*

**fame** Fame is a figment of a pigment. It comes and goes
It changes with every generation. There were never tw
fames alike. One fame is precious and luminous; anothe
is a bubble of a bauble. *Carl Sandbur*

—A fitful tongue of leaping flame;
A giddy whirlwind's fickle gust
That lifts a pinch of mortal dust. *Oliver Wendell Holme*

—The advantage of being known to those who do not kno
us. *Nicholas Chamfor*

—What someone writes on your tombstone.
*Finley Peter Dunn*

—The sunshine of the dead. *Balza*

—Proof that the people are gullible.
*Ralph Waldo Emerso*

—But a hollow echo. *Sir Walter Raleigh*
*A Farewell to the Vanities of the Worl*

—Putting someone high on a pedestal so you can see hi
clay feet.

**family** A spending unit. *Anon. economis*

—A unit composed not only of children, but of men, women
an occasional animal and the common cold. *Ogden Nas*

—Too often a commonwealth of malignants. *Alexander Pop*

FAMILY TREE A genealogical chart listing the decent an
cestors from whom one has descended.

—A mythological tree.

**famous** Conspicuously miserable. *Ambrose Bierc*

**fan** An instrument used by ladies to move the air and coo
themselves. *Dr. Sam'l Johnso*

—A device or person used for the distribution of hot air.

FANS People who live in an orgy of local religion.
*V. S. Pritchet*

FAN DANCER A hot hoofer with a cooling system.

**fanatic** One who will stick to his guns whether they're
loaded or not. *Franklin P. Jones*

—A fellow with such a large chip on his shoulder that it
makes him lose his balance.                    *Cy N. Peace*

—A man who does what he thinks the Lord would do if He
knew the facts of the case.              *Finley Peter Dunne*

**fancy-free** A fancy way to say: "Playing the field."

**fanfare** The prelude to a disappointment.

**fangle** A fashion, such as old-fangled, gold-fangled, star-
fangled, finger-fangled.

**far cry** Disparity measured in decibels.

**farce** A dramatick representation written without regularity,
and stuffed with wild and ludicrous conceits.

*Dr. Sam'l Johnson*

—A type of play that critics laugh at and then pan.

**farewell appearance** Much adieu about nothing.

**farm** A section of land on which if you get up early enough
mornings and work late enough nights, you'll make money
—if you strike oil.                              *Inklings*

FARMER A man who has a TV set in the privy.

SUCCESSFUL FARMER One who holds the summer stock
company over an extra week in his barn. *Jack Herbert*

FARMER'S DAUGHTER The girl who has met all the rakes.

**farrago** A mixture of cattle food.  *Original Latin meaning*

**fascinate** To bewitch; to enchant; to influence in some
wicked and secret manner.              *Dr. Sam'l Johnson*

**fashion** A despot whom the wise ridicule and obey.

> A king there was who lost an eye
>     In some excess of passion;
> And straight his courtiers all did try
>     To follow the new fashion.
>
> Each dropped one eyelid when before
>     The throne he ventured, thinking
> 'Twould please the king. That monarch swore
>     He'd slay them all for winking.
>
> What should they do? They were not hot
>     To hazard such disaster;
> They dared not close an eye—dared not
>     See better than their master.
>
> Seeing them lacrymose and glum,
>     A leech consoled the weepers;
> He spread small rags with liquid gum
>     And covered half their peepers.

The court all wore the stuff, the flame
  Of royal anger dying
That's how court-plaster got its name
  Unless I'm greatly lying. *Ambrose Bierce*

—Never beautiful, it makes everything that just preceded it
  look ugly. *Françoise Giraud*
—That by which the fantastic becomes for a moment universal. *Oscar Wilde*
—Gentility running away from vulgarity, and afraid of being
  overtaken. *William Hazlitt*
—What a her does to a hem to get a him. *Changing Times*
—A forecast as to what women's dresses will be up to.
—This year's leaves.
  FASHIONS Induced epidemics, proving that epidemics can
  be induced by tradesmen. *Bernard Shaw*
fastidious A person that's fast and hideous. *Anon., Jr.*
fat The density that ends our shapes.
fatalism Being reconciled to your own fatality.
father In today's family a kind of public utility. Instead of
  being head of the house, he has succumbed to the notion
  he must be a "friend" to his son or daughter. But the plain
  fact is that father doesn't need friends of kindergarten age,
  and the kids don't need a middle-age pal. They need a
  father, a man to respect, to imitate and to take orders
  from. They need a man who will inspire them, not just
  "understand" them. It is time to cut the hooey and put Dad
  back at the head of the family, in charge of the minors,
  Momma, money and the mortgage. *Samuel Grafton*
—A fellow who has replaced the currency in his wallet with
  snapshots of his kids. *Mike Forrest*
—A man who won't listen to his children because he remem-
  bers what fools they were when they were babies.
                                          *Bernard Shaw*
—A man who, in praising his son, extols himself.
                                          *Chinese proverb*
—The children's mother's husband. *Margaret Mead*
—The next worse thing to a mother. *Bernard Shaw*
—A thing that is forced to endure childbirth without an
  anesthetic. *Paul Harvey*
—What early to bed and early to rise makes a man.
  FATHER'S DAY Any day on which the family buys nothing.
                                          *Changing Times*

**fatty** One who exceeds the feed limit.

—A calorie-fighter who spends too much time fraternizing with the enemy. *Oren Arnold*

**Fawkes, Guy** An Englishman who was penalized for his drastic attempts at Parliamentary reform.

**fear** A great inventor. *French proverb*

—The long, thin shadow of ignorance. *Arnold H. Glasow*

—The only universal passion. *Bernard Shaw*

**feast** A religious celebration usually signalized by gluttony and drunkenness, frequently in honor of some holy person distinguished for abstemiousness. *Ambrose Bierce*

**February** The birth month of Washington and Lincoln, those great patriots whom the politicians find so handy to wish for and whom they would find so embarrassing to have around. *Bill Vaughan*

**feel** A parcel of ground devoted to sports: "Every night is by him a Feel Day." *New Yorkese*

**felon** A person of greater enterprise than discretion, who in embracing an opportunity has formed an unfortunate attachment. *Ambrose Bierce*

**female** A gimmie pig.

FEMALE COLLECTION AGENTS Great successes, because a woman's dun is never work. *Phil Leslie**

**femme fatale** A gal who can make a bum out of a guy faster than white shoes in winter.

**fest** Quick, as in: "We went to Coney Island for a fest couple hours." *New Yorkese*

**fetish** The other guy's good-luck piece.

**feudal system** If one man killed another, the man in the family of the murdered could kill the murderers. *Anon., Jr.*

**fiacre** A French cab, named after the Hôtel de St. Fiacre in Paris where the first cab-stand stood. St. Fiacre was a seventh-century Irish prince who founded a monastery at Breiul and performed miracles unrelated to finding cabs in the rain.

**fib** A lie that has not cut its teeth. *Ambrose Bierce*

—A prevarication that starts out as a harmless white lie and winds up as a double feature in Technicolor.

**fiddle** To trifle; to shift the hands often, and do nothing, like a fellow that plays upon a fiddle. *Dr. Sam'l Johnson*

—An instrument to tickle human ears by friction of a horse's tail on the entrails of a cat.

To Rome said Nero: "If to smoke you turn

I shall not cease to fiddle while you burn."
To Nero, Rome replied: "Pray do your worst,
'Tis my excuse that you were fiddling first."

*Ambrose Bierce*

**fidelity** A virtue peculiar to those who are about to be betrayed. *Ambrose Bierce*

**fifth column** Macbeth in modern dress.
—Squealduggery.

**fight fan** A man with a television set who wouldn't pay a nickel to attend a fight. *Jimmy Cannon*

**figure skating** The Palmer method on ice. *Jimmy Cannon*

**filing cabinet** A place where you can lose things systematically. *T. Harry Thompson*

**film festival** An ocular orgy based on the mistaken notion that the cinema is not a grubby business.

**final decision** The one you arrive at before your spouse decides.

**finance** The art or science of managing revenues and resources for the best advantage of the manager. The pronunciation of this word with the i long and the accent on the first syllable is one of America's most precious discoveries and possessions. *Ambrose Bierce*

FINANCIAL WORRIES What distinguishes man from animals.
*Jules Renard*

FINANCIER A pawnbroker with imagination.
*Arthur Wing Pinero*

**fine** A tax you have to pay for doing wrong.

TAX A fine you have to pay for doing okay.
*Lowell Nussbaum*

**finesse** Artifice; stratagem; an unnecessary word which is creeping into the language. *Dr. Sam'l Johnson*

**fingers** Basic computers (see Toes). *Robert Levinson*

**fink** A cowboy who kisses.
—Someone who turns in an alarm when the school is on fire.
*Mad Magazine*

**fireman** A man of violent passions. *Dr. Sam'l Johnson*

**fiscal** If it's under a million, it's money; if it's over a million, it's fiscal. And if it's over a billion, it's a deficit.
*Wall Street Journal*

**fish** An animal that inhabits the water. *Dr. Sam'l Johnson*

FISHERMAN A fellow who thinks nothing of spending $10 a pound for fish. *Vesta M. Kelly*

FISHIFY To turn to fish: a cant word. *Dr. Sam'l Johnson*

—Here comes Romeo
   Without his roe, like a dried herring;
   O flesh, flesh, how art thou *fishified!*

                         Shakespeare, *Romeo and Juliet*

FISHING  A sport that consists of lying about and later
   lying about it.

—The art of dunking worms.

fit  More than one foot.                    *New Yorkese*

5 & 10 cent store  A mercantile enterprise which now carries tools powerful enough to open its safe.

5:30 p.m.  What it would be if all the autos in town were
   placed end to end.

flam  To deceive with a lye. Merely cant. *Dr. Sam'l Johnson*

Flanders, Moll  The story of a Belgian gun-girl.  *Anon., Jr.*

flattergasted  The sensation of being astounded by admiration.                                       *Newords*

flattery  Like cologne water, to be smelt of, not swallowed.
                                             *Josh Billings*

—The applause that refreshes.

—The food of fools.                       *Jonathan Swift*

—It rarely enlarges
   My head, but flattery
   Surely recharges
   My ego's battery!        *Georgie Starbuck Galbraith*

—Warming yourself by an artificial fireplace.

—The infantry of negotiation.            *Lord Chandos*

flaw  What you spread a cap-it on; i.e., "I made a speech
   from the flaw of the Senate."             *Bostonese*

flesh  Grass.                              *The Bible*

FLESHQUAKE  A tremor of the body; a word formed by
   Jonson in imitation of earthquake.  *Dr. Sam'l Johnson*

flight  The only victory over love.       *French proverb*

flipp  (A cant word.) A liquor much used in ships, made by
   mixing beer with spirits and sugar.  *Dr. Sam'l Johnson*

flirt  A girl who doesn't see what she wants but is asking
   for it.

FLIRTATION  Paying attention without intention.
                                         *J. Réne Mazer*

FLIRTING  The gentle art of making a man feel pleased
   with himself.                         *Helen Rowland*

flogging  A form of debauchery.           *Bernard Shaw*

florid  Productive of flowers; covered with flowers.
                                       *Dr. Sam'l Johnson*

**Florida** A place you go for the winter—and by God, that's where you usually find it. *Anon. Californian*

**florists** Petal pushers.

**flow** A place where you put a ruck or a coppet. *New Yorkese*

**flower girl** One who has not yet been through the mill.

**flowers** The sweetest things that God ever made and forgot to put a soul into. *Henry Ward Beecher*

—The reproductive organs of the plants they grow on.
*Logan Pearsall Smith*

**fluorescent lighting** A ghastly type of illumination which makes everyone look like he is having a hangover.

**flying buttress** A lady butler on airplanes. *Anon., Jr.*

**fog** Rain that is barely mist.

**folk listeners** That which there are fewer of than folk singers.
*Theodore Bickel*

FOLK SINGERS Rich college kids who get together and sing about poverty. *Mary Wells*

FOLK MUSIC Man, I don't know any kind of music but folk music. I ain't never heard a hoss sing a song.
*Louis Armstrong*

**folly** Anger without power. *German proverb*

—Worth whatever you pay for it. *George Ade*

**fondle** Permissible molesting.

**fool** The first sheep through the fence.

—Someone who has been found out.

—One more endurable than half a fool. *Arabic proverb*

—Someone more dangerous than a rogue. *Bernard Shaw*

**foot** A portable pedestal.

**football** Where you watch the figures on sweaters, instead of in them. *Arnold H. Glasow*

—A game where the spectators have four quarters in which to kill a fifth. *Earl Wilson*

**Ford, Henry** The inventor of perpetual motion. *Anon., Jr.*

**foreclosure** A fate worse than debt.

**foreign cars** The ones that have odd shapes before your wife drives them. *Arthur Maisel's press agents*

**Foreign Office (London)** A cross between a Renaissance palace and a Turkish bath. *V. S. Pritchett*

**foreign policy** A synthesis of conflicting interests played by ear. *Dr. Harry Bretton, Professor of Political Science, University of Michigan*

**forever** In a love affair, today, and possibly tomorrow.

**forger** A fellow who writes things you can't bank on.
*Walt Streightiff*

**forgetfulness**  A gift of God bestowed upon debtors in compensation for their destitution of conscience.
*Ambrose Bierce*

**forget-us-not**  The plural of forget-me-not.  *Anon., Jr.*

**forgiveness**  The noblest revenge.  *Salada Tea*

—The secret of forgiving everything is to understand nothing.
*Bernard Shaw*

**fork**  An instrument used chiefly for the purpose of putting dead animals into the mouth. Formerly the knife was employed for this purpose, and by many worthy persons is still thought to have many advantages over the other tool, which, however, they do not altogether reject, but use to assist in loading the knife.  *Ambrose Bierce*

**form**  What makes bookmakers rich.  *Jimmy Cannon*

**formal**  A term that no longer means white tie, or even black tie. Just tie.  *Bill Vaughan*

**fortune**  The way the Chinese cookie crumbles.

FORTUNETELLER  One who cheats common people by pretending to the knowledge of futurity. *Dr. Sam'l Johnson*

**foul play**  One that closes quickly.

**four**  That trying age when a boy can't go from the living room to the dining room without getting on his tricycle.
*Changing Times*

**four-piece dress**  If you remove the bodice, you have a playsuit. If you remove the skirt, you have a sunsuit. If you remove anything else, you have a lawsuit. *Anon. salesgirl*

**4:00 p.m.**  The hour at which a wedding breakfast is normally served.  *Balzac*

**fox**  A wolf who gives mink.

—All tail, as women are all tongue.  *Italian proverb*

**France**  Ambiguity enveloped by ambivalence wrapped in an artichoke.  *Joseph Barry*

—De Gaulle's little acre.  *Joseph Barry*

—Long a despotism tempered by epigrams.  *Carlyle*

—The first day we are infatuated, the second we criticize, the third we are indifferent.  *La Harpe*

**Francescatti, Zino**  A good violinist, though when it comes to playing jazz, no Ziggy Elman—but then, neither is Mischa.

**Franklin, Benjamin**  A writer who expounded the saving of the penny and got his bust on the half dollar.

—The man who discovered the electricity in Washington was D.C. instead of A.C.  *Anon., Jr.*

**Franz Joseph I** The last emperor who ruled Austria-Hungary with despotism tempered by inefficiency.    *Anon.*

**free** The price is concealed.

   FREE DELIVERY The errand boy lives on his tips.

   FREEBOOTER A conqueror in a small way of business whose annexations lack the sanctifying merit of magnitude.    *Ambrose Bierce*

   FREE SOCIETY A society where it is safe to be unpopular.    *Adlai Stevenson*

   FREE SPEECH Long-distance phone calls on other people's phones.

   FREE VERSE The triumph of mind over meter.
           *Anon. poet*

   FREE-LANCER A rolling stone who gathers no boss.

**French** Wiser than they seem.

   SPANIARDS Seem wiser than they are.    *Francis Bacon*

   FRENCH GOVERNMENT An absolute monarchy moderated by popular songs.    *Nicholas Chamfort* (1741–94)

**friend** A speaking acquaintance who also listens.
           *Arnold H. Glasow*

—He is a fine friend. He stabs you in the front.

—A friend in need is not a friend, indeed; he is merely a borrower.    *Schopenhauer*

—A second self.    *Cicero*

—A father's a treasure; a brother's a comfort; a friend is both.    *Benjamin Franklin*

—One who laughs at your stories even if they aren't very good and sympathizes with your troubles even when they aren't so bad.    *Changing Times*

—Come to think of it, that's a good definition for "wife," too.

   FRIENDS He had friends, choosing them as one chooses pieces of furniture for one's house.    *Saint-Simon*

   FRIENDLESS Having no favors to bestow. Destitute of fortune. Addicted to utterance of truth and common sense.    *Ambrose Bierce*

   FRIENDSHIP The relationship some women accept with men they'd rather knot.    *Safe Worker*

—A ship big enough to carry two in fair weather, but only one in foul.

> The sea was calm and the sky was blue;
> Merrily, merrily sailed we two.
>     (High barometer maketh glad.)

On the tipsy ship, with a dreadful shout,
The tempest descended and we fell out.
    (O the walking is nasty bad!)     *Ambrose Bierce*

—A compact by which we undertake to do someone small
favors in expectation of receiving big favors.
               *Montesquieu*

**fright**    Cooked in hot oil; e.g., "One udder fright potatoes."
               *New Yorkese*

FRIGHTFUL    A cant word among women for any thing
unpleasing.            *Dr. Sam'l Johnson*

**frock**    A tailless amphibian. "The frock's lakes are nice tonight."                  *New Yorkese*

**frog**    A wet toad.

—A reptile with edible legs.        *Ambrose Bierce*

**front tea ah**    A border; e.g., "The nation faces a New Front
tea ah."                *Bostonese*

**frumious**    Furiously fuming.       *Lewis Carroll*

**frump**    A female dump.

**frustrate**    Frustrate a German and he will shoot you; frustrate a Dane and he will shoot himself. A frustrated Frenchman will drink himself into the grave, an Englishman will
die of an ulcer, and an Irishman of hypertension.
               *Nora Ephron*

**FUBB**    Fouled Up Beyond Belief.      *Pentagonese*

**fugue**    What you get in a room full of people when all the
windows and doors are shut.    *Anon., Jr. (British Division)*

**fumble**    Shaking the bottle when you've already taken the
medicine.

RECOVERY    Shaking yourself, instead.

**fun**    (A low cant word.) Sport; high merriment; frolicksome
delight.             *Dr. Sam'l Johnson*

**fund**    Lightly loving, as: "I'm fund of the whole family."
               *New Yorkese*

**funeral**    A pageant whereby we attest our respect for the
dead by enriching the undertaker.    *Ambrose Bierce*

**furbelow**    A vacation for soldiers.      *Anon., Jr.*

**furies**    Three fearful maidens, Allecto, Megaera and Tisi-
phone whose purpose was to punish men for such crimes
as perjury, murder and lack of hospitality.
           *Cecil Hunt, Word Origins*

**Furness, Betty**    The one thing that both major political parties have in common every four years.    *Changing Times*

**furniture**  The stuff between the carpet and the ceiling that does not move.                    *Robert Paul Smith*

**furthermore**  Much farther than further.            *Anon., Jr.*

**future**  That period of time in which our affairs prosper, our friends are true and our happiness is assured.

*Ambrose Bierce*

—An empty-handed ghost that promises all things and has nothing.                              *Victor Hugo*

—Something everyone reaches at the rate of sixty minutes an hour, whatever he does, whoever he is.      *C. S. Lewis*

# G

**gad**  A protector. Also in the sense of the Republican Old Gad.                                *Bostonese*

**gain**  In football, what happens when two halves make a hole.

**gaiter**  Many above-hay dinner is gaitered.    *New Yorkese*

**gallows**  A stage for the performance of miracle plays, in which the leading actor is translated to heaven.

*Ambrose Bierce*

**galumph**  To go galloping in triumph.        *Lewis Carroll*

**gambler**  (A cant word, I suppose, for *game* or *gamester*.) A knave whose practice it is to invite the unwary to game and cheat them.                    *Dr. Sam'l Johnson*

—A term erroneously applied to operators of sure-thing games in which the house odds preclude any gambling by the house.

GAMBLING  Any wagering on haphazard chance. A term erroneously used to describe the activity of losers at numbers, bookmaking and Las Vegas.

**games**  Diversion for people who can neither read nor think.

*Bernard Shaw*

**gang**  A number herding together; a troop, a company; a tribe; a herd. It is seldom used but in contempt or abhorrence.                            *Dr. Sam'l Johnson*

**Ganymede**  A busboy for the gods.

**gaol** A prison; a place of confinement. It is always pronounced and too often written jail, and sometimes, goal.
*Dr. Sam'l Johnson*

**garage** A storage place for cars where there is always room for one mower.      *Woodmen of the World Magazine*

GARAGE MECHANIC A professional who views with alarm, so he can point with pride—just like a doctor or a politician.      *Robert F. Jacobus*

**garbage** Food for thought.

GARBAGE CAN An after-dinner pail.

**Garbo, Greta** Every man's harmless fantasy mistress . . . If your imagination has to sin, it can at least congratulate itself on its impeccable taste.      *Alistair Cooke*

—What when drunk, one sees in other women, one sees in Garbo sober.      *Kenneth Tynan*

**gardener** A worker who goes from daybreak to backbreak.

—Love of flowers and vegetables is not enough to make a man a good gardener. He must also hate weeds.
*Eugene P. Bertin*

—Don't throw away your empty seed packages. They are often just the right size for storing your crop.
Graham (Tex.) Rotary Club *Scandal Sheet*

**gardening** Callousthenics.      *Gerald Jacobson*

**gargle** Hoarse liniment.      *Edward Nietupski*

**gargoyle** A rain-spout projecting from the eaves of mediaeval buildings, commonly fashioned into a grotesque caricature of some personal enemy of the architect or owner of the building.      *Ambrose Bierce*

**garlickeater** A mean fellow.      *Dr. Sam'l Johnson*

**garter** An elastic band intended to keep a woman from coming out of her stockings and desolating the country.
*Ambrose Bierce*

**gastric juices** The imagination of the stomach.

**De Gaullism** Pétainism minus Nazism.

**gavel** A hammer to silence hemmers and hawers.

**gay-yet** Opening in a faince.      *Charlestonese*

**gee-gee** A horse. Remember?

**geese** A low heavy bird which is most meat and feathers. Geese can't sing much on account of the dampness of the water. He ain't got no between-his-toes and he's got a little balloon in his stummick to keep him from sinking. Some geese when they are big has curls on their tails and is called ganders. Ganders don't have to sit and hatch, but just eat and loaf around and go swimming. If I was a goose, I'd rather be a gander. *Anon., Jr.*

**gelding** A stallion who had his tonsils taken out so he would have more time to himself. *Anon., Jr.*

**genealogy** Tracing yourself back to people better than you are. *John Garland Pollard*

**General Custer** To put it mildly, this was an odd ball.
*James Warner Bellah*

**generation** All the people who were born at approximately the same time, wear approximately the same type of clothes and do exactly the same stupid things.
*Schweizer Illustrierte*

—The period between the time when a town tears down a historic landmark and the time when it has a fund-raising to build an authentic reproduction of it. *Bill Vaughan*

**generosity** The ability to accept ingratitude. *G. Martin*

GENEROUS Not of mean birth; of good extraction.
*Dr. Sam'l Johnson*

**genial** That which contributes to propagation.
*Dr. Sam'l Johnson*

—Creator Venus, *genial* pow'r of love,
The bliss of men below and gods above! *Dryden, Fables*

**genius** Mainly an affair of energy. *Matthew Arnold*

—It is patience. *Buffon*

—An infinite capacity for taking pains. *Jane Ellice Hopkins*

—One per cent inspiration and ninety-nine per cent perspiration. *Thomas A. Edison*

—Talk not of genius baffled.
Genius is master of man.
Genius does what it must,
And Talent does what it can.

Owen Meredith, *Last Words of a Sensitive
Second-Rate Poet*

—A man who can figure his own income tax.
*Cynic's Cyclopaedia*

—A perception of the obvious which nobody else sees. *Anon.*

—A man who solves a problem you didn't realize you had in a manner you can't understand. *F. G. Kernan*

—A fellow who gets into trouble; then some moron comes along and gets blamed. *Anon., Jr.*

—An artist who is worth more dead than alive.

—The ability to evade drudgery by doing something right the first time it has to be done.

—A masculine quality, just as a beard is or strong muscles are.                                    *Elie Metchnikoff*

FINANCIAL GENIUS   A man who can pay his family's Christmas bill in January.                                    *Nuggets*

gentility   A sieve without holes for delicate ladies who don't want to strain themselves.

gentle   A lovely word until they began using it on radio to describe the action of laxatives.                                    *William Feather*

gentleman   One who refuses to make an issue out of every difference of opinion.                                    *Arnold H. Glasow*

—A man who leaves the lawn mower where his wife can find it.                                    *Puck*

—A man who holds the door open so his wife can carry in $25 worth of groceries in two small sacks.                                    *Anon.*

—One who never strikes a woman without provocation.
                                    *H. L. Mencken*

—A wolf with his ears pinned back.                                    *Leon Aikman*

GENTLEMEN'S AGREEMENT   A deal that neither party cares to put in writing.                                    *Changing Times*

GENTLEMAN FARMER   One whose house looks as good as his barn.                                    *Ibid.*

—One who tips his hat every time he passes a likely looking tomato.                                    *G. Norman Collie*

geologist   A scientist who won't take Noah for an answer.

GEOLOGY   A very important part of geography because without geology, geography would have no place to put itself.                                    *Anon., Jr.*

German   One, a mad scientist; two, a beer parlor; three, a war.                                    *Jerome Lawrence**

germs   Sort of small insecks that swim in you when they can get in. Some are called measles but you can't see them.
                                    *Anon., Jr. (British Division)*

gesundheit!   The new scientific answer to the common cold.
                                    *Anon. doctor*

get well card   What to send a Texan looking for oil.

geyser   A hole in the ground that burps.

gherkin   A native who runs after people with a knife.
                                    *Anon., Jr.*

ghost writer   One a speaker hires when the spirit doesn't move him.

GHOST WRITERS   Spooksmen.                                    *Josephine Hemphill*

Gibson   A grey flannel Martini.                                    *Jim Backus*

**gift shop** A place where they sell things you wouldn't have as a gift.

PERFECT GIFT For a woman, something she can exchange the very next day. *North Vernon (Ind.) Sun*

**gigolo** A fee-male. *Isaac Goldberg*

**gilt** Feeling bad about stealing gold. *Anon., Jr.*

**gimcrack** (Supposed by Skinner to be ludicrously formed from *gin*, derived from *engine*.) A slight or trivial mechanism. *Dr. Sam'l Johnson*

**gimmick** Something you look for while you ignore the main point.

**ginger ale** A drink that tastes like bees sound. *Diana Meyers*

**giraffes** A rich source of necks.

*Anon., Jr., overheard by Art Linkletter*

**girdle** The difference between facts and figures.

*Rotary Spoke*

—What women use to keep their figures down.

*Changing Times*

—Figures may not lie, but they sometimes push the truth a little out of position. *Morrie Gallant*

—Reinforcements for the battle of the bulge.

—A waist basket. *Pete Stickney*

**girl, smart** One who can hold a man at arm's length without losing her grip on him. *Anon.*

**girl sprinter** One who enjoys a run in her stockings.

**girls** Like newspapers. They have great forms; they always have the last word; back numbers are not in demand; you can't believe everything they say; they are thinner than they used to be. And, finally, every man should have his own and not try to borrow his neighbor's. *Bill Dufty*

—All it takes to separate the men from the boys. *Playboy*

—What women over forty call each other. *Charley Jones*

**give** A word for which a miser has so great an aversion that he never says, "I give you good day," but, "I lend you good day." *Molière, L'Avare*

**glacier** A man who goes along the street putting glass in windows. *Anon., Jr.*

**glamor** When a man knows a woman is a woman.

*Gina Lollobrigida*

—That certain indefinable something about a girl who has a large bosom. *Abe Burrows*

GLAMOR GIRL One whose clothes fit her as if they appreciated the opportunity. *John Evans*

—One who is able to get more out of a dress than she puts in. *Ray Fine*

—One who hasn't much upstairs, but gad what a stairway! *Clubhouse Quotes*

GLAMOROUS All you have to do is stand still and look stupid.

glee Joy; merriment; gayety. It anciently signified musick played at feasts. It is not now used, except in ludicrous writing, or with some mixture of irony and contempt. *Dr. Sam'l Johnson*

glutton A person who escapes the evils of moderation by committing indigestion. *Ambrose Bierce*

goatee A bored beard. *Carol Weld*

God The John Doe of philosophy and religion. *Elbert Hubbard*

—Someone who is not primarily interested in religion. *Anon.*

—But a word invoked to explain the world. *Lamartine*

—The caterer of the little birds of the field. *Cervantes*

—Simply the word that comes next to "gocart" to the lexicographer. *Samuel Butler*

HONEST GOD The noblest work of man. *Robert Green Ingersoll*

Goethe The wandering Aryan. *Paul West*

gold The most useless thing in the world. *Henry Ford*

golddigger A gal who likes to go places and sue things. *Frank Kane*

golden rule Give unto others the advice you can't use yourself. *Anon.*

golf A sport for liars, drinkers and cussers who like to walk two or three miles belaboring an object 1/45th their size with a loaded cane.

—What men do to relax when they are too tired to mow the lawn. *Vesta M. Kelly*

—A form of work made expensive enough for rich men to enjoy. It is physical and mental exertion made attractive by the fact that you have to dress for it in a $200,000 clubhouse. Golf is what letter-carrying, ditch-digging and carpet-beating would be if these tasks could be performed on the same hot afternoon in short pants and colored socks by gouty-looking gentlemen who required a different implement for every mood. Golf is the simplest-looking game in the world when you decide to take it up, and the toughest, after you've been at it for a dozen years. *Essex Golf and Country Club News*

—A lot of walking, broken up by disappointment and bad arithmetic. *Earl Wilson*

—A sport that keeps you on the green, in the pink and in the red.

GOLFER A gardener digging up someone else's lawn. *Changing Times*

GOLF BAG An elderly female golfer.

*Fred Beck, 89 Years in a Sand Trap*

good clean fun A couple taking a bath together. *Playboy*

good company One who can kill an evening by keeping it alive. *Changing Times*

good driver One who can wear his automobile out without any assistance from other drivers. *Ibid.*

good manners Being able to put up pleasantly with bad ones. *Changing Times*

good neighbor policy Thou shalt not bear faults witness.

*Imogene Fry*

good old days When policemen didn't hide at the side of a busy road, but took their chances in traffic like anyone else. *Terry McCormick*

—When kids used to cut classes instead of teachers!

*Mike Connolly*

—Those when one's chief thought was of the years that lay ahead. *Changing Times*

—When you got the landlord to fix anything by just threatening to move. *F. G. Kernan*

—The time when inflation was just something you did to a balloon. *Anon.*

—When you kissed a girl and all you tasted was girl.

—When the political campaign speeches reached you a week later.

—A time so long ago that you've forgotten how awful it was. *Changing Times*

good-bye The most difficult thing for some people to say in twenty-five words or less. *Tony Pettito*

Good-Will Industries Carpet beggers.

goose A large waterfowl proverbially noted, I know not why, for foolishness. *Dr. Sam'l Johnson*

gooseberry A sour grape.

Gorki, Maxim Hemingway with heartburn. *Time*

gossip An ill wind that blows nobody good.

—The art of saying nothing in a way that leaves practically nothing unsaid. *Walter Winchell*

—What you hear.

  NEWS  What you tell.

—What no one claims to like—but everybody enjoys.

*Joseph Conrad*

—Gossip always travels faster over grapevines that are slightly sour.                                                        *Brushware*

—A person who creates the smoke in which other people assume there's fire.                                    *Dan Revello*

—One who can't leave bad enough alone.

—A person who turns an earful into a mouthful.

*Cy N. Peace*

—A person who can make a mountain out of a little dirt.

*Changing Times*

**gourmandism**  The belief that the seat of emotion is in the liver.

  ALCOHOLISM  The belief that the seat of emotion is in the kidneys.

  GOURMET  A guy who carefully ages and seasons a steak before putting it on his black eye.                          *Anon.*

—An eater who avoids unfashionable restaurants because he doesn't want to gain weight in the wrong places.

*Journeyman Barber*

**government**  An art consisting in taking as much money as possible from one class of citizens to give to the other.

*Voltaire*

  GOVERNMENT BOND  A scheme to get back some of the dough you paid in taxes.

  SOUND GOVERNMENT  To the Republicans it is the kind of government where the President makes nice sounds while the Vice President snarls.        *Harry S Truman*

**gown, evening**  An alleged dress named after Eve, who didn't wear anything, either.

*Paul and Helen Martin Denis**

**grabity**  The Earth's pull.                    *Ann Nicholas*

**gracious living**  In describing a new high-rent apartment, means "no children allowed."                      *Dan Kidney*

**grandchildren**  The ones who seem to get the most out of middle age.                                        *Pep Mealiffe*

**gratitude**  The most exquisite form of courtesy.

*Jacques Maritain*

—The feeling one has that one can get more from the same source.                                        *Ivar Kreuger*

—A word only imbeciles use; you find it in the dictionary, but not in the human heart. *Balzac*

grave A place in which the dead are laid to await the coming of the medical student. *Ambrose Bierce, 1881*

gravity What you get when you eat too much and too fast. *Anon., Jr.*

—That which if there were none, we should all fly away. *Anon., Jr. (British Division)*

great-fruit A low-calorie eyewash. *New Yorkese*

Greece A land of no secrets but many mysteries. *C. L. Sulzberger*

Green Giant A swollen leprechaun.

green persimmons A rich source of indigestion. *Anon., Jr.*

green thumb A physical condition which is usually accompanied by black and blue knees.

grey The color of truth. *André Gide*

grindstone Father's birthstone.

groan Increasing in size. *Charlestonese*

gross injustice One hundred forty-four times as bad as plain injustice.

growing pains An affliction of middle-aged gardeners. *Frances Rodman*

growing up The period spent in learning that bad manners are tolerated only in grownups. *Changing Times*

grubstreet Originally the name of a street in Moorfields in London, much inhabited by writers of small histories, dictionaries, and temporary poems; whence any mean production is called grubstreet. *Dr. Sam'l Johnson*

gruesome A little bit taller. *Junior Scholastic*

guano The product of manurous birds. *Anon., Jr. (British Division)*

guest towel A piece of lint entirely surrounded by waterproof embroidery.

—The only place most of us make our mark in the world.

—Something else untouched by human hands.

—What guests stand in front of and look at while they wait for the air to dry their hands. *Changing Times*

—A towel stolen while you were a guest at a hotel. *Anon., Jr.*

Guggenheim Museum A monster, a jewel, a flash of light, a descent into darkness. *William Feather*

—Short of insisting that no pictures at all be shown, Wright could not have gone much farther to create a structure

sublime in its own right but ridiculous as a museum of
art.                                              *Lewis Mumford*
—A reject from Disneyland.                    *Caskie Stinnett*
**guide**  A guy who knows where to find whiskey in the jungle.
                                                   *John Wayne*

**gun**  A thing it's impolite to point with.
—A machine for throwing balls.            *Oliver Winchester*
**gusting**  Enjoying, reveling in.                   *Newords*
**gymnasium**  To exercise naked.     *Original Greek meaning*

# H

**habille**  The dress of a strip-tease artist when she starts to
work.                                              *Newords*
**habit**  A shackle for the free.            *Ambrose Bierce*
—A shirt that we wear until we die.          *Russian proverb*
  HABITS  About the only servants that will work for you
  for nothing. Just get them established and they will operate even though you are going around in a trance.
                                               *Frederic Whitaker*
**hacienda**  A Spanish house, not necessarily a home.
                                                   *Fred Beck*
  HALF-HACIENDA  One half of a Spanish duplex. *Fred Beck*
**hag**  An elderly lady whom you do not happen to like.
                                               *Ambrose Bierce*
**hail**  The abode of integrationists, some damyankees and
other evil spirits.                            *Charlestonese*
**hair**  The current status symbol, long for boys, short for
girls, any for older men.
**Halloween**  The night when pumpkins are thrown through
the front window.
**halo**  Properly a luminous ring encircling an astronomical
body, but not infrequently confounded with "aureola," or
"nimbus," a somewhat similar phenomenon worn as a
headdress by divinities and saints. The halo is a purely
optical illusion, produced by moisture in the air, in the
manner of a rainbow; but the aureola is conferred as a sign
of superior sanctity, in the same way as a bishop's mitre,

or the Pope's tiara. In the painting of the Nativity, by Szedgkin, a pious artist of Pesth, not only do the Virgin and the Child wear the nimbus, but an ass nibbling hay from the sacred manger is similarly decorated and, to his lasting honor be it said, appears to bear his unaccustomed dignity with a truly saintly grace. *Ambrose Bierce*

**ham** Injury, hurt, e.g., "The opposition patty has done the nation great ham." *Bostonese*
—Another actor.

**hamburger** A food on which you could live for a week during a depression if you were broke, but now, if you lived on it for a week, you'd be broke.

**"Hamlet"** Among Shakespeare's plays, though rather less bawdy than *Othello,* much bawdier than *Macbeth* and approximately as bawdy as *King Lear.* *Eric Partridge*
—A play about a man who couldn't make up his mind. *Anon.*
—The tragedy of tackling a family problem too soon after college. *Tom Masson*

**Hamlet** A hoop through which every eminent actor must, sooner or later, jump. The eminent actor may not have any natural impulse to jump through it, but that does not matter. However unsuited to the part he may be in temperament or physique, his position necessitates that he play it.
*Max Beerbohm*

**hand** A singular instrument worn at the end of a human arm and commonly thrust into somebody's pocket.
*Ambrose Bierce*

**handicapper** A tout with press credentials. *Jimmy Cannon*
—A pauper who creates horseplayers in his own image.
*Jimmy Cannon*

**handerchief** A small square of silk or linen, used in various ignoble offices about the face and especially serviceable at funerals to conceal the lack of tears. The handkerchief is of recent invention; our ancestors knew nothing of it and intrusted its duties to the sleeve. Shakespeare's introducing it into the play of "Othello" is an anachronism: Desdemona dried her nose with her skirt, as Dr. Mary Walker and other reformers have done with their coattails in our own day—an evidence that revolutions sometimes go backward.
*Ambrose Bierce*

**hangover** The wrath of grapes. *Playboy*
—When you don't want to leave your room because you think your head won't fit through the door. *Milton Herman*

**happify**  To make yourself, and therefore others, joyous.
*Newords*

**happily married couple**  A husband out with another man's wife.　　*Playboy*

**happiness**  A good bank account, a good cook, and a good digestion.　　*Jean Jacques Rousseau*

—The sum total of misfortunes avoided.　　*Alphonse Karr*

—A state of mind caused by a release of tension. *Anon. doctor*

—Not something you search for like a collar button that has rolled under the radiator.　　*Dr. W. Beran Wolfe*

—The perpetual possession of being well deceived.
*Jonathan Swift*

—The most tedious thing in the world to me. Should I be what I am if I cared for happiness?
*Napoleon in The Man of Destiny, by Bernard Shaw*

—Watching TV at your girl's house during a power failure.
*Some of Bob Hope's less happy writers*

—An agreeable sensation arising from contemplating the misery of another.　　*Ambrose Bierce*

—Like potato salad—share it, and you have a picnic.
*Sam N. Hampton*

—The estate of an idiot.　　*Harry Ruby*

—The only thing one should ever be resigned to. *Alfred Capas*

—The art of forgetting the things you can't have.

—The absence of pain.　　*Schopenhauer*

—And being aware of it.

—To open the window and let a wasp out. *Chinese writer*

—The three great essentials are something to do, something to love, and something to hope for.　　*Puck*

—A pawnticket which you have to redeem by suffering.
*Paul Tabori*

—The great secret is never to suffer your energies to stagnate. The old adage of "too many irons in the fire" conveys an abominable lie. You cannot have too many; poker, tongs, and all—keep them all going.　　*Adam Clarke*

**harbor**  A place where ships taking shelter from storms are exposed to the fury of the customs.　　*Ambrose Bierce*

**hard times**  When hitchhikers are willing to go either way.
*Industrial Press Service*

—When they come, a Frenchman changes his government, an Englishman votes new taxes, the Russian switches his propaganda line, but an American just trades in his old car on a new model.　　*Harold Coffin*

**harms** (1) The upper limbs, also known as four-harms. (2) Weapons. Example: "Two harms! Two harms!"
*New Yorkese*

**harness racing** Horse and buggy bingo. *Jerry Mitchell*

**harp** Steinway in the nude. *Louise H. Kunkel*

—A piano after taxes. *Tom O. Horgan*

**harpy** A virgin from the waist up. *Anon., Jr.*

**hash** The connecting link between the animal and vegetable kingdoms. *Anon., Jr.*

**hatchet** A young axe, known among Indians as a Thomashawk.

"O bury the hatchet, irascible Red,
For peace is a blessing," the White Man said.
The Savage concurred, and that weapon interred,
With imposing rites, in the White Man's head.
*Ambrose Bierce*

HATCHET-FACE An ugly face; such, I suppose, as might be hewn out of a block by a hatchet. *Dr. Sam'l Johnson*

**hate** The number between seven and nine. *New Yorkese*

—The other day, by a little lake,
——— ———[1] was bit by a snake.
What was the sequel? Needless to say,
The snake, not ———, passed away. *Voltaire*

HATRED An emotion so durable and obstinate that reconciliation on a sickbed is the surest sign of death.
*La Bruyère*

**hattie** Vigorous; e.g., "I got a hattie loff from the platform of the opposition patty." *Bostonese*

**have id** A university across the Charles River from Boston.
*Ann Ronell\**

**Hawaiian Islands** The loveliest fleet of islands that lies anchored in any ocean. *Mark Twain*

**hay** Something it is smart to make between the time you crawl out of it and the time you hit it again. *June Collier*

**H-bomb** The invention to end all inventions. *Robert Orben*

**head** Something hair today and gone tomorrow. *Anon.*

HEAD OF THE FAMILY The one who can spend five dollars without explaining it to the rest. *Changing Times*

SWELLED HEAD The vulgar ailment that afflicts only those whose minds are so preoccupied with the few things they know that there is no room left for the innumerable things they don't know. *Bernard Shaw*

[1] Fill in name of your favorite enemy.

**head cold**   Rheum at the top.      *Jerome Beatty, Jr.*

**headsman**   An official who parts your hair with an axe.

**headwaiter**   One guy who makes a successful career out of putting other people in their places.    *Changing Times*

**hearsay**   Eavesdroppings you can repeat in court.

**hearse**   Death's baby carriage.      *Ambrose Bierce*

**heart**   An automatic, muscular blood pump. Figuratively, this useful organ is said to be the seat of emotions and sentiments—a very pretty fancy which, however, is nothing but a survival of a once universal belief. It is now known that the sentiments and emotions reside in the stomach, being evolved from food by chemical action of the gastric fluid. The exact process by which a beefsteak becomes a feeling—tender or not, according to the age of the animal from which it was cut; the successive stages of elaboration through which a caviar sandwich is transmuted to a quaint fancy and reappears as a pungent epigram; the marvelous functional methods of converting a hard-boiled egg into religious contrition, or a creampuff into a sigh of sensibility —these things have been patiently ascertained by M. Pasteur, and by him expounded with convincing lucidity.

     *Ambrose Bierce*

BROKEN HEART   A very pleasant complaint for a man in London if he has a comfortable income. *Bernard Shaw*

HEARTBREAK   The end of happiness and the beginning of peace.      *Bernard Shaw*

**heat**   One of the more useful by-products of fire.

     *Anon., Jr. (Art Linkletter Dept.)*

**heathen**   A benighted creature who has the folly to worship something that he can see and feel.    *Ambrose Bierce*

**heaven**   Eating *pâté de foie gras* to the sound of trumpets.

     *Sydney Smith*

—Christmas morning for ever and ever.

—The dull monotony of forever arranged for those who denied themselves heaven on earth.

**heavyweight contender**   Any pug with a license who weighs over 175 pounds.      *Jimmy Cannon*

**Hecht, Ben**   A veteran exhibitionist.    *Mary McCarthy*

**Hector**   A noble Trojan whose name has been reduced to a bully verb.

**hedonism**   The proverbial eat, drink and be married.

     *Walla Walla high school student*

**Hefner, Hugh**   The papa of the only Playboy that paid off.

**heirloom** Something old nobody liked well enough to wear out. *Anon.*

—A hand-me-down weaving outfit. *Anon., Jr.*

**hell** A place where the French are the engineers, the British are the cooks, the Germans are the police, the Russians are the historians and the Americans are the lovers. *Anon. Japanese*

—and the Japanese are the inventors.

—Where dullness is unopposed. *Eli Siegel*

—Love no longer, Madame. *Georges Bernanos*

—A place with forty fireplugs to the block.

—Living in a world of poor and unhappy people. *Bernard Shaw*

—A perpetual holiday. *Bernard Shaw*

—Yourself. *Tennessee Williams*

—A place where you have nothing to do but amuse yourself. *Bernard Shaw*

    CHURCH A place where we must on no account enjoy ourselves, and where ladies are trained in the English art of sitting in rows for hours, dumb, expressionless, and with elbows turned in. *Bernard Shaw*

**hemp** A plant from whose fibrous bark is made an article of neckwear which is frequently put on after public speaking in the open air and prevents the wearer from taking cold. *Ambrose Bierce, 1900*

**hen** It takes all our leavings and turns them into fresh eggs. *Anon., Jr.*

    HEN-KISS The plural of handkerchief. *New Yorkese*

**henpecked** A man who has to wash and iron his own aprons.

—A man who controls his wife the way a weather vane controls the weather. *Art Semle*

**heredity** A theory you believe in when your child's report card is all A's. *E. E. Kenyon*

—When a teen-age boy winds up with his mother's big brown eyes and his father's long yellow convertible. *Automotive Service Digest*

—An omnibus in which all our ancestors ride, and every now and then one of them puts his head out and embarrasses us. *Oliver Wendell Holmes*

**heretic** One who has a private opinion. *Jacques-Benigne Bossuet*

    HERETICS The less numerous party. *Edward Gibbon*

**hermaphrodite** The wedding of Hermes and Aphrodite in one word . . . and person.

**hermit** A dropout from the School of Hard Knocks.

**hero** One who views death as going home. *Chinese proverb*

—One who believes all women are ladies.
*George Jean Nathan*

—One who does what he can. The others don't.
*Romain Rolland*

HERO-MAKING, U.S. STYLE Our insistence that our leaders
—whether in politics, science or other fields of endeavor
—be shown to us as Huck Finn grown taller.
*Clifton Fadiman*

HERO WORSHIP What society is founded on.
*Thomas Carlyle*

**Herod** One of the great characters in history. He got rid of
babies. There are too many babies in this area.
*Sir Thomas Barlow*

**herring** The national fish of the Bronx.

**hiccoughs** Messages from departed spirits.

**hick town** One in which, if you see a girl dining with a man
old enough to be her father, he is. *Anon.*

—One where the all-night restaurant closes at 4:30 P.M.
*Pat Henry*

**high cost of living** These days, the cost of high living.

**high dudgeon** A big-wheeled vehicle in which cooks depart.
*Rev. Remsen B. Ogilby*

**highbrow** A person who thinks he has found something
more interesting than women. *Homestead*

—One who can quote from Shakespeare without attributing
it to the Bible. *Frances Rodman*

**high lethality** A characteristic of a gun with a press agent.

**highway** A road you could go fast on—if it wasn't torn up.
*Leonard Neubauer**

**hindsight** How a mistake looks from the rear.
*Changing Times*

—A fat lady in a bikini.

**hippogriff** An animal (now extinct) which was half horse
and half griffin. The griffin was itself a compound creature,
half lion and half eagle. The hippogriff was actually, therefore, only one-quarter eagle, which is two dollars and fifty
cents in gold.[2] The study of zoology is full of surprises.
*Ambrose Bierce*

**hired girls** The principal exports of Sweden. *Anon., Jr.*

**hiss** To utter a noise like that of a serpent and some other

---

[2] In Bierce's time a ten-dollar gold piece was called an eagle.

animals. It is remarkable, that this word cannot be pronounced without making the noise which it signifies.

*Dr. Sam'l Johnson*

**historian**   A broad-gauge gossip.    *Ambrose Bierce*
—A prophet looking backwards.   *August W. von Schlegel*
—A prediction-monger after the event.

HISTORICAL NOVELS

> A lot of historical novels,
>> I've found,
> Are apparently written to sell
>> by the pound!    *Georgie Starbuck Galbraith*

**history**   The story of the world's crime.    *Voltaire*
—What succeeds.    *R. D. Charques*
—A fable agreed upon.    *Napoleon*
—Merely gossip.    *Oscar Wilde*
—Reportage plus hindsight.
—But the nail on which the picture hangs.

*Alexandre Dumas, père*

—Fiction with the truth left out.    *Anon.*
—Fiction written without imagination.   *Konrad Bercovici*
—A novel that happened.

NOVEL   History as it might have happened.

*The Goncourt brothers*

—A nightmare from which I am trying to awake.

*James Joyce*

—The follies of the majority.    *Lindsay Rogers*
—Just gossip that has grown old gracefully. *Sydney J. Harris*
—A prejudiced account of events written by persons who
weren't present when they happened.    *Maxwell Droke*
—An excitable and lying old lady.    *De Maupassant*
—An account mostly false, of events mostly unimportant
which are brought about by rulers mostly knaves, and
soldiers mostly fools.    *Ambrose Bierce*
—If you don't speak the truth, how can history know what
happened? Let me give you an example: Who would ever
imagine that the final plan for the invasion of Sicily was
made in an Algerian lavatory? Nobody would believe it,
but it is true. I was there myself.

*Field Marshal Viscount Bernard Law Montgomery*

—A register of the crimes and miseries that man has inflicted
on his fellow man.    *Washington Irving*
—Like an iceberg, most of it lives under the surface.

*Bruce Catton*

—Great men laid end to end between a frontispiece and a colophon.

—Something that happens elsewhere. *Bernard Taper*

—With history being made all the time, every day now seems to be the first anniversary of something awful. *Puck*

—Cut off the human race from the knowledge and comprehension of its history, and its government will just turn into a monkey cage. We need the guidance of history. All our yesterdays, it is true, have only lighted fools the way to dusty death. But we need at least the dates of the yesterdays and the list of the fools. *Stephen Leacock*

—Philosophy learned from examples.
        *Dionysius of Halicarnassus, paraphrasing Thucydides*

—A pageant, not a philosophy. *Augustine Birrell*

—The essence of innumerable biographies. *Thomas Carlyle*

—There is properly no history, only biography.
        *Ralph Waldo Emerson*

—The science of things that do not repeat themselves.
        *Paul Valéry*

—The short trudge from Adam to atom.

**Hitler** A despotic neurotic.

**hi-ya, honey** The original Mason-Dixon line.
        *George DeWitt**

**hobby** Hard work you wouldn't do for a living. *Anon.*

—An activity which gives you something to do when you should be worrying.

**hocus pocus** (The original of this word is referred by Tillotson to a form of the Romish church. Junius derives it from *hocced*, Welsh, a cheat, and *poke* or *pocus*, a bag, jugglers using a bag for conveyance. It is corrupted from some words that had once a meaning, and which perhaps cannot be discovered.) A juggle; a cheat. *Dr. Sam'l Johnson*

**hod** (1) Difficult. (2) Obdurate. *New Yorkese*

   HOD TAG A cardiac seizure. *New Yorkese*

**hog caller** A communications expert with a pig following.

**holdupmen** Gents who know how to meet a payroll and where.

**hole** The accident of the day; but a darn is premeditated poverty. *Ned Shuter*

**holiday season** That time of year when every home looks Christmussy. *Anna Herbert*

**Hollywood** The place where they put beautiful frames in pictures. *Armed Forces Press Service*

—A plaster of Paris.

—A plastered Paris.

—A place where diplomacy is the art of putting your foot down without treading on anyone's toes or getting it into your mouth. *Sidney Skolsky*

—The place where all the girls are looking for husbands and all the husbands are looking for girls. *Guy Lepre*

—The most beautiful jail in the world. *Max Gordon*

—A risk business trying to act like an insurance agency. *Robert Daniel Graff*

—The most sensational merry-go-round ever built. *Tony Curtis*

—Malice in Wonderland. *Tom Jenks*

—A place where a kid actor can grow up to be the leading man for an actress who once played his mother. *Frank DeVol*

—Potter's field in neon lights. *Jerry Asher*

—A locality where people without reputation try to live up to it. *Tom Jenk*

—Where you know it's spring when the smog gets greener. *Sidney Skolsky*

HOLLYWOOD BOULEVARD  A backdrop in "one." *Laurette Taylor*

**Holmes, Oliver Wendell**  A writer who always considered his face a convenience rather than an ornament.

**holocaust**  From two Greek words signifying burning altogether and meaning a sacrifice of cattle which are totally consumed. Thus a holocaust is even worse than a barbecue.

**holy cow**  An Irish papal bull. *Anon., Jr.*

**home**  A place to stay whenever the car is being repaired. *Anon.*

—Where you hang your head. *Groucho Marx*

HOME LIFE  No more natural to us than a cage is natural to a cockatoo. *Bernard Shaw*

HOME REMEDY  The best is a good wife. *Frank McKinney Hubbard*

**homework**  Skull-drudgery. *V. Tubazio*

—A thing that kids don't have any of when it's time for their favorite TV program and have heaps of when it is time to go to bed. *Changing Times*

**homicide**  The slaying of one human being by another. There are four kinds of homicide: felonious, excusable, justifiable and praiseworthy, but it makes no great differ-

ence to the person slain whether he fell by one kind or another—the classification is for advantage of the lawyers.
*Ambrose Bierce*

**hominy**  A corny saying sung by two or more.
*Anon., Jr. (New Yorkese Division)*

**honesty**  The only virtue left to humble folk.  *Stendhal*
—It's strange that men should take up crime when there are so many legal ways to be dishonest.  *Sunshine Magazine*

**honeymoon**  A short period of doting between dating and debting.  *Ray Bandy*
—The time during which the bride believes the bridegroom's word of honor.  *H. L. Mencken*
  HONEYMOON COTTAGE  A small structure in which the loving room is the most important.

**Hong Kong**  China's Switzerland.

**hooky**  When a small boy lets his mind wander—and then follows it.  *Circle Arrow Retailer*
  UNAUTHORIZED ABSENTEEISM  Adult hooky playing.

**Hoover, J. Edgar**  A man with a self-made halo. *Rex Stout*

**hope**  The nurse of desire.  *Charles S. Finger*
—Desire and expectation rolled into one.  *Ambrose Bierce*
—The highest form is despair overcome.  *Georges Bernanos*

**Hoppe, Willie**  A perennial billiard champion who always won because his opponent was always playing Willie, and Willie was always playing billiards.

**hors d'oeuvre**  Out of work.  *Anon., Jr.*

**horse**  A neighing quadruped, used in war, and draught and carriage. Joined to another substantive, it signifies something large or coarse; as, a *horseface*, a face of which the features are large and indelicate.  *Dr. Sam'l Johnson*
  HORSE SENSE  Nothing more than stable thinking.  *Anon.*

**hospital**  A pain factory.  *Frank Scully\**
—A place where a private room has nothing to do with privacy.
  HOSPITALS  Places populated with people who are overly suspicious, according to an eminent psychologist. This generalization, however, does not apply to maternity hospitals.  *Changing Times*

**hospitality**  The virtue which induces us to feed and lodge certain persons who are not in need of food and lodging.
*Ambrose Bierce*

**host**  The guy at the party who keeps reminding the guests to only make local phone calls.  *Bob Hope*

HOSTESS   A woman with the difficult problem of giving the impression that the family always eats that well, and still make the guests feel that she has gone to a lot of extra trouble.   *Changing Times*

—A lady who greets you with hostility.   *Anon., Jr.*

**hostage**   A big bird with four legs and a long neck.
*Anon., Jr. (British Division)*

**hot**   An internal organ which, in every red-blooded Charlestonian, beats quicker when the band strikes up "Dixie."
*Charlestonese*

**hot dog**   A poached pooch.

**hotel (Las Vegas)**   Five miles of free parking surrounded by losers.   *Dick Sharon*

**house**   The beginning of an inquiry, as in "House Bayou?"
*New Yorkese*

—A hollow edifice erected for the habitation of man, rat, mouse, beetle, cockroach, fly, mosquito, flea, bacillus and microbe.   *Ambrose Bierce*

HOUSE OF GOD   A building with a steeple and a mortgage on it.   *Ambrose Bierce*

HOUSE DOG   A pestilent beast kept on domestic premises to insult persons passing by and appal the hardy visitor.
*Ambrose Bierce*

HOUSEMAID   (Obsolete) A youngerly person of the opposing sex employed to be variously disagreeable and ingeniously unclean in the station in which it has pleased God to place her.   *Ambrose Bierce*

HOUSE OF LORDS   The British Outer Mongolia for retired politicians.   *Anthony Wedgewood Benn*

HOUSEKEEPING   Work which husbands are expert at but unfortunately don't have time for.   *Changing Times*

HOUSEWIFE   A woman who can lick her weight in trading stamps.

**hovering**   The chief occupation of a captain of waiters.

**hug**   A roundabout way of expressing affection.   *Anon.*

**Hugo, Victor**   A genius without frontiers.   *Baudelaire*

**hula**   A shake in the grass.   *Playboy*

—A wild-waist show.   *Bruce Patterson*

**human**   The class-conscious animal.

HUMAN BRAIN   A most unusual instrument of elegant and as yet unknown capacity.   *Stuart Luman Seaton*

HUMAN LIFE   The rarest, most complex and most precious of all the prizes in the universe.   *Norman Cousins*

—Also the cheapest.

HUMAN NATURE   What we have; other people have faults.
                                                *Akiko Sullivan*

—What makes you swear at a pedestrian when you are
  driving and at the driver when you are a pedestrian.
                                                *Oren Arnold*

**humanitarian**   A guy who collects from the rich and gives
  to the poor and is thanked by both sides.

**humility**   The mean between arrogance and self-abasement.
                                         *Twelfth-century rabbi*

—I have spent seventy years finding out that I am not God.
                                       *Oliver Wendell Holmes*

—Wet air.                                        *Anon., Jr.*

**humor**   A defense from insanity.

—The result of kicking someone so courteously that he is
  happy about it, since he thinks it was the next fellow who
  got kicked.                             *Conrado Nale Roxlo*

—An antibiotic against hate.                 *Felix Weltsch*

—The sense that makes you laugh at something which would
  make you mad if it happened to you.     London *Telegraph*

—Strange, when you come to think of it, that of all the count-
  less folk who have lived before our time on this planet,
  not one is known in history or in legend as having died of
  laughter.                                   *Max Beerbohm*

—A declaration of man's superiority to all that befalls him.
                                               *Romain Gary*

—When a thing is funny, search it for a hidden truth.
                                              *Bernard Shaw*

FRESH HUMOR   Old, sure-fire jokes told by a young comedian.                                       *Milton Berle*

HUMORIST   A writer who shows us the faults of human
  nature in such a way that we recognize our failings and
  smile—and our neighbors' and laugh.            *Anon., Jr.*

—A man who feels bad but who feels good about it.
                                                *Don Herold*

**hunch**   What you call an idea that you're afraid is wrong.
                                             *Carter Dickson*

**hunger**   The father of art.                *Russian proverb*
**hurry**   The dispatch of bunglers.          *Ambrose Bierce*
—The exact opposite of poise.                *Fred De Armond*
—No man in a hurry is quite civilized.          *Will Durant*
**husband**   A man who started handing out a line and finished
  walking it.                                      *Playboy*

—A bachelor who lost his liberty in the pursuit of happiness.

—A man who firmly believes he can eat his breakfast; read his newspaper, listen to his wife talk and not miss anything important. *F. G. Kernan*

—The male of animals. *Dr. Sam'l Johnson*

—From man-about-town to mouse-around-the-house.

—A man who has to grow old alone.

—Nothing is more debasing for a real man than a plastic apron. *Viscountess Lewisham*

—Some are comforters, while others are just wet blankets. *Paula Thorne*

MODERN HUSBAND  A do-it-yourself man with a get-it-done wife. *Jim Kelly*

PERFECT HUSBAND  One about whose improvement there is no particular hurry. *Kodiak (Alas.) Nugget*

SMART HUSBAND  One who isn't so busy bringing home the bacon that he forgets the applesauce. *Changing Times*

hustle  Any New York friend can get it for you hustle. Hustle costs only slightly more than riddle; but then, the merchandise you get is vastly inferior. *New Yorkese*

huswife  A bad manager; a sorry woman. It is common to use *housewife* in a good, and *huswife* or *hussy* in a bad sense. *Dr. Sam'l Johnson*

Huxley  The greatest antagonist of the nineteenth century. *Anon., Jr.*

hybrid  A pooled issue. *Ambrose Bierce*

hydrant  What you put in the middle of a word like waterworks. *Anon., Jr.*

hydraulics  The writing of Ancient Egypt. *Anon., Jr.*

hydroelectric damns  What you'd hear if a man stepped in a puddle while using an electric shaver. *Anon., Jr.*

hygiene, public  A science which seeks to make morons immortal. *H. L. Mencken*

Hymen  The god of Chaos. *H. L. Mencken*

hypochondriac  A person with an infinite capacity for faking pains. *Modern Medicine*

—One who gets symptoms by reading and may die of a typographical error.

—A bed bug.

hypochondriantiquarian  One who tries to buy a stained glass thermometer. *Newords*

hypocrite  One who, professing virtues that he does not respect, secures the advantage of seeming to be what he despises. *Ambrose Bierce*

—A person who prays on Sunday and preys the rest of the week.

—A person who talks about his principles but makes capital of his interests.

—A person who preaches by the yard but practices by the inch.                                    Detroit *Free Press*

—An actor.                                    *Original Greek meaning*

HYPOCRISY   Leading a double life: pretending to be wicked and being really good all the time.          *Oscar Wilde*

hysterics   Letters in sloping type.                    *Anon., Jr.*

# I

**I**   Is the first letter of the alphabet, the first word of the language, the first thought of the mind, the first object of affection. In grammar it is a pronoun of the first person and singular number. Its plural is said to be "We," but how there can be more than one myself is doubtless clearer to the grammarians than it is to the author of this incomparable dictionary. Conception of two myselves is difficult, but fine. The frank yet graceful use of "I" distinguishes a good writer from a bad; the latter carries it with the manner of a thief trying to cloak his loot.

                    Ambrose Bierce, *The Devil's Dictionary*

—Our favorite word—used 450 times more than any other.
                                                   *Pageant*

**Ibid**   A famous Latin poet.                    *Ibid., Jr.*

**ice**   Plural of I, meaning two organs to see through.
                                                   *New Yorkese*

—One of the most useful by-products of cold.      *Anon., Jr.*

ICE CREAM   Freezy kid stuff.                    *W. E. Piece*

**icicle**   An eaves-dripper.                    *Ann Herbert*

**Idaho**   A nice place to be if you are a potato. *Fred Beck*°

**idea**   Something you can see better with your eyes shut.

IDEAS   One of the most hazardous of human occupations is the transferring of an idea from one mind to another. It's hazardous because you presuppose the existence of a second mind.                    *Christian Burckel*

—Like beards: men do not have them until they grow up.
                                                   *Voltaire*

**ideals** The mirage that draws travelers a little further into the desert.

**IDEALISM** A principle which increases in direct proportion to one's distance from the problem. *John Galsworthy*

**IDEALIST** One who tries to keep politics out of politics. *Patuxent River Tester*

**PRACTICAL IDEALIST** A sort of hard-boiled egghead. *Anon. chairman introducing Adlai Stevenson*

**TOUGH IDEALIST** Nature's noblest creation. *Eli J. Schleifer*

**idiot** A member of a large and powerful tribe whose influence in human affairs has always been dominant and controlling. *Ambrose Bierce*

—A private person. *Ancient Greek meaning*

**idleness** Leisure gone to seed. *Eli J. Schleifer*

—The mother of mischief. *Col. Thomas H. Perkins*

—The mother of want. *Greek saying*

—and of children.

**IDLING** Inactivity it is impossible to enjoy unless one has plenty of work to do. *Jerome K. Jerome*

**IDLER** A learned man who kills time by study. *Bernard Shaw*

**ignoramus** A person unacquainted with certain kinds of knowledge familiar to yourself, and having certain other kinds that you know nothing about. *Ambrose Bierce*

**ignorance** The trouble with most folks isn't so much their ignorance as knowing so many things that ain't so. *Josh Billings*

—Everybody is ignorant, only on different subjects. *Will Rogers*

—How soft, how gentle a pillow to rest a well-composed head upon. *Montaigne*

—Like a delicate exotic fruit; touch it, and the bloom is gone. *Oscar Wilde*

—Not knowing something and someone finds it out. *Anon., Jr.*

—What you don't know won't hurt you. It's what you suspect that causes all the trouble.

**illegible** The mark of a true executive. *Leo J. Farrell, Jr.*

**illegible writing** Script tease. Walden, N.Y., *Citizen Herald*

**ill-fortune** Being knifed in the back and then arrested for carrying a concealed weapon.

**illiterate** One who reads medical books.

**illiterature** The current sick writing. *Newords*

**illusion** The first of all pleasures. *Voltaire*

—That blessed bread of miserable souls.     *Claude Debussy*

—Something that has not yet been proven false.

*Edward Albee*

ILLUSIONED  Looking at the world through Disney-colored glasses.

**image**  What you think people think of you when you think they're thinking of you.     *Changing Times*

**imagination**  Getting a larger view of life than the one we can get through the keyhole of reality.

—A warehouse of facts, with poet and liar in joint owner-ship.     *Ambrose Bierce*

—The eye of the soul.     *Joubert*

—Imagination is more important than knowledge.

*Albert Einstein*

—What makes you think you are having a wonderful time when you are only spending money.     *Supervision*

**imbalance**  Difference between inflow and outflow. As at home, the outflows have it, every time. *Wall Street Journal*

**imbecile**  (From the adjective. This word is corruptly writ-ten *embezzle*.) To weaken a stock or fortune by clandestine expences or unjust appropriations.     *Dr. Sam'l Johnson*

IMBECILITY  A kind of divine inspiration, or sacred fire affecting censorious critics of this dictionary.

Ambrose Bierce, *The Devil's Dictionary*

**imitation**  The sincerest form of plagiarism.

*Quoted by David Ogilvy*

**immigrant**  An unenlightened person who thinks one country better than another.     *Ambrose Bierce*

**immodest**  Having a strong sense of one's own merit, coupled with a feeble conception of worth in others.

*Ambrose Bierce*

**immorality**  Conduct, mischievous or not, which does not conform to current ideals.     *Bernard Shaw*

**immortality**

A toy which people cry for,

And on their knees apply for,

Dispute, contend and lie for,

  And if allowed

  Would be right proud

Eternally to die for.     *Ambrose Bierce*

—The genius to move others long after you yourself have stopped moving.     *Frank Rooney*

**immure**  To stick someone in jail.     *Anon., Jr.*

**immune**  To do it with a needle.                    Anon., J

**immunity**  The ability to catch a disease without the aid of a physician.                                Anon., J

**imp**  A son; the offspring; progeny.    Dr. Sam'l Johnso

**impartial observer**  A glass eye at a keyhole.

**impeccable**  Exempt from possibility of sin.

                                        Dr. Sam'l Johnso

—The way the typewriter was when it got back from th repair shop.      Bill Manhoff, *The Owl and the Pussyca*

**imperialism (British)**  The unforgivable sin is not exploita tion but that it has made life dull.    *Tanganyika offici*

**impervious**  Saturated without overflowing, like a drunkar or a sponge before they are squeezed.

                            Anon., Jr. (British Division

**impetus**  Something that makes you move. One of the mai impetuses of modern times is the automobile.

                            Anon., Jr. (Art Linkletter Dept

**impiety**  Your irreverence toward my deity. *Ambrose Bier*

**impossible**  A word to be found only in the dictionary of fools.                                    *Napoleo*

**imposter**  A rival aspirant to public honors. *Ambrose Bierc*

**impractical**  Writing sliding trombone solos to be played i telephone booths.

**imprisonment**  As it exists today, a worse crime than any of those committed by its victims.          *Bernard Sha*

**improvidence**  Provision for the needs of today from th revenues of tomorrow.              *Ambrose Bierc*

**impunity**  Wealth.                            *Ambrose Bierc*

**in**  The hardest thing to give.    *Douglas B. Netherwoo*

**incense**  The odor of sanctity.

—To fume or perfume.

—An aromatic preparation burned in self-defense by wome who just love the smell of a good cigar.

**incentive pay**  A ploy employed when threat of discharg no longer works.

**incinerate**  To cook your goose by telling on somebody.

                                        Anon., Jr

   INCINERATOR  A person who hints bad things instead of coming right out and telling you.          Anon., J

**income**  What you make.  Anon., Jr. (Art Linkletter Dept

   OUTGO  What the government takes.

                            Anon., Jr. (Art Linkletter Dept

—The amount of money, no matter how large it is, that you spend more than. *Anon.*

INCOME TAX   The fine you pay for reckless thriving. *Anon.*

**incommunicado**   A place where big shots are.   *Anon., Jr.**

**incompatability**   Inability to find a mate with the aid of a computer-Cupid.   *Judy Michaels*

—In matrimony, a similarity of tastes, particularly the taste for domination.   *Ambrose Bierce*

**incongruous**   Where our laws are made and how they appear.
Philadelphia *Bulletin*

**inconstancy**   The only thing in this world that is constant.
*Jonathan Swift*

**incubation**   Sleeping in a temple for curative purposes.
*Original Latin meaning*

**incumbent**   A person of the liveliest interest to the outcumbents.   *Ambrose Bierce*

**independent**   When a person refuses to do the things he doesn't like to do, so he can work himself to death doing what he likes, he's independent.   *Anon.*

**Indian**   The American Untouchable.   *Henry Miller*

INDIAN SUMMER   About the only decent thing we ever said about the Indian.   *Changing Times*

INDIAN WOLF   A paw-knee.   *Robert Orben*

WOODEN INDIAN   The only good Indian.
*Alvin Josephy III**

**Indiana**   The home of more first-rate second-class men than any other state in the Union.   *Thomas R. Marshall*

**indigestion**   A disease which the patient and his friends frequently mistake for deep religious conviction and concern for the salvation of mankind. As the simple Red Man of the western wild put it, with, it must be confessed, a certain force: "Plenty well, no pray; big bellyache, heap God."
*Ambrose Bierce*

—That inward fate which makes all Styx through one small liver flow.   *Don Juan, Canto 9, Stanza 15*

**individualist**   What *you* are.   *Russell Baker*

—A man whose wife is away for a few days.
*Mannie Manheim*

**indolence**   Freedom from pain.   *Dr. Sam'l Johnson*

**inertia**   That which tends to have a uniform motion in a state of rest.   *Anon., Jr. (British Division)*

**inexpedient**   Not calculated to advance one's interests.
*Ambrose Bierce*

**infancy**  The period of our lives when, according to Wordsworth, "Heaven lies about us." The world begins lying
about us pretty soon afterward.          *Ambrose Bierce*

**infidelity**  The awkward situation of being caught while being untrue.

**inflation**  When money to burn is the cheapest fuel.

—When you look at that nest egg and it's chicken feed.

—The time when people who used to say money isn't everything say it's hardly anything.          *Fletcher Knebel*

—What makes balloons bigger and candy bars smaller.
                                         *Changing Times*

—Paying $250 for an auto and then five years later paying
$500 for an overhaul.                    *George N. Hall*

—That period when a man can lose his shirt not only in the
stock market but also in the supermarket. *Changing Times*

—Something similar to looking at your lifetime savings
through the wrong end of a telescope.
                    *Counselor, Securities Acceptance Corp.*

—Instead of not having the money you haven't, you have
twice as much, but it is worth only half of what you
haven't got now.                         *Anon.*

—When you read that inflation will make your money worth
less, it's no relief to reach into your pocket and discover
that you have nothing to worry about.    *Supervision*

—When everybody is so rich that no one can afford anything.
                                         *Changing Times*

—Being broke with a lot of money in your pocket.
                                  *Industrial Press Survey*

—A state of affairs when you never had it so good or parted
with it so fast.                         *Anon.*

—One of the benefits of inflation is that kids can no longer
get sick on a nickel's worth of candy. *Journeyman Barber*

—The reason you can't take it with you—it all goes before
you do.

—An economic condition when, by the time you get a raise,
it won't be enough.                      *Pearson*

—Like sin, something to be deplored, but public measures
to abate it are to be avoided, lest they hurt business.
                                         *Changing Times*

—Something we thought we had five years ago.      *Ibid.*

**ingenue**  A pigeon who gets billing by cooling.
                                         *Judith Johnson**

**ingenuity**  Man's cleverness in getting out of spots his stupidity got him into.                     *Changing Times*

—Reading the handwriting on the wall when you're got your back to it.

—The art of turning stumbling blocks into stepping stones.

**ingratitude** The mark of the true actor.

**injury** An offense next in degree of enormity to a slight.
*Ambrose Bierce*

**injustice** A burden which, of all those that we load upon others and carry ourselves, is lightest in the hands and heaviest upon the back. *Ambrose Bierce*

**ink** A villainous compound of tanno-gallate of iron, gum-arabic and water, chiefly used to facilitate the infection of idiocy and promote intellectual crime. *Ambrose Bierce*

—The black liquor with which men write. *Dr. Sam'l Johnson*

**in-law** A law you'd like to repeal.

**innocence** The best makeup. *Russian proverb*

**inquisitiveness** A great curiosity, but actually not such a great curiosity.

**insane** Out of step with the parade.

**insects** Bugs that are found in many sizes, shapes and cup-boards. *Anon., Jr.*

**insincerity** The soul of discussion. *Roqueplan*

—Merely a method by which we can multiply our personalities. *Oscar Wilde*

**insomnia** The triumph of mind over mattress. *Anon.*

—What a person has when he lies awake all night for an hour.
*Roger Price*

—When you can't sleep even on the job. *Cy N. Peace*

**INSOMNIAC** A person who keeps a flock of sheep jumping over a fence all night just because he can't sleep.
*Changing Times*

**inspiration** At its best means breath, and only too frequently means wind. *G. K. Chesterton*

—Breath; which may account for so many inspirational books being full of hot air. *Sydney Harris*

**instant** The length of time it takes a supermarket cash register to reach $10. *Changing Times*

**instead** At once; e.g., "A cuppa instead coffee."
*New Yorkese*

**insurrection** An unsuccessful revolution. *Ambrose Bierce*

**intellectual** A man who takes more words than are necessary to tell more than he knows.
*Heard by Dwight D. Eisenhower*

—A man who carries a book. *Tom Crimmins**

**interior decorating**   Spending money you haven't got, to buy things you don't want, to impress people you can't stand.
*Judith Beach\**

**interior decorator**   A person who turns your flowerpots into lamps and fills your lamps with plants!   *Bert Bacharach*
—A color schemer.

**interjection**   A sudden explosion of mind.
*Anon., Jr. (British Division)*

**International Association of Marble, Slate and Stone Polishers, Rubbers and Sawyers, Tile and Marble Setters Helpers and Terrazzo Helpers Union**   One of the smallest international unions in the AFL–CIO.

**interne**   A ward-healer.

**interpreter**   One who enables two persons of different languages to understand each other by repeating to each what it would have been to the interpreter's advantage for the other to have said.   *Ambrose Bierce*
—The hardest to be understood of the two.
*Richard Brinsley Sheridan*

**interrogation**   'Tis a little crooked thing that asks questions.
*Anon., Jr.*

**intersection**   One place where two wrongs can make a rite.
*Julian Brown*

**interval**   (In music) The distance from one piano to the next.   *Anon., Jr.*

**intimate dining room**   Real Estatease for, "It can only hold two people at once. How intimate do you want to get?"
*William V. Shannon*

**intoxicated**   What you have to get so you won't get a disease.
*Anon., Jr.*

**introvert**   One who spends all his time minding his own business.   *Anon.*

**intuition**   Reason in a hurry.   *Holbrook Jackson*
—A method whereby women draw false conclusions from a lack of facts.
—Simply a matter of reading between the lyings.
*Spring Byington*
—What tells a wife her husband has done something wrong before he thinks of doing it.   *John J. Plomp*

**invention**   The mother of necessity.   *Samuel Butler*
    INVENTOR   A person who makes an ingenious arrangement of wheels, levers and springs, and believes it civilization.
*Ambrose Bierce*

—An old-fashioned creator almost entirely supplanted by research and development departments.

**investments**   In investing money, the amount of interest you want should depend on whether you want to eat well or sleep well.                                    *J. Kenfield Morley*

INVESTOR   A man who turns his money over to men he has never seen and expects to get it back at least twice.

**I.Q.**   What a man looks for in a woman after he's looked at everything else.                                    *Changing Times*

**iris**   The pleasant part of the eye, like in iris eyes are smiling.
                                                        *Anon., Jr.*

**Irish**

> For the great Gaels of Ireland
> Are the men that God made mad,
> For all their wars are merry,
> And all their songs are sad.                    *G. K. Chesterton*

—Still, a clever Irishman is better than the usual alternative: a mediocre Englishman.                                    *Bernard Shaw*

IRISH BULL   A male cow.                                    *Anon., Jr.*

—Mr. Speaker, I smell a rat; I see him forming in the air and darkening the sky; but I'll nip him in the bud.
                                    *Sir Boyle Roche, Irish Parliament*

**irrigate**   To disturb.                    *Anon., Jr. (British Division)*

**irritant, counter**   A woman who shops all day and buys nothing.                                    *Wilcox Antenna*

**irritants, harsh**   All the ingredients of a competitor's products.                                    *Ballyhoo*

**isinglass**   A whitish substance made from the bladders of surgeons.                                    *Anon., Jr.*

**island**   A spot where the ocean floor has been pushed up out of the water.

**isolationist**   A man who prefers making money by himself.
                                    *Anon., Jr. (British Division)*

—A person who doesn't care what happens so long as it doesn't happen to him.   *Paul and Helen Martin Denis**

**italics**   A primitive method of soliciting attention.
                                                        *H. W. Fowler*

**Italy**   A whole country that is a theatre and the worst actors are on the stage.                                    *Bernard Shaw*

—A nation of actors, the worst of whom go on the stage.
                                                        *Orson Welles*

**itinerary**   A list of the places you intend visiting if your money holds out.

# J

**J** Is a consonant in English, but some nations use it as a vowel—than which nothing could be more absurd. Its original form, which has been but slightly modified, was that of the tail of a subdued dog, and it was not a letter but a character, standing for a Latin verb, *jacere*, "to throw," because when a stone is thrown at a dog the dog's tail assumes that shape. This is the origin of the letter, as expounded by the renowned Dr. Jacolpus Bumer, of the University of Belgrade, who established his conclusions on the subject in a work of three quarto volumes and committed suicide on being reminded that the "j" in the Roman alphabet had originally no curl. *Ambrose Bierce*

**jail** A place where they keep the litter of the law.

**James, Henry** An author who writes fiction as if it were a painful duty. *Oscar Wilde*

**Jamestown, Virginia** The most tragic spot in all America. *Henry Miller*

**Jantzen** President. *Bostonese*

**January** The beginning of a disappointment.
*Bill Manville* (See "December")

—The month named for Janus, who had forward and backward faces, to observe the Christmas bills and the delayed payments.

—Snowy; February flowy; March blowy; April show'ry; May flow'ry; June bow'ry; July moppy; August croppy; September poppy; October breezy; November wheezy; December freezy. *Richard Brinsley Sheridan*

**jargon** Pro's prose.

**jealous** Unduly concerned about the preservation of that which can be lost only if not worth keeping.
*Ambrose Bierce*

**JEALOUSY** Poison envy. *Changing Times*

**Jehovah** The most fascinating character in all fiction.
*Oliver Herford*

**Jerusalem** Besides being one of the most profoundly depressing of the earth's cities, one of the strangest and, in its own way, one of the most beautiful. *Aldous Huxley*

**jester** An officer formerly attached to a king's household, whose business it was to amuse the court by ludicrous actions and utterances, the absurdity being attested by his motley costume. The king himself being attired with dignity, it took the world some centuries to discover that his own conduct and decrees were sufficiently ridiculous for the amusement not only of his court but of all mankind. The jester was commonly called a fool, but the poets and romancers have ever delighted to represent him as a singularly wise and witty person. *Ambrose Bierce*

**jet age** Swift transportation that permits you to eat an early breakfast in New York and fly to San Francisco in time to find nobody up yet. *Woman's Day*

JET SET A gang of sophisticates who never arrive at a party until everybody is there.

JETS Planes that have passed the speed of sound and will soon dare to approach the speed of gossip.
*Arcadia (Wis.) News Letter*

—Planes which have eliminated distant relatives.

**jiggumbob** A trinket; a knick-knack; a slight contrivance in machinery. *Dr. Sam'l Johnson*

**jigsaws** What the people of Japan ride about in. *Anon., Jr.*

**jilted** Learning that you have just been a passing fiancé.

—What happens when the wedding goes off without a hitch.

**job** Death without the dignity. *Dylan Thomas*

JOB SEEKER A want addict.

STEADY JOB A rocking chair—it keeps you busy, but you don't get anywhere.

**Johnson, Dr. Sam'l** This permanent London object.
*James Boswell*

**joint account** Where you send your wife to the bank and kiss your money good-bye.

**journalism** Organized gossip. *Oscar Wilde*

—Bad manners make a journalist. *Oscar Wilde*

—That which is unreadable. *Oscar Wilde*

LITERATURE That which is unread. *Oscar Wilde*

**journalists** People who always say what they know is untrue, in the hope that if they go on saying it long enough, it will come true. *Arnold Bennett*

**joycamp** Forced labor camp.
*George Orwell's "Newspeak," 1984*

**Joyce, James** A writer with whom the pen is mightier than the word. *W. Y. Tindall*

—He was a man who in order to breathe felt he had to break
all of the windows. *Rebecca West*

—A Shaw without opinions. *Arland Ussher*

**judge** A man who is paid 5,000 pounds a year to be wicked.
*Bernard Shaw*

—Credit; e.g., "Is this a cash or a judge?" *New Yorkese*

**judo** Mayhem with a gentle touch. *Charles Miller*

**juke box** Edison's answer to Beethoven.

—A slot-machine that pays off in decibels.

**jump** The last word in parachuting.

**juncate** A furtive or private entertainment. It is now improperly written *junket* in this sense, which alone remains
much in use. *Dr. Sam'l Johnson*

**June** That exciting month when the kids are almost finished
with school, the vacation plans are all set and the road
gangs are all out ripping up the highways.

—The month the kids get out of school and into your hair.
*Changing Times*

—The month when a girl gets a Lohengrin on her face.
*Paul Vandervoort II*

—The act of mastication, or that which is masticated, as in:
"What flavor june gum you want?" *New Yorkese*

**junk** Anything that has outlived its usefulness.
*Oliver Herford*

**justice** A commodity which in a more or less adulterated
condition the State sells to the citizen as a reward for his
allegiance, taxes and personal service. *Ambrose Bierce*

—A piece of gold that can be hammered out into many thin
plates. *Russian proverb*

**juvenile** What King Saul threw at David when he was playing the harp to him. *Anon., Jr.*

JUVENILE DELINQUENCY The result of parents trying to
train children without starting at the bottom.
*G. G. Kinvin*

—When a youngster stops asking his parents where he
came from and tells them where to go. *Jackie Kannon*

JUVENILE DELINQUENT A boy whose parents give him a
free hand, but not in the proper place.

—A teenager who wants what he wants when he wants it
and won't wait to get it. *Survey Bulletin*

—The kind of a boy his mother wouldn't let him run
around with. *Changing Times*

—Child hood. *Eugene H. Lehman*

# K

**K**  A Roman numeral for 250; in chemistry, it is the symbol for potassium; in mathematics, a symbol for constant; in meteorology, a symbol for cumulus. In assaying, it stands for carat (also spelled Karat).

*Webster's New World Dictionary*

**Kaffirs**  A very savage African race. In time of war they beat their tum-tums and can be heard for many miles around.

*Anon., Jr.*

**kangaroo**  A leaping pedestrian, with patch pockets.

**Kate Canaveral**  The most famous woman scientist. *Anon., Jr.*

**Kazan (Russia)**  A slave city with a Tartar sauce.

*Negley Farson*

**Kennedy, Robert**  There is something pathetic about a man who turns on the charm when he has none.  *John O'Hara*

**kicksy-wicksey**  A made word in ridicule and disdain of a wife.  *Hanmer*

**kids**  Whys guys.  *Anon. parent*

**kill**  To create a vacancy without nominating a successor.

*Ambrose Bierce*

**kilt**  A costume sometimes worn by Scotchmen in America and Americans in Scotland.  *Ambrose Bierce*

—In Scotland a pair of short pants with one leg. Also past tense of *kill,* as in "MacTavish has kilt his pint."

*Fred Beck, 89 Years in a Sand Trap*

**kind**  Self-defeating.  *Bill Manville*

**kindred**  Fear of relatives.

**king**  A place in the sun for shady people.  *Old saying*

—A male person commonly known in America as a "crowned head," although he never wears a crown and has usually no head to speak of.  *Ambrose Bierce*

**kink**  A ruler that has two feet.  *New Yorkese*

**Kipling**  A snapshot Balzac.  *Anon.*

**kipper**  The masculine of heroine.

*Anon., Jr. (British Division)*

**kiss**  An oath of allegiance taken in close proximity. A promise more precise, a seal on a confession, a rose red dot upon the letter I in loving; a secret which elects the mouth for ear; an instant of eternity murmuring like a fee; balmy communion with a flavor of flowers; a fashion of inhaling each other's heart; and of tasting on the brink of the lips each other's souls!

Edmond Rostand, *Cyrano de Bergerac*

—An application for a better position. *Playboy*

—"I love you" in one syllable.

—A method of procedure, cunningly devised, for the mutual prevention of speech at a time when words are superfluous.

*Don Carlson*

KISSES What's left of the language of Paradise.

*Joseph Conrad*

—Many a miss would not be a missus if liquor would not add spark to her kisses. *E. L. C.*

**knees** Not the prettiest things in the world but . . . they're functional. *Norman Norell*

**knish** A delicacy that looks like half a ladyfinger and weighs two hundred pounds. *Fred Allen*

**knot net** The profit a minister earns from performing marriages. *Kenneth J. Shively*

**know-how (American)** A condition that has produced so many push-button gadgets that we may become the first people in history with muscle-bound knuckles.

*Changing Times*

**knowledge** When you know a thing, to hold that you know it, and when you do not know a thing, to acknowledge that you do not know it. *Confucius*

—The small part of ignorance that we arrange and classify.

*Ambrose Bierce*

—The struggling for knowledge hath a pleasure in it like that of wrestling with a fine woman. *Marquis of Halifax*

—Even a professor soon discovers how little he knows when a child begins asking questions. *Good Impressions*

**Kodak** The Bible of the Mohammedans. *Anon., Jr.*

# L

**labor leaders**  Those who seem to suffer least from exposure, along with girls.  *Cy N. Peace*

**labor pains**  Forcing the issue.  *Anon.*

**labor saving**  Money-costing.

**labor union**  An organization of wage earners for the aid, protection and benefit of Jimmy Hoffa.

**labyrinth**  The original blueprint for crowd control.

**lack**  Enjoy; e.g., "I lack fried chicken."  *Charlestonese*

LACK OF MONEY  The root of all evil.  *Bernard Shaw*

**Lady Macbeth**  A woman with only one consistent characteristic, which is, that she thinks everything her husband does is wrong and that she can do it better. *Bernard Shaw*

**ladyfinger**  A stick of sponge cake used by a society woman to point.  *Anon., Jr.*

—The reward a chivalrous man usually gets.

**ladies club**  A room full of loose tongues and tight girdles.  *George Gobel*

**Ladies' Day**  The day the old man gets cold cuts for dinner.  *Jimmy Cannon*

**laissez faire**  Let the farmers pay the taxes.  *Anon., Jr.*

**landloper**  A landman; a term of reproach used by seamen of those who pass their lives on shore.  *Dr. Sam'l Johnson*

**landlord**  A man who profits from the ground up.

**language**  (There are) over 600,000 words in *Webster's Unabridged Dictionary*; a million possible if technical terms were admitted. . . . The first dictionary in English compiled by Dr. Samuel Johnson and published in 1755, contained but 58,000 words; and the first dictionary of English in America, edited and published by Noah Webster in 1828, offered only 70,000. The size of English vocabulary has thus increased almost ten-fold in slightly over one hundred years. And now we face the sobering prospect, according to Prof. Albert H. Marckwardt of the University of Michigan, that the next two centuries may bring us a total English vocabulary of over two million words.

   *Charles W. Ferguson, senior editor, The Reader's Digest*

—The American language has become so inflated that even

the strongest words have lost half their purchasing power. The spiral of good-better-best has, over the years, invaded not only advertising but almost all speech and writing to the point where even the unsophisticated listener and reader automatically cuts the adjectives in half, believing only the remainder. Like the penny and the nickel, ordinary simple words that mean exactly what they say are well on their way toward obsolescence. *Public Relations Newsletter*

—Much of the world's traffic is conducted along rivers of words. *Anon.*

—The music with which we charm the serpents guarding another's treasure. *Ambrose Bierce*

**Laocoön** A famous piece of antique sculpture representing a priest of that name and his two sons in the folds of two enormous serpents. The skill and diligence with which the old man and lads support the serpents and keep them up to their work have been justly regarded as one of the noblest artistic illustrations of the mastery of human intelligence over brute inertia. *Ambrose Bierce*

**lap** One of the most important organs of the female system— an admirable provision of nature for the repose of infancy, but chiefly useful in rural festivities to support plates of cold chicken and heads of adult males. *Ambrose Bierce*

**Las Vegas** A Hollywood set they're going to pull down next week.

—A town where you can do so well that you arrive in a $7,000 Cadillac and leave in a $35,000 bus. *Anon.*

**lasslorn** Forsaken by his mistress. *Dr. Sam'l Johnson*

**last year** The best time to buy anything. *Marty Allen*

**"Late, Late Show"** The one that features an early, early movie. *Harold Coffin*

**Latin** The language of marble. *Browning*

**laughter** An interior convulsion, producing a distortion of the features and accompanied by inarticulate noises. It is infectious and, though, intermittent, incurable.

*Ambrose Bierce*

—The revolt of the intelligence.

—The only way you can destroy evil without malice and affirm good fellowship without mawkishness. *Bernard Shaw*

—Not a bad beginning for a friendship, and it is the best ending for one. *Oscar Wilde*

—Sudden glory. *Thomas Hobbes*

**laundromat** Automated rubadub-dub.

**laureate** Crowned with leaves of the laurel. In England the

Poet Laureate is an officer of the sovereign's court, acting as dancing skeleton at every royal fest and singing-mute at every royal funeral. Of all incumbents of that high office, Robert Southey had the most notable knack at drugging the Samson of public joy and cutting his hair to the quick; and he had an artistic color-sense which enabled him so to blacken a public grief as to give it the aspect of a national crime.
*Ambrose Bierce*

**Laurie, Annie** She's backit like the peacock,/ Her breast is like the swan;/ She's jimp around the middle,/ Her waist ye weel nicht span—/ Her waist ye weel nicht span;/ And she has a rollin' e'e./ And for Bonnie Annie Laurie/ I would lay me doon and die.
*William Douglas, a rejected suitor*

**law** A set of rules that permits society to sleep peacefully.
—A protection for the mighty and a punishment for the small.
*Russian proverb*
—In its majestic equality, forbids the rich as well as the poor to sleep under bridges, to beg in the streets, and to steal bread.
*Anatole France*

**LAWS** Spider webs that catch little flies but cannot hold big ones.
*Balzac*
—The conventions of an older generation. *Hippias*
—It's hard to explain to kids why a nation that spends billions for nuclear bombs is still trying to outlaw firecrackers.
*Lebanon (Ind.) Reporter*

**LAW OF GRAVITY** One of the first laws passed by Congress. It says no fair flying without an airplane. *Anon., Jr.*

**LAWYER** One skilled in circumvention of the law.
*Ambrose Bierce*
—A man who knows where the law errs.
—A man who earns his living by the sweat of his browbeating.
*James Huneker*
—When there's a rift in the lute, the business of the lawyer is to widen the rift and gather the loot.
*Arthur Garfield Hays*

**PHILADELPHIA LAWYER** An heir-splitter.

**LAWYERS** The only persons in whom ignorance of the law is not punished.
*Jeremy Bentham*

**lawn mower** The one thing that permits a man to run things around the house.

**NEW LAWN** The gay young blades. *Robert Lambert*

**Lawrence, D. H.** A plaster gnome on a stone toadstool in some suburban garden. At the same time he bore some resemblance to a bad self-portrait by Van Gogh. He had a rather matted, dank appearance. He looked as if he had just returned from spending an uncomfortable night in a very dark cave, hiding perhaps, in the darkness, from something which, at the same time, he was hunting.

*Dame Edith Sitwell*

**Lawrence, T. E.**  A kind of sandy Rover Boy. *Lowell Thomas*

**laymen**  The greatest single frozen asset of the kingdom of God.  *Bishop Richard C. Raines*

**Lazier Susan**  The whirligig gadget known as the Lazy Susan, now powered by electricity.

**laziness**  Unwarranted repose of manner in a person of low degree.  *Ambrose Bierce*

**Leacock, Stephen**  The kind of man who would never notice an oriole building a nest unless it came and built it in his hat in the hat room of the club.  *Stephen Leacock*

**lead**  A heavy blue-gray metal much used in giving stability to light lovers—particularly to those who love not wisely but other men's wives.  *Ambrose Bierce*

**leaf, dead**  Jack Frost's card.  *O. Henry*

**learner's permit**  What they should give you before you get a marriage license, too.  *Alan King*

**learning**  The kind of ignorance distinguishing the studious.  *Ambrose Bierce*

**leaving**  Being alive and breeding. Not to be confused with "living," about to depart.  *New Yorkese*

**leftovers**  Bits of food kept in the refrigerator until they are old enough to be thrown away.  *Changing Times*

**legacy**  A dead giveaway.

**legislative logrolling**  An aye for an aye.  *Robert G. Crooks*

**legislator**  An official who spends half his energies making laws and the other half helping his friends evade them.

**Legree, Simon**  The original efficiency expert.

**leisure**  Freedom from business or hurry; vacancy of mind; power to spend time according to choice. *Dr. Sam'l Johnson*
—Time you spend on jobs you don't get paid for.
*Changing Times*
—The bane of our time.  *R. F. Lucas*

**leotard**  A feminine undergarment—long stockings and panty in a single unit. They provide attractive cover for the legs and at the same time keep the backside cosy.
*Canadian Financial Post*
*New Yorkese*

**less**  Contraction of "let us."

**LESSER**  A barbarous corruption of *less,* formed by the

vulgar from the habit of terminating comparatives in *er;* afterwards adopted by poets, and then by writers of prose.                                     *Dr. Sam'l Johnson*

**lesson**   Not as much as.                               *New Yorkese*

**Lethe**   One of the rivers of Hades from which the souls of the dead had to drink to secure oblivion and forgetfulness. The living can get the same effect out of a bottle of highly-taxed spirits.

**Levant, Oscar**   A court jester in a society without any aristocracy.                                     *Clifton Fadiman*

—A pianist who has taken the mystery out of psychiatry.

—A man on such unfriendly terms with himself that he can dispense with enemies.                         *Clifton Fadiman*

**Levinson's Law No. 1**   If it was easy, everybody would be doing it.

**Levinson's Law No. 2**   When a man says "Honesty compels me . . ." it's a safe bet that Honesty lost the struggle.

**Levinson's Law No. 3**   If anything can possibly go wrong, it will.

**Levinson's Law No. 4**   If both shoes feel uncomfortable, maybe you've got them on the wrong feet.

**Levinson's Law No. 5**   We won't realize how wonderful today is until tomorrow.

**Levinson's Law No. 6**   In choosing a wife, visualize how she would look if she weren't a blonde.

**Levinson's Law No. 7**   If the smell that greets you as you enter a restaurant isn't a pleasant one, turn on your heel and leave.

**Levinson's Law No. 8**   If you get a bad waiter, do what you would do with a bad dish—call the manager and insist on another one.

**Levinson's Law No. 9**   If she pans her last boyfriend, later on how will she speak of you?

**Levinson's Law No. 10**   Sometimes the view is so great because you can't see the building you're looking from.

**Levinson's Law No. 11**   Every second drum majorette should be taken out and shot.

**Levinson's Law No. 12**   No matter how well a toupee blends in the back, in the front it always looks like hell.

**Levinson's Law No. 13**   If the paper carton of milk is damp at the bottom and the grocer assures you it won't leak—take another one.

**Levinson's Law No. 14**   The longer the key chain, the lousier the conductor.

**Levinson's Law No. 15**  You never hear the piano teach
upstairs until after you've signed the lease.

**Levinson's Law No. 16**  If you check your coat at t
theatre, there will be ten empty seats around you wh
you sit down.

**Levinson's Law No. 17**  The time when you win at the rac
is when you don't need it.

**Levinson's Law No. 18**  When you yank off the "Made
Japan" label, the whole article falls apart.

**lexicographer**  A writer of dictionaries; a harmless drud,
that busies himself in tracing the original, and detaili
the signification of words.            *Dr. Sam'l Johns*

—A pestilent fellow who, under the pretense of recordi
some particular stage in the development of a langua,
does what he can to arrest its growth, stiffen its flexibil
and mechanize its methods.            *Ambrose Bier*

—The slave of science, the pioneer of literature, doom
only to remove rubbish and clear obstructions from t
paths of Learning and Genius.            *Dr. Sam'l Johns*

—A literary surveyor trying to give words a sense of sen

—A reporter who works on a dictionary.

**liar**  One who tells an unpleasant truth.        *Oliver Herfo*

—A lawyer with a roving commission.        *Ambrose Bier*

—One who needs a good memory.            *Quintili*

**BIGGEST LIAR**  The one who talks most of himself.

*Chinese prove*

**liberal**  Not mean; not low in birth; not low in mind.

*Dr. Sam'l Johns*

—One who wants to spend the conservative's money.

*Changing Tim*

—One who gives away what he has not got.

—A congressman who gives people's money away.

**CONSERVATIVE**  One who wants to keep what he shou
not have.            *Rabbi Stephen W*

**RADICAL**  One who throws it away.

*Republican congressm*

**liberty**  One of Imagination's most precious possessions.

The rising People, hot and out of breath,
Roared round the palace: "Liberty or death!"
"If death will do," the King said, "let me reign;
You'll have, I'm sure, no reason to complain."

*Ambrose Bier*

—The inalienable right to stick your nose in the gove
ment's business.

—The right to be in the wrong.     *Harry Delmar\**
—The right to meddle with the affairs of others. *Abbe Galiani*

**library** A collection of books to match the curtains.

*Harry Martin\**

—A place where someone can find what he wants to know if he can find someone who knows the place where it is.
—This Arcadian silo of books.     *Ray Bradbury*

**libretto** The husband of Othello.     *Anon., Jr.*

**license number** The first thing you should take when you're run down.     *Anon.*

**lie** A truth nobody wants to believe.     *Charles Haas*
—'Tis but the truth in masquerade.     *Lord Byron*
—There are four kinds: lies, white lies, damned lies and statistics.     *Anon.*

**lie-berry** A ridding rum.     *New Yorkese*

**lie-detector** A complicated long-drawn-out electronic method of ascertaining what the ordinary wife detects instantly by woman's intuspicion.

**lieutenant commander** A lieutenant's wife. *Calgary Alberton*

**life** A game of continuous salesmanship.

*Dr. George W. Crane*

—Helplessly we arrive in this world, add what we can to the general confusion and then depart—with equal helplessness. The impression left behind by most of us usually just about equals the hole left in a bucket of water after a clenched fist is withdrawn.     *Arthur Godfrey*

—A gift so meretricious it can be given only to infants.

*Bill Manville*

—A house which we all burgle. We enter it uninvited, take all we can lay our hands on and then go out again.

*P. G. Wodehouse*

—We come in, we scream.

DEATH We yawn and go out.     *De Chancel*

—There is no cure for birth and death save to enjoy the interval.     *George Santayana*

—A jest, and all things show it, I thought so once, but now I know it.     *John Gay*

—A ladder—full of splinters and they always hurt the most when you're sliding down.     *William L. Brownell*

—A game played with marked cards.     *Anon.*

—A tissue woven of wind.     *Joseph Joubert*

—A disease from which sleep gives us relief every sixteen hours.     *Chamfort*

—A spiritual pickle preserving the body from decay.

*Ambrose Bierc*

—A foreign language: all men mispronounce it.

*Christopher Morle*

—A voyage that's homeward bound. *Possibly Herman Melvil*

—A badly written play.                    *Stella Adler*

—A fine thing, they say. *Toulouse-Lautrec, on his deathbe*

—An endless parade over an unfamiliar road—in the dar

—Stepping down a step or sitting in a chair and it isn't ther

*Ogden Nas*

—A search for truth—and there is no truth.

*Chinese proverb quoted by Norton Simo*

—A mental journey from believing anything to believin
nothing.

—A grindstone. Whether it grinds you down or polishes yo
up depends on what you're made of.            *Ano*

—A banquet, but most poor sons-of-bitches are starving t
death.                    *Auntie Mam*

—A condition that would be tolerable but for its amus
ments.            *Adapted from Bernard Sha*

—The art of drawing sufficient conclusions from insufficien
premises.                    *Samuel Butl*

—An L of a thing with a big if in the middle.    *Ano*

—A hospital in which every patient is possessed by the desi
to change his bed.                    *Baudelai*

—A gun. It can be aimed in only one direction at a tim

*Alison Fowler Sho*

—Not a bowl of cherries but a bunch of raisins—raisin' hec
raisin' kids or raisin' money!            *S. S. Bidd*

—A compromise with realities.            *William Feath*

—A hard, unceasing battle between man and his enemie
between woman and her friends.    *Schweizer Illustrier*

—Is too short and the time we waste in yawning never ca
be regained.                    *Stendh*

—A sheet of paper white
Whereon each one of us may write
His word or two, and then comes night.

*James Russell Lowe*

—But a walking shadow; a poor player
That struts and frets his hour upon the stage,
And then is heard no more.    Shakespeare, *Macbet*

—The thing that really happens to us while we are makir
other plans.            *Robert Lawrence Balze*

—A series of inspired follies. The difficulty is to find them to do. Never lose a chance: it doesn't come every day.
                    *Higgins in* Pygmalion, *by Bernard Shaw*

—This dream which lasteth but a day, wherein are many things on which to stumble and many things at which to laugh, and others like unto a stony path along which one goeth leaping.     *Aztec prayer, quoted by Adlai Stevenson*

—Like an onion; you peel off layer after layer and then you find there is nothing in it.          *James G. Huneker*

—And all the time you keep crying for no reason at all.

—Something that most people go through expecting to be disappointed.                    *Thomas Dreier*

—Hardens what is soft within us and softens what is hard.
                    *Dr. Joseph Fort Newton*

—An automobile. To run it a man must put in oil, water, gas and air. Some men leave out the oil and make enemies. Some leave out the water and ruin their physical ability. Some leave out the gas and get nowhere. Some leave out the air and complain what a rough road life is.
                    *Atlas Auto Finance Co.*

—Twenty years of having a man's mother asking him where he is going, forty years of having his wife ask the same question; and at the end, the mourners are wondering, too.
                    *Weekly Animator*

—Easier to take than you'd think; all that is necessary is to accept the impossible, do without the indispensable and bear the intolerable.            *Kathleen Norris*

—Far too important a thing ever to talk seriously about.
                    *Oscar Wilde*

"LIFE"  A magazine for people who move their lips when they look at pictures.

—The triumph of the Brownie over intelligence.

—A weekly of wide-eyed sophistication.

LIFETIME  Until the new model comes out.     *Ballyhoo*

LOVE OF LIFE  Man's greatest weakness.     *Molière*

light  Something which travels at incredible speed until it enters the brain.                    *Anon.*

LIGHT YEAR  One where there isn't too much homework.
                    *Anon., Jr.*

lighthouse  A tall building on the seashore in which the government maintains a lamp and the friend of a politician.
                    *Ambrose Bierce, 1881*

lightning  Free electricity.

**limb** What most of us are away out on when we discover that money doesn't grown on trees. *Cy N. Peace*

**limerick**

> Said an envious, erudite ermine,
> "There's one thing I cannot determine:
>   When a dame wears my coat,
>   She's a person of note;
> When I wear it, I'm called only vermin!"

—A certain young fellow named Beebee
Wished to wed with a lady named Phoebe.
  "But," he said, "I must see
  What the clerical fee
Be before Phoebe be Phoebe Beebee."

—There was a young lady of Kent
Who said that she knew what it meant
  When men asked her to dine,
  Gave her cocktails and wine,
She knew what it meant—but she went!

—There was a young salesman of Leeds
Rashly swallowed six packets of seeds.
  In a month, silly ass,
  He was covered with grass,
And he couldn't sit down for the weeds.

—The bottle of perfume that Willie sent
Was highly displeasing to Millicent;
  Her thanks were so cold
  They quarreled, I'm told,
Through that silly scent Willie sent Millicent.

—A maiden at college, Miss Breeze,
Weighed down by B.A.'s and Ph.D.'s.
  Collapsed from the strain.
  Said her doctor, "It's plain
You are killing yourself—by degrees!"

—There was a young fellow named Hall,
Who fell in the spring in the fall;
  'Twould have been a sad thing
  If he'd died in the spring,
But he didn't—he died in the fall.

—A young fellah of Tomahawk Bluff
  Carried pistols to make him look tough.
    When they asked, "Do you chew?"
    He said, "Yeth, I do,
  I'm a wegular wip-snortin' wough."

**linen** Jantzen's first name.    *Bostonese* (See "Jantzen")

**lingerie** Gay nighties.    *Jacob M. Brande*

**lipstick** The definition of a woman's mouth.

**Lipton** The capital of Ceylon.    *Anon., Jr.*

**lipwisdom** Wisdom in talk without practice.

          *Dr. Sam'l Johnson*

**liquor** The oldest of medicines.    *Morris E. Chafey, M.D.*

**lisp** To limp when you talk.    *Anon., Jr.*
—To thskip with the tongue.

**literary style** Language inside language.    *George Steiner*

**literati (Hollywood)** Those who can read and write.

**literature** News that stays news.    *Ezra Pound*

  ESCAPE LITERATURE What today's writers seem determined to do.    *Ivern Boyett*

  GREAT LITERATURE The creation, for the most part, of
  disreputable characters, many of whom looked rather
  seedy, some of whom were drunken blackguards, a few
  of whom were swindlers or perpetual borrowers, rowdies,
  gamblers or slaves to a drug.    *William Dean Howells*

**litigant** A person about to give up his skin for the hope of
retaining his bones.    *Ambrose Bierce*

**little** Smaller than average; as a little mountain, a little
cinder. When urged to allow "a little inflation" during
World War II, President Roosevelt said: "That's like 'a
little pregnant.' "

**little Willie**

    Willie saw some dynamite,
    Couldn't understand it quite.
    Curiosity never pays;
    It rained Willie seven days.

—Willie fell down the elevator—
Wasn't found till six days later.
Then the neighbors sniffed, "Gee whizz!
What a spoiled child Willie is!"

—Into the cistern little Willie
Pushed his little sister Lily.
Mother couldn't find our daughter:
Now we sterilize our water.

**liquidate** To drink up the profits. *Charlotte Holicke*
**live** To think. *Cicer*
**liver** A large red organ thoughtfully provided by nature t
be bilious with. *Ambrose Bierc*
**living, modern** The development in many different fields c
techniques for keeping clean at a cost so low that prac
tically everybody can afford the luxury of not being di
gusting. *Aldous Huxle*
**living room** Where the line forms for an enraptured c
envious look at the new kitchen. Cincinnati *Enquire*
**load** As much drink as one can bear. *Dr. Sam'l Johnso*
—There are those that can never sleep without their *loac*
nor enjoy one easy thought, till they have laid all thei
cares to rest with a bottle. *L'Estrang*
**loafer** A poor man impersonating a millionaire.
—Nowadays about the only person who knows what he
doing. *Rex Moble*
**loan shark** A rapacious fish that attacks people when the
are beyond their financial depth. *Ano*
**lobbyist** A man trying to get people to do something yo
don't like. If you like what he is pushing, he is not
lobbyist. Then he is just a nice fellow going to Washingto
to let them know there what the folks back home thin
*Arthur T. Hadle*
**local express** A train that doesn't stop long at all station
**locksmith** A Beatle hairdresser. *James Dav*
**locomotive** The only thing that's not afraid of a teen-age
in a hot rod. *Ano*
**loft** Past tense denoting merriment; e.g., "Our opponen
loft when we promised the country prosperity, but . .
*Bostones*
**logic** The art of thinking and reasoning in strict accordanc
with the limitations and incapacities of the human mi
understanding. The basic of logic is the syllogism, consis
ing of a major and a minor premise and a conclusion—thu
    Major premise: Sixty men can do a piece of work sixt
times as quickly as one man.
    Minor premise: One man can dig a post-hole in sixt
seconds; therefore—

Conclusion: Sixty men can dig a post-hole in one second. This may be called the syllogism arithmetical, in which, by combining logic and mathematics, we obtain a double certainty and are twice blessed.                    *Ambrose Bierce*

**London**  The metropolis New York thinks it is.

—The swinging city today.                    *Walter Shenson*

—A place where we are all mongrels together, mainly on leash, but let out for short, mad daily scampers in the park.                    *V. S. Pritchett*

LONDONER  An individual who loves to be in the park with his arms around his girl to the scandal of puritanic foreigners who see miles of park treated as a public bedroom.                    *V. S. Pritchett*

LONDONERS  A people kippered by the variable fogs and smogs of ten thousand bad days and nights.

**lone guile and**  A sleeping subcontinent stretching east of New York City.                    *New Yorkese*

**loneliness**  Not so much a matter of isolation as of insulation.                    *Harold W. Ruopp*

—A prison that can be opened only from the inside.                    *Annabelle, Zurich*

**long run (Broadway)**  It's like a housewife having to cook the same meal every night—and then having to eat it.                    *Rex Harrison*

**long shot**  Any bet you cash.                    *Jimmy Cannon*

LONG SHOT (HOLLYWOOD)  Any scene without sex.                    *Groucho Marx*

**longevity**  The postponement of senility.

—An achievement to which there is no short-cut.

—Uncommon extension of the fear of death.                    *Ambrose Bierce*

**loquacity**  A disorder which renders the sufferer unable to curb his tongue when you wish to talk.                    *Ambrose Bierce*

**lord**  In American society, an English tourist above the state of a costermonger.                    *Ambrose Bierce*

LORD CHESTERFIELD  The fourth earl, whose letters to his natural son taught him "the morals of a whore and the manners of a dancing master." *Dr. Sam'l Johnson, who couldn't get Chesterfield to back his Dictionary.*

**lorgnette**  Spectacles made for women who make spectacles of themselves.

—A dirty look you can hold in your hand.                    *Fibber McGee*

**Los Angeles**  A town where you can watch night baseball almost any afternoon.                    *Changing Times*

—The Cassius Clay of municipalities.

                    Charles Denton in the San Francisco *Examiner*

—Oklahoma City with an overactive pituitary gland.

**LOS ANGELES SOCIETY GIRL**  Someone who's been through high school.                    *Ethel Barrymore*

**lost and found department**  Where people bring things they've found and can't use.                    *Peter Nero*

**love**  Ah, sweet mystery of life.                    *Anon.*

—The feeling that you feel when you feel you are going to feel a feeling that you never felt before.  *College Humor*

—A great teacher.                    *St. Augustine*

—Being stupid together.                    *Paul Valéry*

—The tie that blinds.                    *Maxwell Shane*

—Selfishness for two.                    *Mme. de Staël*

—An invention of death.                    *Claude Roy*

—Happiness given back and forth.                    *Freundin*

—Having the wool pulled over your sheep eyes.

—A flower.

**FRIENDSHIP**  A vegetable.                    *Paul-Jean Toulet*

—Love is like those second-rate hotels where all the luxury is in the lobby.                    *Paul-Jean Toulet*

—A conflict between reflexes and reflections.

                    *Magnus Hirschfeld*

—Let the man who does not wish to be idle fall in love. *Ovid*

—The sweet tussle.                    *Jean Antoine de Baif*

—The same old, sad sensation.

                    Larry Hart, *Bewitched, Bothered and Bewildered*

—A credulous thing.                    *Ovid*

—Like an electric blanket with someone else controlling the switch.                    *Kathy Carlyle*

—The pleasure of the heart.

                    *Jean Anouilh, possibly quoting Marivaux*

—The exchange of two fancies and the contact of two skins.

                    *Nicholas Chamfort*

—A disease that begins with a fever and ends with a yawn.

                    *Cynic's Cyclopaedia*

—A temporary insanity curable by marriage or by removal of the patient from the influences under which he incurred the disorder. The disease, like *caries* and many other ailments, is prevalent only among civilized races living under artificial conditions; barbarous nations breathing pure air

and eating simple food enjoy immunity from its ravages.
It is sometimes fatal, but more frequently to the physician
than to the patient.                        *Ambrose Bierce*
-The delusion that one woman differs from another.
                                              *H. L. Mencken*
-The delightful interval between meeting a beautiful girl
and discovering that she looks like a haddock.
                                              *John Barrymore*
-The only fire against which there is no insurance.
                                                  *Edith Piaf*
-The strange bewilderment which overtakes one person on
account of another person. *James Thurber and E. B. White*
-Veneral gymnastics dished up with a touch of sentimentality.                                          *Gautier*
-The only big difference in the game of love over the last
few thousand years is that they've changed trumps from
clubs to diamonds.                        Indianapolis *Star*
-The Frenchman intends to love many women; the Italian
desires to love all women; the Englishman will love only
himself and the Austrians we meet don't seem to love anybody at all. The American wants to love one woman all his
life. We're for him!                        *Else Lachmann*
-An alliance of friendship and lust; if the former predomi-
nates, it is passion exalted and refined; but if the latter,
gross and sensual.                        *Godey's Lady's Book*
-An emotion based on a view of women that is impossible
to those who have had any experience with them.
                                              *H. L. Mencken*
-Religion has done love a great service by making it a sin.
                                              *Anatole France*
-People fall in love with themselves almost immediately
after birth. This is invariably the beginning of a life-long
romance. There is no record of infidelity, separation or
divorce between humans and their egos.    *Henry Singer*
ADOLESCENT LOVE  Water in a basket.      *Spanish saying*
LOVE STORY  A comedy of Eros.                    *Anon.*
SELF-LOVE  The flaw of consciousness.
—He that falls in love with himself will have no rivals.
                                          *Benjamin Franklin*
TRUE LOVE  Like a ghost; everybody talks about it, but
   few have seen it.                      *La Rochefoucauld*
—Marrying the girl even though she doesn't have a steady
   job.                                    *G. Norman Collie*

UNDYING LOVE  The kind you wouldn't die for.

LOVER  A man who tries to be more amiable than it is possible for him to be.    *Nicholas Chamfort*

—A romantic person who thinks almost as much of another person as he does of himself.

LOVER'S LANE  A stretch of road where a fellow parks his car to try out his clutch.

—A secluded place with indoor outdoor car-petting.

LOVER'S LEAP  The distance between twin beds. *Playboy*

NATURE LOVER  A man who goes into the woods without a girl.

LOVING  The finger of God on a man's shoulder.
                                                *Charles Morgan*

low-calorie food  Something you eat to fool your mind that your stomach is full.

Luce, Henry  The Printer's Devil.    *Harvard Lampoon*

luck  Good planning, carefully executed. *American Salesman*

luggage  Now that porters are a disappearing lot, that which you lug about.

—Any thing cumbrous and unwieldy that is to be carried away; any thing of more weight than value.
                                                *Dr. Sam'l Johnson*

LUMBER  Any thing useless or cumbersome; any thing o more bulk than value.    *Dr. Sam'l Johnson*

lunacy  A condition where dreams overflow into life.
                                                *Connolly Norman*

LUNATICS  What they will call the first men who volunteer to be rocketed to the moon.

lunarian  An inhabitant of the moon, as distinguished from Lunatic, one whom the moon inhabits.    *Ambrose Bierce*

lunch, luncheon  As much food as one's hand can hold.
                                    *Dr. Sam'l Johnson* (See "Bit")

LUNCHEON  The feminine of lunch.    *Anon., J*

lungs  Those wonderful windbags.    *J. D. Ratcl*

Lunt, Alfred  An actor with his head in the clouds and h feet in the box office.    *Noel Cowar*

luscious  Sweet, so as to nauseate.    *Dr. Sam'l Johnso*

lush  One who pours ale on troubled vodkas.    *Ano*

lustre  The space of five years.    *Dr. Sam'l Johnsc*

Luther, Martin  A man who died a horrible death. He wa excommunicated by a bull.    *Anon., J*

luxury  The things that make death terrible.
                                                *Dr. Sam'l Johnso*

—Something that makes life richer and the buyer poore

**LXXX**   Love and kisses.              *Anon., Jr.*

**lynching bee**   A noose conference.     *Frank A. Knapp*

**lyric**   A poem to be sung accompanied by a lyre.

**lyre**   An ancient instrument of torture.   *Ambrose Bierce*

# M

**Macao**   About as racy as Albany.     *Caskie Stinnett\**

**"Macbeth"**   A play about a man who saw ghosts.

**mad**   Affected with a high degree of intellectual independence; not conforming to standards of thought, speech and action derived by the conformants from study of themselves; at odds with the majority; in short, unusual. It is noteworthy that persons are pronounced mad by officials destitute of evidence that themselves are sane. For illustration, this present (and illustrious) lexicographer is no firmer in the faith of his own sanity than is any inmate of any madhouse in the land; yet for aught he knows to the contrary, instead of the lofty occupation that seems to him to be engaging his powers he may really be beating his hands against the window bars of an asylum and declaring himself Noah Webster, to the innocent delight of many thoughtless spectators.     *Ambrose Bierce*

**madam**   One for whom the belles toil.     *Playboy*

**Madison Avenue**   Where they took the padding out of the shoulders and put it in the expense account.

**madman**   One who suffers from absence of mind.

  —We want a few mad people now. See where the sane ones have landed us!     *Bernard Shaw*

**madrigal**   A nonreligious motet.     *Aldous Huxley*

**magazine**   Derived from two Arabic words, *makhazin,* meaning warehouse, and *khazana,* meaning to store up. Brought to England by sixteenth-century travelers, the word gradually came to mean, a storehouse or treasury of information. It was first used in a literary sense in 1731, when it appeared as a name on the still-flourishing *Gentleman's Magazine,* which described itself as a fine collection of subjects "to treasure up."     *Sunshine Magazine*

—A large pamphlet issued at regular intervals, usually bulg
ing with coupons. Used to cover coffee tables.

**Magdalene** An inhabitant of Magdala. Popularly, a woma
found out. This definition of the word has the authorit
of ignorance. *Ambrose Bierc*

**magic** An art of converting superstition into coin. There ar
other arts serving the same high purpose, but the discree
lexicographer does not name them. *Ambrose Bierc*

—A word about to join "new," "best," and "quick" as s
worn out that they have become invisible to the public i
ads. *Advertising Diges*

—Pulling a rabbit out of a hat.

STUPIDITY Letting the cat out of the bag.

**magnesium** The best food for babies. It will stop almos
anything. *Anon., Jr. (British Division*

MAGNESIUM SILICATE Another name for talc. We call i
talc because who would want to put magnesium silicat
on a little baby? *Anon., J*

**magnificent** Having a grandeur or splendor superior to tha
to which the spectator is accustomed, as the ears of an as
to a rabbit, or the glory of a glowworm to a maggot.
*Ambrose Bierc*

**maidenhead** A thing oft smothered in bed.
*Merry Drollerie (166*

**mail order** A method of purchasing disappointment by post

**makeabuck** The Eleventh Commandment. *Neword*

**mal de mer** A French expression meaning "mother-in-law.
*Anon., J*

**male** The lord of the home—if he's under three years ol
*Anon*

**malefactor** The chief factor in the progress of the huma
race. *Ambrose Bierc*

**man** The unknown. *Dr. Alexis Carre*

—An animal that cooks his victuals. *Bark*

—An animal who looks for home cooking in a restauran
and restaurant service at home.

—The animal who gets pleasure from doing those thing
which give him no pleasure. *Latap*

—Merely a successful animal. *Remy de Gourmor*

—The only animal that can be a fool. *Holbrook Jackso*

—A religious animal. *Edmund Burk*

—An unfinished animal. *Anor*

—The only animal that plays poker. *Don Herol*

—A higher species of animal that produces poems and philosophical systems in much the same way silkworms produce cocoons and bees hives. *Hippolyte Taine*

—That creature who should not be mourned at his death, but at his birth. *Baron de Montesquieu*

—By no means an ideal creature. Nature holds no brief for the human experiment; it must stand or fall by its results. If Man will not serve, Nature will try another experiment. *Bernard Shaw*

—A creature who cannot make a worm, and yet makes gods by the dozen. *Montaigne*

—A compassionate creature who has done away with the horse and put himself in the harness.

—A wild species, breeding at random and always propagating his kind to the limit of available food supplies. *Aldous Huxley*

—An embodied spirit. *Aldous Huxley*

—An ape that has learned to talk. *Aldous Huxley*

—If it were not for language, we would only be hairless chimpanzees.

—An educated chimpanzee.

—An animal so lost in rapturous contemplation of what he thinks he is as to overlook what he indubitably ought to be. His chief occupation is extermination of other animals and his own species, which, however, multiplies with such insistent rapidity as to infest the whole habitable earth and Canada. *Ambrose Bierce*

—His own greatest enemy, and as it were, his own executioner. *Sir Thomas Browne*

—A mean between nothing and everything. *Pascal*

—But a breath and a shadow. *Euripides*

—Only a reed, the weakest in Nature; but he is a thinking reed. *Pascal*

—A fallen god who remembers heaven. *Lamartine*

—A god playing the fool. *Ralph Waldo Emerson*

—One of God's blunders, or is God one of man's blunders? *Nietzsche*

—God's most noticeable mistake. *Anon.*

—The only animal that chews tobacco.

—Our Heavenly Father invented man because he was disappointed in the monkey. *Mark Twain*

—The inventor of stupidity. *Remy de Gourmont*

—The glory, jest and riddle of the world. *Alexander Pope*

—Of all created creatures man is the most detestable. Of the entire brood he is the only one . . . that possesses malice. . . . Also . . . he is the only creature that has a nasty mind.
*Mark Twain*

—It is not necessary to wear trousers and smoke big cigars to live a man's life. Preface to *St. Joan,* by Bernard Shaw, who didn't smoke and who wore knickerbockers.

IDEAL MAN   The first husband of a widow.

MAN OF THE HOUR   One you've got to watch every minute.

POOR MAN   One who has nothing but money.
*American Salesman*

THOUGHTFUL MAN   One who gives his wife a birthday present without mentioning her birthday past.
*Frank G. McInnis*

OUTDOOR MAN   A fellow who hammers on the radiator for more heat while he is dressing to go skiing. *Jack Herbert*

SELF-MADE MAN   One who would have done better if he had let out the contract.

—The result of cheap labor and long hours.

WELL-INFORMED MAN   One whose wife has just told him what she thinks of him.                    *Ray Fine*

MANKIND   The diminutive of man.
*Anon., Jr. (British Division)*

—Entirely determined by hunger and love.
*Anatole France*

—A human species with a most conspicuous failing: an inability to stay quiet.          *Walter Bagehot*

managed abundance   A campaign to make the U.S. eat its way to agriculture stability.

manager, beloved   An old guy who hasn't any more fighters.
*Jimmy Cannon*

Manhattan   A body of land consisting of four million square males, completely surrounded by women.
Opening line of *The Opposite Sex*

manicurist   A woman who makes money hand over fist.
*Anon.*

—One who has made a cult of the extremities.

Mann, Thomas   A writer stiffened by the public solemnity of his performance.          *George Steiner*

manners   Like the zero in arithmetic, may not be much in themselves, but they are capable of adding a great deal to the value of everything else.          *Freya Stark*

map   A piece of paper to help you get lost.          *Anon., Jr.*

ROAD MAP   The only thing that doesn't fold up after a long trip.   *Changing Times*

**March**   Time to put away the snow shovel but not yet time to get out the lawn mower.   *Ibid.*

—The month that comes in like a lion and hangs around like a polar bear.   *Bill Vaughan*

**Mare Nostrum**   Quack horse medicine.   *Anon., Jr.*

**market**   A place marked off for the purpose of cheating.
   *Anarcharses, 600 B.C.*

**marquee**   An actor's idea of heaven. *Anon. theatre manager*

**marriage**   Mutual misunderstanding.   *Oscar Wilde*

—Two toothbrushes with a single tube of paste.

—A three-ring circus: engagement ring, wedding ring and suffering.   *Roger Price*

—One long stupidity.   *Nietzsche*

—The worst punishment.   *Russian proverb*

—Mate service.   *Myra Garst**

—The only adventure open to the cowardly.   *Voltaire*

—A status of antagonistic cooperation.   *Anon. Chicagoan*

—An entrapment into penury.   *Harry Golden*

—Formerly a man wondered if he could afford to marry; now he wonders if he can get along without a working wife.   *Carl Ellstam*

—Anyone who thinks it is a 50–50 proposition doesn't understand women or fractions.   *Danny Thomas*

—A cage. The birds without try desperately to get in, and those within try desperately to get out.
   *Montaigne (1533–1592)*

—A feast where the grace is sometimes better than the dinner.   *Charles Caleb Colton*

—A long banquet with the dessert served first.   *Playboy*

—A highly sanitary institution.   *H. L. Mencken*

—When a man gets billed for the times he cooed.

—Love parsonified.   *Anon.*

—The process of finding out what sort of guy your wife would have preferred.   *Sundial*

—An institution that entitles women to the protection of strong men who steady the stepladder for them while they paint the kitchen ceiling.   *Wall Street Journal*

—Like a violin. After the beautiful music is over, the strings are still attached.   *Irish Independent*

—Oceans of emotions surrounded by expanses of expenses.
   *Circle Arrow Reader*

—A condition where no wife gets what she expected and no husband expected what he's getting. *Schweizer Illustrierte*

—A triumph of habit over hate. *Oscar Levant*

—The triumph of inertia over irritation. *Gene Raskin**

—A man needs a wife because sooner or later something is bound to happen that he can't blame on the government.

—An obedience school for many a gay dog. *Frank J. Pepe*

—The man who said you can't teach an old dog new tricks obviously was not married. *Raymond Duncan*

—What a howl would go up if people had to pay the preacher as much for marrying them as they have to pay a lawyer for getting a divorce. *Employment Counselor*

—A throwback to the Victorian Age. I've always contended that the marriage license should be issued the same as a driver's license—subject to expiration and renewal.

*George Sanders*

—Like a tango: it takes two, and sometimes one has to bend over backward to keep the dance going.

*Margaret T. White*

—A condition which breaks down the natural barrier between the sexes. *Sarah Palfrey*

—The end of love at first sight.

—The distance between Niagara Falls and Reno.

—The original duet-yourself project. *Kenneth J. Shively*

—If the current proverb is true, it has two good days—the first and the last. *Piron (1689-1773)*

—The institution with probably the poorest public relations in the world. However, its business is only slightly short of spectacular. *Douglas Meador*

—Not only another mouth to feed, but a great big one to listen to.

—A system of producing motors for tricycles. *Harold Orben*

MARRIAGE LICENSE  A certificate that gives a woman the right to drive a man. *Joseph Gancher*

MARRYING  Playing the fool all one's life long.

*William Congreve*

Mars  A plant that has planet life. *Anon., Jr.*

Marshall Plan  A G.I. Bill for countries. *Art Buchwald*

martinet  Borrowed from Jean Martinet, Louis XIV's Inspector General of Infantry, an autocratic drill-master killed by his own artillery while leading the infantry, some say accidentally.

martyr  One who moves along the line of least reluctance to a desired death. *Ambrose Bierce*

—Something like a bachelor.                        *Anon., Jr.*

MARTYRDOM   The only way in which a man can become
    famous without ability.                *Bernard Shaw*
    (Of course this was before rock 'n' roll.)

**Marx, Karl**   One of the Marx Brothers.          *Anon., Jr.*

**mascara**   What the redskins do to the settlers when they get
    on the warpath.                       *Anon., Jr.*

**master of ceremonies**   A guy who tells you what is coming
    next—but not how to avoid it.          *Milton Berle*

**mastication**   What the Italians do with their hands when
    they talk English.                    *Anon., Jr.*

**Mata Hari**   Suicide in Japanese.                *Anon., Jr.*

**matchbooks**   The one kind of book where the U.S. outshines
    the rest of the world by about ten billion a year.

**maternity dress**   A slip cover.

**maternity shop**   A business where accidents are covered.

**maternity ward**   The only place in the world where there
    isn't a chance of evading the issue.    *Superior Cirkuts*

**matrimony**   The only life sentence which is suspended for
    bad behavior.                         *Anon.*

—A place where souls suffer for a time on account of their
    sins.                                 *Anon., Jr.*

**mature**   Voting the same way as I do.   *Adlai Stevenson*

MATURING   The journey into disillusionment.

MATURITY   The rusty trickle of the fountain of youth.

—The time of life when, if you had the time, you'd have
    the time of your life.                *Changing Times*

**maudlin** (*Maudlin* is the corrupt appellation of *Magdalen*,
    who being drawn by painters with swoln eyes, and dis-
    ordered look, a drunken countenance, seems to have been
    so named from a ludicrous resemblance to the picture of
    *Magdalen*.) Drunk; fuddled.        *Dr. Sam'l Johnson*

**Maugham, W. Somerset**   Like blotting paper, he took in
    everything and all of it came out as fiction treated with
    superlative skill.   *Alexander S. Frere, his literary executor*

**mausoleum**   Originally the elaborate, 100-foot-high tomb of
    Mausolus, King of Caria, erected in 353 by his widow.

—The final and funniest folly of the rich.   *Ambrose Bierce*

**max**   Causes or creates; as in: "Max no difference."
                                         *New Yorkese*

**mayonnaise**   One of the sauces which serve the French in
    place of a state religion.[1]            *Ambrose Bierce*

---

[1] See De Gaullism.

**M.C.** Not Member of Congress, but Master of Confusion.
*Abraham J. Multer (D-N.Y.) M.C.*

**me** The objectionable case of I. The personal pronoun in English has three cases, the dominative, the objectionable and the oppressive. *Ambrose Bierce*

**meadow** Substance, as in: "What'sa meadow with you?"
*New Yorkese*

**meander** To proceed sinuously and aimlessly. The word is the ancient name of a river about one hundred and fifty miles south of Troy, which turned and twisted in the effort to get out of hearing when the Greeks and Trojans boasted of their prowess. *Ambrose Bierce*

**meany** A guy who would put tacks on an electric chair.

MEANIE The fellow in the middle between Eenie and Moe. *Anon., Jr.*

**meat** A food you now get at a supermarket in a cardboard tray, fat side down. *Harry Golden*

**mediator** A man who says, "Punch me instead."
*Anon., Jr. (British Division)*

**medicare** What is about to replace sex in Hollywood. *Time*
—Dr. Johnson (Lyndon B., that is).

**medicine** A stone flung down the Bowery to kill a dog in Broadway. *Ambrose Bierce*

—We've made great medical progress in the last generation. What used to be merely an itch is now an allergy.
*Sunshine Magazine*

—The desire to take medicine is perhaps the greatest feature which distinguishes man from animals.
*Sir William Osler, M.D.*

—The troubled calling. *Selig Greenberg*

—Medical specialization has reached such a state today that patients have to learn to diagnose themselves before they know which specialist to call. *Two Minutes with You*

—A business to prevent people from dying natural deaths.
*Anon.*

—An art that consists of amusing the patient while nature cures the disease. Doctors pour drugs of which they know little, to cure diseases of which they know less, into human beings of whom they know nothing. *Voltaire*

GROUP MEDICINE Where twenty-five kind relatives and thoughtful friends pitch in with a cure apiece for the cold in your head. *Wayfarer*

SOCIALIZED MEDICINE Giving free diagnoses at parties.
*Anon. doctor*

**meekness** Uncommon patience in planning a revenge that is worth while.         *Ambrose Bierce*

**melancholy** The pleasure of being sad.       *Victor Hugo*

**Melba** A peach dessert named after Nellie Porter Mitchell, the Australian soprano who named herself after the City of Melbourne.

—An island where Napolean was imprisoned.     *Anon., Jr.*

    MELBA, NELLIE A coloratura who never bothered much about acting. She did not need to, with her throat full of larks.         *Lawrence Gilman*

**memento** The keepsake of an event, such as a hotelroom Bible.

**memoirs** Books usually written by people who remember very little or have done little worth remembering.

        *Oscar Wilde*

**memory** What tells a man his wife's birthday was yesterday.         *Mario Rocco*

—What makes you wonder what you've forgotten to do.

        *Franklin P. Jones*

—What keeps telling you that you know the guy without giving you any idea of whom he is.     *Franklin P. Jones*

—The diary that we all carry about with us.   *Oscar Wilde*

—A great memory does not make a mind any more than a dictionary is a piece of literature.     *John Henry Newman*

—A nursery in which children who have grown old play with their broken toys.         *Claude Houghton*

**men** People who are always wondering what the future holds in store. Women always wonder what the store will hold in the future.         *Anon.*

—Only little boys.

With more expensive toys.

—Animals.

    PRINCES Animals whom no one has tied up. *Montesquieu*

    AD MEN The fellows with charcoal gray hearts.

        *Milton Berle*

    GREAT MEN The apparent freaks of nature. *Bernard Shaw*

    —Ones who not only leave footprints in the sands of time, but also leave statues in the park.     *Vesta M. Kelly*

    MARRIED MEN Merely bachelors who weakened under the strain.         *George Ade*

**Mencken, H. L.** A writer who denounces life and makes you want to live.         *Walter Lippmann*

—The kettle-drummer of the revolt of the twenties.

        *Gerald W. Johnson*

—Disturber of the peace.    *William Manchester*

—The Baltimore aureole.    *Paul H. Oehser*\*

**menstruation**    The weeping of a disappointed uterus.
*Anon. doctor*

**mental health**    It isn't so much mental illness that gets people into an institution. It's the neighbors finding out about it.
*Dr. William L. Grover, superintendent,*
*Cleveland State Hospital*

**Mephistopheles**    A devil of a fellow.

**Mercedes-Benz**    The rich man's Volkswagon.
*Hans Koningsberger*

**Mercer, Mabel**    A singer who can make you nostalgic for days you never knew.    *Sidney Zion*

**merchant**    One who trafficks to remote countries.
*Dr. Sam'l Johnson*

—One engaged in a commercial pursuit. A commercial pursuit is one in which the thing pursued is a dollar.
*Ambrose Bierce*

—A peddler without a horse.    *John Gunther*

**mercurial**    Easy glum, easy glow.    *Safe Driver*

**mercurichrome**    A medicine you put on a cut to make it look worse.

**Mercury**    The messenger god of commerce. The two associations are doubtless the reason why the name Mercury is incorporated in many newspaper titles, not the fact that Mercury was the patron of rogues and vagabonds.
*Cecil Hunt*

—The God of weather.    *Anon., Jr.*

**mercy**    An attribute beloved of detected offenders.
*Ambrose Bierce*

**Meredith, George**    A prose Browning, and so is Browning; he used poetry as a medium for writing in prose.
*Oscar Wilde*

**merger**    What happens in business when an irresistible force meets an immovable object.    *Changing Times*

**mermaid**    Not enough fish to fry and not enough woman to love.    *Art Ryon*

**merry-go-round**    The way of the whirled.

**metabolism**    A way of changing matter into energy without having to mess around with atoms.
*Anon., Jr. (Art Linkletter Dept.)*

**metallurgist**    A man who can look at a platinum blonde and tell whether she is virgin metal or common ore. *Playboy*

**metaphor**    A thing you shout through.    *Anon., Jr.*

**metaphysics** Reasoning from zero to get infinity.
—The finding of bad reasons for what we believe on instinct.
*F. H. Bradley*

**metatarsals** A race of people who lived in the foot of Italy.
*Anon., Jr.*

**meteors** Stars that are so hot that they have to leave in a hurry.
*Anon., Jr.*

**Methodist** A physician who practises by theory. One of a new kind of puritans lately arisen, so called from their profession to live by rules and in constant method.
*Dr. Sam'l Johnson*

**Methuselah** The oldest man recorded in the Bible; died at the age of 969 in the year of the Deluge, which was just as well, since he couldn't swim.

**metropolis** A stronghold of provincialism. *Ambrose Bierce*
—A town with a traffic problem.

**Mets** A baseball team that specializes in disaster.
*Rex Lardner*

—In a telephone call to a newspaper, a Mets fan asked the sports desk:
"How many runs did the Mets make today?"
"Nineteen," was the answer.
"Did they win or lose?"
(Actually, they beat the Cubs 19-1 that day, their finest hour.)

**middle age** That time in life when one wishes there were some other way to start the day than by getting up.
YOUTH Same definition.
OLD AGE Same definition.

—When each day makes you feel two days older.
*Gordon E. Thatcher*

—An average between the 18 you feel tonight and the 118 you'll feel tomorrow morning. *Quitman (Ga.) Free Press*

—When you start out with your spirits up and end with a rub down.
*Jules Henry Marr*

—When a man is warned to slow down by a doctor instead of a policeman.
*Sidney Brody*

—When you don't care where your wife goes, just so you don't have to go along.
*Anon. husband*

—When you begin to feel on Saturday night the way you used to feel on Monday morning.
*Changing Times*

—When a man can get exhausted simply by wrestling with his conscience.
*O. A. Battista*

—When a man feels he gets less for his money each time he goes to the barber. *O. A. Battista*

—When a man starts talking about what a fool he used to be. *Changing Times*

—When you begin to smile at things that used to cause you to laugh. *Puck*

—When a man returns a wink with a blink. *Dan Bennett*

⌐—When a man dreams about a banker saying "yes" instead of a girl. *Anon.*

—When the hardest thing to raise in your garden is your knees. *O. A. Battista*

—When you'd rather pay the piper than dance. *Ivern Boyett*

—When you want to see how long your car will last instead of how fast it will go. *National Safety News*

—When you are too young to take up golf and too old to rush up to the net. *Franklin P. Adams*

—Being too old to be fired but too young to be retired. *Changing Times*

—That difficult period between juvenile delinquency and senior citizenship when you have to take care of yourself. *In a Nutshell*

—When you begin to exchange your emotions for symptoms. *Irvin S. Cobb*

—When your idea of getting ahead is just to stay even. *Puck*

—When you use all the new wrinkles you can buy to get rid of the old ones. *Florence Clum*

—When you are impressed not with the fact that the grass is greener on the other side of the fence but rather how difficult the fence looks to get over.

North Vernon (Ind.) *Sun*

—When a man looks back and discovers that the mountain he's been climbing is only a molehill. *Changing Times*

—When you can't decide which there is most of—age or middle. *Anon.*

—Later than you think and sooner than you expect.

—When you burn the midnight oil about 9 P.M. *Robert Ryan*

—The uncomfortable feeling that perhaps your gray hair isn't premature. *Jim Harget*

—When a lot of dreamboats give up the shape. *Dan Bennett*

—Nothing is so apt to turn a middle-aged woman's hair gray as running out of rinse. *Franklin P. Jones*

MIDDLE-AGED WOMAN  One who has either made a hit or is a miss. *Anon.*

**middleman** A man who bamboozles one party and plunders the other. *Benjamin Disraeli*

**midwest** A grand reservoir for our excess population. *Boston clergyman*

**mid-yam** Not well-done, but still not roar. *New Yorkese*

**mile** Only six seconds long in the jet age of air transport. *Planes*

MILER A man who runs around in circles.

**military justice** To justice what military music is to music. *Georges Clemenceau*

**milker** A person with butterfingers.

**Miller, Henry** A panhandler on the street of life.

—That old boudoir Bolshevik—the Lenin of the dirty-word revolution. *Time*

**millionaire** A man with enough lettuce to choose his own tomatoes. *Red Skelton*

**mince pie** The stuff that dreams are made of. *Changing Times*

**mind** A mysterious form of matter secreted by the brain. Its chief activity consists in the endeavor to ascertain its own nature, the futility of the attempt being due to the fact that it has nothing but itself to know itself with. *Ambrose Bierce*

MINDS Like parachutes, only function when open. *Thomas R. Dewar*

**mink** Something you don't get from strangers. *Anon. showgirl*

**minor** Less objectionable. *Ambrose Bierce*

MINOR LEAGUES A group of ball clubs whose paying customers stay home to listen to the Game of the Day on television. *Jimmy Cannon*

**minute** A very short time unless you are holding your breath. *Anon., Jr.*

**miracle drug** Any one that doesn't cost a fortune.

**mirror** The best place for an ad to catch a woman's eye. *James Joyce*

**misanthrope** A person who hates what other people say; a hermit hates what he himself says. *Thornton Wilder*

**miscasting** Calvin Coolidge played by Arthur Godfrey.

**misdemeanor** An infraction of the law having less dignity than a felony and constituting no claim to admittance into the best criminal society. *Ambrose Bierce*

**miser** One who is only happy when he is miserable.
—One who lives poor to die rich. *Anon.*

**miserable les** The beatnik version of *Les Misérables*.
*Will Jones*

**mishmash** A low word. A mingle or hotchpotch.
*Dr. Sam'l Johnson*

**mishuga** The opposite of Miss No-Cal. *New Yorkese*

**miss** A title with which we brand unmarried women to indicate that they are in the market. Miss, Missis (Mrs.) and Mister (Mr.) are the three most distinctly disagreeable words in the language, in sound and sense. Two are corruptions of Mistress, the other of Master. In the general abolition of social titles in this our country they miraculously escaped to plague us. If we must have them, let us be consistent and give one to the unmarried man. I venture to suggest Mist. abbreviated to Mst.
*Ambrose Bierce*

**Mississippi** A desolate area of nothing with the bottom out.
*H. L. Mencken*

**mistake** A way to get maximum attention that is hard to beat. Hanover (N.H.) *Gazette*

**Mr. Meaner** The public prosecutor. *Anon., Jr.*

**mistletoe** Greenery bad for trees but good for two's.
*Arnold H. Glasow*

—A man who hates all mankind. *Anon., Jr.*

**mistresses** Surreptitious dishes.

**mitt** Edible flesh, as: "Today the spatial is mitt loaf."
*New Yorkese*

**mob** A group of people who can't remain calm and cool when collected.

**mockumentary** An unpretentious documentary film.

**moderate progressivism** Republicanese for "Don't just do something. Stand there." *Adlai Stevenson*

**moderation** A policy either neglected or pursued to excess.

**modern age** The time when the envy of the neighborhood is the man who has so many automatic conveniences in his house that he adds a spare room for the serviceman.
*Changing Times*

**modern apartment house** One in which both the landlord and the tenant are trying to raise the rent. *Cy N. Peace*

**modern composer** A baker who prepares a luscious-looking moist chocolate cake and then instead of flavoring it with sugar, uses vinegar.

**modern home** Where the bathroom is bigger than the kitchen. *Hugh Allen*

**modern housewife** One who presses buttons instead of clothes. *Earl Wilson*

**modern maid** One who believes that children should be seen and not had.

**modern playwright** One who has sold his birthright for a pot of message.

**modern sculptor** A man who can take a rough block of stone or wood, work on it for months and make it look like a rough block of stone or wood. *Dublin Opinion*

**modern technology** When you can't get the dead horn on your card fixed because the sign in front of the repair shop reads "Blow horn and automatic door will open."

**modern times** The period when man has lost his fear of God and acquired a fear of microbes. *Anon.*

**modernism** Deviation from the ancient and classical manner. A word invented by Swift. *Dr. Sam'l Johnson*

—Scribblers send us over their trash in prose and verse, with abominable curtailings and quaint modernisms.
*Jonathan Swift*

**modest** To shrink from watching.

MODESTY A characteristic that comes from awareness of one's own strength. *Cézanne*

—The one thing Texas hasn't got more of.

—An artificial emotion for an actor—like love to a call girl. *Jackie Gleason*

**Mohock** The name of a cruel nation of America given to ruffians who infested, or rather were imagined to infest, the streets of London. *Dr. Sam'l Johnson*

—A similar gang of well-born youths who infested the canals of Venice at night. *Casanova*

**moky** Dark; as *moky* weather. Ainsworth. It seems a corruption of murky; and in some places they call it muggy; dusky. *Dr. Sam'l Johnson*

**Mona Lisa** A picture puzzle.

**monastery** A place where they make money.
*Anon., Jr. (British Division)*

**Monday** In Christian countries, the day after the baseball game. *Ambrose Bierce*

**monetary expert** One who talks for an hour about money and makes you listen and when he's through, you ask yourself, "What's he talking about?" *Anon. senator*

**money** The principal export of the United States. *Ben Roth*
—The root of evil, all right; but lack of it is almost as bad.
La Habra (Cal.) *Star*

—Money isn't everything. In fact, the way things are going,
it soon won't be anything. *Changing Times*

—Maybe it isn't everything, but it's a wonderful substitute.
*Ibid.*

—A material which speaks sense in a language all nations
understand. *Aphra Behn*

—The most expensive thing. *Juliette Greco*

—The most convenient thing in the world. One of the most
useful contrivances ever invented: it is not its fault that
some people are foolish or miserly enough to be fonder of
it than of their souls. *Bernard Shaw*

—The most important thing in the world. It represents health,
strength, honor, generosity, and beauty as conspicuously
and undeniably as the want of it represents illness, weakness, disgrace, meanness, and ugliness. Not the least of its
virtues is that it destroys base people as certainly as it
fortifies and dignifies noble people.
Bernard Shaw, *The Gospel of St. Andrew Undershaft*

—A commodity that does not grow on trees. You've got to
beat the bushes for it. *Changing Times*

—The only substance which can keep a cold world from
nicknaming a citizen "Hey, you!" *Wilson Mizner*

—Something that gives a man wings that can take him everywhere except to heaven. *Russian proverb*

—That element which makes stupidity shine.
*Russian proverb*

—The theatre's sweet music. *Lewis Funke*

—The best passport. *Anon.*

—Something that things run into and people run out of. *Anon.*

—There was a time when a fool and his money were soon
parted. Now it happens to everybody.

—The poor man's credit card. *Playboy*

—A commodity that eliminates waiting, ends billings and is
even handier than a credit card. *Changing Times*

—Something that brushes by you on its way to Washington.
*Ibid.*

—The best tranquilizer.
—Still the most efficient labor saving device.
*Franklin P. Jones*

—Something that doesn't grow on trees.
*Gov. Nelson Rockefeller*

**MONEY IN THE BANK** Like a tube of toothpaste—easy to take out, but hard to put back in.     *Robert Ackerstrom*

**PUBLIC MONEY** Like holy water: everyone helps himself to it.     *Italian proverb*

**SPENDING MONEY** The only kind I earn.

         *Leonard K. Schiff*

**monocle** Mode in your eye.

**monkey** An organized sarcasm upon the human race.

         *Henry Ward Beecher*

**MONKEY WRENCH** A farm where apes live.     *Anon., Jr.*

**monologophobe** A guy who would rather walk naked in front of Saks Fifth Avenue than be caught using the same word more than once in three lines of type.

         (See "Synonymania") *Theodore M. Bernstein*

**monologue** A dialogue for one person.

         *Anon., Jr. (British Division)*

**monotonize** To act like a son of a bee and drone on and on.

         *Newords*

**monsieur** A term of reproach for a Frenchman.

         *Dr. Sam'l Johnson*

**monsoon** French for Mister.     *Anon., Jr.*

**Monte Carlo** A town full of old women, like Pasadena with a gambling casino.     *Marlene Dietrich*

**Montreal** The city saved by the French for the English from the Canadians.     *Anon.*

**mooers** A nation of people who worshipped sacred cows.

         *Anon., Jr.*

**moon** Something formerly promised by politicians, now by scientists.     *Jack Lambert*

**MOONLIGHTER** An employee who has two bosses trying to please him.

**morale** When your hands and feet keep on working when your head says it can't be done.

         *Southern Baptist Brotherhood Journal*

**MORALITY** The residue left after our cravings are satisfied.

         *Anon.*

**more** The comparative degree of too much. *Ambrose Bierce*

**morisco** A dancer of the morris or moorish dance.

         *Dr. Sam'l Johnson*

       I have seen

Him caper upright like a wild morisco,

Shaking the bloody darts, as he his bells.

         Shakespeare, *Henry VI*

MORRIS, MORRIS-DANCE   A dance in which bells are gingled or staves or swords clashed, which was learned by the Moors, and was probably a kind of Pyrrhick or military dance. *Dr. Sam'l Johnson*

**Mormonism**   A society of puritanical but theatre-going and music-loving polygamists. *Aldous Huxley*

**mortgage**   That which makes the months seem shorter and the years seem longer. *Changing Times*

**mortician**   A man whose life is a grave undertaking.

**Moses**   The inventor of the ten most universally broken laws.

**moth**   A worm that has turned.

**mother**   A kid's bosom friend.

—A person who, seeing there are only four pieces of pie for five people, promptly announces she never did care for pie. *Tenneva Jordan*

—Cook, chauffeur, maid, nurse and household manager all in one. She is the invention of necessity. *Changing Times*

MOTHER NATURE   A combination of two of the world's leading goddesses. The creator and destroyer.

—A providential process that gives us twelve years to develop a love for our children before turning them into teen-agers. *William A. Galvin*

MOTHER'S DAY CARDS   Greetings with poems printed in imitation handwriting, so that if Mom were in her second childhood she might be duped into believing that the sentiment was not a reach-me-down but custom-made, a lyrical outpouring from the sender's overflowing heart. *Aldous Huxley*

SMART MOTHER   One who knows a pounce of prevention is worth a pound of cure. *Imogene Fe*

MOTHER-IN-LAW   The other woman in many a domestic triangle.

—One who frequently goes too far by remaining too near. *Changing Times*

—It is impossible to please the whole world and your mother-in-law as well.

**motion pictures**   Stories written by the half-educated for the half-witted. *St. John Ervine*

ARTISTIC MOVIE   An accident that happened in a camera.

**motorcycle beatnicks**   Little-read riding hoods. *Harry C. Bau*

**motorist**   One who keeps pedestrians in good running condition. *Clarence Shir*

—A person who, after seeing a wreck, drives carefully for
several blocks.                                          *Anon.*

—A tourist with a heavy tan on his left forearm.

**Mt. Vernon**  A country place they're done all over in early
American.

**mountain climber**  One who wants to take just one more
peak.                                          *Scholastic Magazine*

**mountebank**  A doctor that mounts a bench in the market,
and boasts his infallible remedies and cures.
                                          *Dr. Sam'l Johnson*

**mourn**  Greater than.                                          *New Yorkese*

**mouse**  An animal which strews its path with fainting
women.                                          *Ambrose Bierce*

**mouth**  What catches no flies if it is closed.

—In man, the gateway to the soul; in woman, the outlet of
the heart.                                          *Ambrose Bierce*

MOUTH-FRIEND  One who professes friendship without in-
tending it.                                          *Dr. Sam'l Johnson*

**mum**  (Of this word I know not the original; it may be
observed, that when it is pronounced it leaves the lips
closed.) A word denoting prohibition to speak, or resolu-
tion not to speak; silence; hush.                                          *Dr. Sam'l Johnson*

—The citizens are *mum,* say not a word.
                                          Shakespeare, *Richard III*

**mumbo jumbo**  An elephant that doesn't speak clearly.
                                          *Anon., Jr.*

**mummies**  Egyptians that were pressed for time.
                                          *Ralph Mitchel*

**mundane**  The day following a heavenly weekend.
                                          *Ray Southworth*

**murder**  Always a mistake; one should never do anything
that one cannot talk about after dinner.                                          *Oscar Wilde*

**muscles**  What helps your bones stay together.
                                          *Anon., Jr. (N.Y. Division)*

—The difference between man and gorilla.

**muses**  There were nine: Calliope, Clio, Euterpe, Thalia,
Melpemone, Terpsichore, Erato, Polyhymnia and Urania.

MUSEUM  Home of the Muses. The first one, built by
Ptolemy about 300 B.C., was at Alexandria.

**museum piece**  An old tart.                                          *Robert Levinson\**

**museums**  Graveyards of the arts.                                          *De Lamartine*

**mushroom**  An upstart; a wretch risen from the dunghill; a
director of a company.                                          *Dr. Sam'l Johnson*

—What happens if you eat a toadstool and don't die.

*Anon., J*

**music** Communication that exposes us to the work of grea
minds that were dissatisfied by the limits of the spoke.
language. *Martin Tolchi*

—Dear noise.

—Much more enjoyable if you listen to it with your eyes shut
It is also more enjoyable if the people sitting near yo
listen to it with their mouths shut. *Instrumentali*

—The food of love. Shakespeare, *Twelfth Nigh*

—Moody food of us that trade in love.

*Cleopatra, according to Shakespear*

—The only language in which you cannot say a mean o
sarcastic thing. *John Erskine, who died before rock 'n' ro*

MUSICAL IGNORAMUS One who doesn't know his bras
from his oboe.

MUSICAL NOTATION Scarcely more than a collection o
extensive hints. *Herbert Weinstoc*

MUSICALE A function which brings out the conversation
abilities of the guests.

**muss-did** A condiment that goes wit mitt. *New Yorke*

**mussle-bound** To go clam digging.

**mustache** The thing that makes a girl feel like she's kissin
her toothbrush good night. *Honor Blackma*

—Mine is my radar. It pulls ideas out of places. Grea
painters need a luxuriant mustache like mine. The point
have to be just under the eyes to get the right perspectiv
*Salvador Da*

**mustachio** A green nut used in making ice cream.
*Laurel and Hard*

**mutter** A female parent, as in: "I'm going home to mutter
*New Yorke*

—A variation of meadow. "Was mutter wit use?"
*New Yorke*

**mystery** A trade; a calling; in this sense it should, accordin
to Warburton, be written *mistery*, from *mestier*, Frenc
a trade. *Dr. Sam'l Johnsc*

**mythology** The body of a primitive people's beliefs concer
ing its origin, early history, heroes, deities and so forth,
distinguished from the true accounts which it invents late
*Ambrose Bier*

—Religion minus faith.

# N

**nab-king** The dry cleaner's greatest enemy. *New Yorkese*

**nail** A small length of metal used for aiming before hammering the thumb.

**namby-pamby** Wishy-washy. Named after Ambrose Phillips, minor poet of insipid verse.

**name** The most personal pronoun.

**nanny goat** A butter from which you get milk.

**nap** All you have to do to get the world to beat a path to your door. *O. A. Battista*

**national debt** What we all seem to be saving for our old age. *Wall Street Journal*

**national gross profit** How much the government thought it made before the bills started coming in. *Anon., Jr.*

**national flower** The concrete cloverleaf. *Lewis Mumford*

**nationalism** A silly cock crowing on its own dunghill. *Richard Aldington*

**nature** The supreme tyrant that can never be slain or deposed. *Bernard Shaw*

—A hard taskmaster. *Bernard Shaw*

**navel** A dimple that wanted to become the center of attention. *Ade Kahn*

**naw** An underdeveloped negative.

**NBC vice president** A man who doesn't know what he's supposed to be doing there, and by the time he finds out, he's not there any longer. *Fred Allen*

**neat** Keen.

KEEN Neat.

NEAT WHEAT One devoid of reasoning powers. *New Yorkese*

**necking** A lofty name for that lowdown feeling.

**neckweed** Hemp. *Dr. Sam'l Johnson*

**neglect** Any time a fellow feels neglected, he should think of Whistler's father. *Midland, Tex., The Rotary Table*

**neighbor** One who wonders when that damned party will end. *Anon.*

NEIGHBORS People who live nearby who may be slow

about returning books, rakes, tools or dry vermouth but when it comes to bringing back your small children from a birthday party they are always right on time.

*Joe McCarthy*

GOOD NEIGHBOR   A fellow who smiles at you over the back fence but doesn't climb over it.   *Arthur "Bugs" Baer*

**neo-orthodoxy**   Calvinism in Bermuda shorts.

*John Alexander Mackay*

**nephews**   What the devil gives a man when God gives him no sons.   *Spanish proverb*

**nepotism**   Togetherness with pay.   *G. Norman Collie*

—Putting on heirs.   *Robert Fitch*

**neurologist**   A twitch doctor.   *Shelby Friedman*

**neurotic**   A person who worries about things that didn't happen in the past—instead of worrying about something that won't happen in the future, like normal people.

*The Reader's Digest*

—A person who thinks the world owes him a loving.

*Changing Times*

—A person who builds castles in the air.

PSYCHOTIC   One who lives in them.

PSYCHIATRIST   The one who collects the rent.

*Jerome Lawrence**

—The sweetheart of Sigmund Freud.   *Anon.*

**neutrality**   The big business in times of war. *Paul Tabori**

**Nevada**   A state with so much nothing that every day Las Vegas sends away hundreds of tourists with their pockets full of it.   *Reported by Josephine Cardamone*

—A state where women are made free.

—A state where the cream of society goes to get separated.

*Anon.*

**New Englander**   A person who talks through his nose to save wear and tear on his teeth.

**New Jersey**   What would be a happy state and a merry one if they could train their mosquitoes to be vegetarian.

**New Year's Eve**   Rolling with the punch.

—The time of year when a man most feels his age and his wife most often reminds him to act it.   *Changing Times*

NEW YEAR'S RESOLUTIONS   What you give up for Lent.

*Dolly Bremner or Anna Herbert*

**New York**   An unfinished mining camp.   *Bat Masterson*

—The wonderful, cruel, enchanting, bewildering, fatal, great city.   *O. Henry*

—A place where it must be against the law to smile.

*Schoolgirl visitor*

—The most horrible place on God's earth.     *Henry Miller*

—A city that specializes in man's immunity to man.

—Where all good little minks go when they die. *Brown Jug*

—Bogusburg on the East River (which is an estuary).

—A mile-high wall of people to be ascended by climbers plunging their knives in the backs of others and pulling themselves up.

—A city where you can get away with murder, unless you're parked alongside a fireplug at the time.     *Anon.*

—A city where everyone mutinies but no one deserts.

*Harry Hershfield*

—The capitol of greed and selfishness that corrupts all who linger here.

NEW YORKER An out of towner who has been sending money home ever since.     *The New Yorker*

**newfangled** Formed with vain or foolish love of novelty.

*Dr. Sam'l Johnson*

**newlywed** A guy who still tells his wife when he gets a pay raise.

**news** The peepshow of misery; literature in a hurry; everything that happens to you and anything you repeat. *Anon.*

BAD NEWS News that is always true.     *Spanish proverb*

**newspaper** A public publication in which the advertisements are 50 per cent truthful, while the reading matter rarely achieves that percentage.

—A journal to expose the faults of the world and the typographical errors of its staff.

—The keyhole of the world.     *Anon.*

—Words were invented to conceal thought; newspapers are a great improvement on a bad invention.

*Henry David Thoreau*

NEWSPAPER EDITOR A man who has convinced himself that he can bang out as good a column himself if he had the time.     *John O'Hara*

**newsreel** A series of catastrophes ending with a fashion show.     *Oscar Levant*

**"Newsweek"** A dull *Time, U.S. News and World Report*.

**Niagara Falls** The toilet bowel of America. *Anon. plumber*

**nice person** One who has more heel marks on him than a subway.     *Walter Winchell*

**nicotine** An important pesticide.

—The man who invented cigarettes.     *Anon., Jr.*

**nidget** (Corrupted from *nithing* or *niding*. The opprobrious term with which the man was anciently branded who refused to come to the royal standard in times of exigency.) A coward; a dastard. *Dr. Sam'l Johnson*

**niggle** The twentieth part of a doll. *New Yorkese*

**nightclub** An eating-drinking-show enterprise that abhors a vacuum of silence or space.

—A den of equality. *Kenneth Taylor*°

NIGHTCLUBS Popular because they are the only places still open by the time your wife gets dressed. *Arnold H. Glasow*

**Nightingale, Florence** A French opera singer, who sang to the soldiers during the French and Indian War. *Anon., Jr.*

—A famous Swedish soprano. *Anon., Jr.*

**nim** To take. In cant, to steal. *Dr. Sam'l Johnson*

**nincompoomp** (A corruption of the Latin *non compos*.) A fool; a trifler. *Dr. Sam'l Johnson*

**ninny hammer** A simpleton. *Dr. Sam'l Johnson*

**no** The adverb of negotiation. *Anon., Jr.*

**no-account** A person without a single credit card.

**Nobel, Alfred** Europe's richest vagabond. *Anon.*

**noise** A stench in the ear. Undomesticated music. The chief product and authenticating sign of civilization.
*Ambrose Bierce*

**nolition** Unwillingness; opposed to volition.
*Dr. Sam'l Johnson*

**nominee** A modest gentleman shrinking from the distinction of private life and diligently seeking the honorable obscurity of public office. *Ambrose Bierce*

**nonchalance** The ability to look like an owl when you have behaved like an ass. *Phi Delta Kappan*

**nonconformist** A free-lance thinker.

**none** Plenty when you're hunting tigers. *Anon.*

**nonsense** The objections that are made against this excellent dictionary. *Ambrose Bierce, The Devil's Dictionary*

**noon gland** Important section of the country believed to favor native Noon Glanders like the Candys. *Bostonese*

**noose** Reports of events, as: "No noose is good noose."
*New Yorkese*

**nose** An unmusical organ that should be seen and not heard.

**nostalgia** The realization that things weren't as unbearable as they seemed at the time. *Mac Benoff*

**Nostradamus** A seer whose predictions were so numerous

and obscure that they can be related to any important subsequent event.

**nostrum**  A medicine not yet made publick, but remaining in some single hand.  *Dr. Sam'l Johnson*

**not guilty**  The best two words in any language.
*Erich Maria Remarque*

**notoriety**  The fame of one's competitor for public honors.
*Ambrose Bierce*

**novel**  A small tale, generally of love.  *Dr. Sam'l Johnson*

—A short story padded. A species of composition bearing the same relation to literature that the panorama bears to art.
*Ambrose Bierce*

—A story that can be told in 500 to 1,000 pages. According to Gary Merrill, Carl Sandburg once wrote a novel in four lines:

"Papa loved Mama,
Mama loved men.
Mama's in the graveyard;
Papa's in the pen."

—A literary effort that must be sin to be appreciated.

—A mirror that strolls along a highway. Now it reflects the blue of the skies, now the mud puddles underfoot. *Stendhal*

NOVELIST  An unnatural phenomenon whose tale comes out of his head.  *Robert Jones*

—A man who tries to live on the fruits of his imagination.

**novelty dealer**  One who lives off the fad of the land.

**November**  The eleventh twelfth of a weariness.
*Ambrose Bierce*

**now**  The good old days you're going to miss in 1979.
*Phi Delta Kappan*

—There isn't any such word. By the time you've said it, "now" is "then."  *Anon. finance company*

**nowhere**  Where you can get without going. *Chinese proverb*

**nude**  Barely proper.

NUDIST  A person who has the advantage of not having to hold out his hand to see if it is raining.  *Tom Pepe*

**nudnick**  One who is naked in the brains.

**No. 1**  Third grade apples. Top grade is Extra Fancy, next is Fancy.  *U.S. Department of Agriculture*

**nurse, practical**  The step before we have Practical Doctors.

**nurse, registered**  A dame who shakes you at 2 A.M. and says: "Wake up—it's time to take your sleeping pill."

**nursery school**  A place parents send children to catch colds from each other so they can stay at home. *Changing Times*

**"o" turn** A new female driving manoeuver, during which they start a "U" turn and then change their minds.
*Royal Neighbor*

**oath** In law, a solemn appeal to the Deity, made binding upon the conscience by a penalty for perjury.
*Ambrose Bierce*

**oats** A grain, which in England is generally given to horses, but in Scotland supports the people. *Dr. Sam'l Johnson*
—And where will you find such men and such horses?
*James Boswell*

**obelisk** A mark of censure in the margin of a book, in the form of a dagger. *Dr. Sam'l Johnson*

**observatory** A place where astronomers conjecture away the guesses of their predecessors. *Ambrose Bierce*

**obsolescence** What happens to your car as soon as it is paid for. *Changing Times*

**obstetriks** A disease my mother catches every year.
*Anon., Jr.*

**Occident** The part of the world lying west (or east) of the Orient. It is largely inhabited by Christians, a powerful subtribe of the Hypocrites, whose principal industries are murder and cheating, which they are pleased to call "war" and "commerce." These, also, are the principal industries of the Orient. *Ambrose Bierce*

**ocean** Where buoy meets gull. *Dell Crossword Puzzles*

**ocean racing** The equivalent of standing under a cold shower in Lapland tearing up $100 bills.
*Reported by Robert P. Sutton\**

**ochrephobia** Fear of being covered with gold paint. (Gilt complex.) *Roger Price*

**Ochs, Adolph** Colorless, odorless and especially tasteless . . . political hermaphrodite capable of intercourse with conservatives of both parties at the same time.
*A. J. Liebling in The New York Times (1923)*

**octopus** An eight-sided cat. *Anon., Jr.*

**odder** Someone else, as: "You want some odder party."
*New Yorkese*

**oddly** Stevenson's first name. *Bostonese*

**Oddessy** One of the authors, along with Illyad, of the Greek epic *Homer*. *Anon., Jr.*

**offending** The aristocratic pleasure. *Robert de Montesquieou*

**office party** One thing an electronic computor can't screw up.

**officeholder** Someone with the arrogance and courage of his connections.

**officials, bad** Ones elected by good citizens who do not vote. *George Jean Nathan*

**official, public** One who frequently forgets that the electorate gave him a mandate and not a charge-a-plate. *Richard Mayer*

**officious** Kind; doing good offices. *Dr. Sam'l Johnson*

**Ohio** "Good Morning" in Japanese.

**okay** Along with terrific, lousy, definitely, racket, gal, honey, swell, contact and impact, the ten most overworked words in the English language. *Wilfred J. Funk*

**old age** The time when you're more interested in pension than passion. *In a Nutshell*

—The time when you are ready to undertake tasks that youth shirked because they would take too long. *Somerset Maugham*

**old days** Before the dime store had a lay-away plan.

**old flame** A sweetheart who made an ash of himself.

**oldthink** Wickedness and decadence. *George Orwell's "Newspeak," 1984*

**old-timer** A man who chases a girl and hopes he won't catch her.

—One who remembers when the telephone was a convenience. *Frances Rodman*

—One who remembers when a bureau was a piece of furniture. *Coronet*

—A person who can remember when the only red menace was long winter underwear. *Changing Times*

—A person who remembers when you bought $5 worth of groceries and had to hold the bag from the bottom. *Ibid.*

—One who remembers when all the vacant lots were full of ballplayers instead of used cars.

—A guy who remembers when the hero only kissed the heroine in the end.

—One who can remember when a day's work took only a day. *Franklin P. Jones*

—A person who can remember when a job was the first thing
you went steady with. *John J. Plomp*

—One who can remember when things in ten-cent stores
were ten cents. *Changing Times*

—One who can recall when wives rocked the cradle instead
of the boat. *Cy N. Peace*

—A man who remembers when women dressed on the
beaches as they now do in supermarkets.

—A man who can remember when it was easy to distinguish
between a bathing beach and a nudist camp. *Al Spong*

—A guy who can remember when a businessman spent his
time trying to corner the market instead of his secretary.
*Dan Bennett*

—One who remembers when it paid to make a lot of money.
*Changing Times*

—One who remembers when unmentionables were also un-
seeables. *Ibid.*

—One who remembers when a kid who got a licking at
school was in for another one when he got home.
*Dan Kidney*

—One who can remember when there was some criticism
of the Government for extravagance in giving away free
garden seeds. *Ohio State Journal*

—A guy who remembers when charity was a virtue instead
of an industry. *Changing Times*

—One who can remember when a girl married a man for his
money instead of divorcing him for it. *F. G. Kernan*

—A person who can remember when you didn't have to buy
what you couldn't afford. *Anon.*

—A guy who can remember when a free plug was a potato
for the spout of the kerosene can. *David O. Flynn*

—One who can remember when "extras" were special nickel
newspaper editions, instead of a thousand dollars added
to the price of a car. *Kenneth J. Shively*

—A man who can remember when both panhandlers and
restaurant owners only asked a nickel for a cup of coffee.
*Dan Revello*

—A fellow who remembers when a baseball game was called
on account of darkness. *Jules Henry Marr*

—A person who remembers when your coffee breaks came
with your meals. *Jules Henry Marr*

—Someone who remembers when only Italians ate pizza.
*Frank J. Pepe*

—One who can remember when a member of the "beat generation" was a lad leaving the woodshed. *Changing Times*

—One who can remember when the law suspended crooks instead of sentences.                    *Cy N. Peace*

—A man who remembers when a new baby was prized as an addition instead of a deduction.         *Changing Times*

—A man who can remember when a woman looked the same after washing her face.           *Russell Newbold*

—One who remembers when the best music heard on radio wasn't in the commercials.           *John J. Plomp*

—A man who can remember when there were other hand-me-downs for the children besides money.   *John J. Plomp*

—One who remembers when being shot from a cannon was considered fast transportation.         *Jack Herbert*

—Fellow who recalls when you could promise a boy the moon without having to buy him a space suit. *Ed Wynn*

—A man who can remember when children learned to count up from one to ten, not down from ten to one.

*Dan Revello*

—A man who remembers when the sky was the limit.

*Frank J. Pepe*

—A guy who remembers when girls walked backward in a high wind.                    *Changing Times*

—A guy who remembers when couples used to go driving in the park instead of parking in the drive.

—A fellow who has made the last payment on his house. *Puck*

—One who scans the menu before the waitress.

Tuscaloosa (Ala.) *Graphic*

—A man who raves about the good old days while riding in an air-conditioned car in ninety-degree weather. *Al Spong*

**Olympic Games** This corruptive mess, this sweaty hypocrisy.

*Roger Kahn*

**omen** A sign that something will happen if nothing happens.

*Ambrose Bierce*

**once** Enough.                    *Ambrose Bierce*

**one-piece bathing suit** The lower half of a bikini.

**opening night** Along with earthquakes, tidal waves, marriages and other natural disasters beyond Man's control—fascinating to observe if you're not involved.

*John Barrymore*

—The night before the play is ready to open.

*George Jean Nathan*

**opera** An exotic and irrational entertainment.
*Dr. Sam'l Johnso*

—A play representing life in another world, whose inhab
tants have no speech but song, no motions but gesture
and no postures but attitudes. *Ambrose Bierc*

OPERA IN ENGLISH In the main, just about as sensible a
baseball in Italian. *H. L. Mencke*

OPERA GLASSES An instrument often only less injurious i
effect to a lady than a double-barreled pistol.
*Henry James, J*

**opinion** Solidified rumor.

—Knowledge in the making. *Milto*

—The queen of the world. *Pasc*

**opium** A Chinese medicine discovered by Dr. Fu Manch
*Anon., J*

**opportunimist** One who has missed his opportunities.
*Neword*

**opportunist** A human kite who gets up in the world usin
wind and pull.

—One who doesn't wait till he hears the knock on the door

—A guy who makes hay out of the grass that grows unde
other guys' feet.

—The chap who keeps up with the Joneses by selling the
new cars. *Pep Mealif*

OPPORTUNITY A favorable occasion for grasping a disap
pointment. *Ambrose Bierc*

—Something more people would recognize if it didn't com
disguised as hard work. *Changing Time*

OPPORTUNITIES Situations that look bigger going tha
coming. *Anor*

**opposition** In politics the party that prevents the Goverr
ment from running amuck by hamstringing it.
*Ambrose Bierc*

**optimism** A mania for maintaining that all is well whe
things are going badly. *Voltai*

—The noble temptation to see too much in everything.
*G. K. Chesterto*

—The doctrine, or belief that everything is beautiful, includ
ing what is ugly, everything good, especially the bad, an
everything right that is wrong. It is hereditary, but fort
nately not contagious. *Ambrose Bierc*

—With the news these days, I tell you it takes a certai
amount of optimism even to be a pessimist. *Jill St. Joh*

OPTIMIST   A man who goes on a fishing trip carrying a camera and a frying pan.                                *Quote*

—A girl who goes into Tiffany's with a shopping cart.

—A man who falls off the top of the Empire State Building and, passing the forty-fourth floor, says to himself, "Well, halfway down, and nothing has happened yet . . ."
                                                *Leo Mishkin**

—A grown man who decides to take up ice skating again, with a bottle on his hip.   *Scripps-Howard Newspapers*

—A driver who thinks that empty space at the curb won't have a hydrant right beside it.   *Changing Times*

—A man who is happy to feel rosy.

—A man who thinks a woman will be right out of the phone booth just because he heard her say good-bye.
                                                *Changing Times*

—A guy who opens a bottle of liquor at a New Year's Eve party and saves the cork.         *Pearl Wilson*

—A man who makes a motel reservation before a blind date.                                        *Playboy*

—A $50-a-week man who marries a girl crazy about kids.
                                                *Changing Times*

—A person who can plan what to do with the money he'll have left over after taxes. *Paul and Helen Martin Denis**

—A man who thinks the dry cleaners are shrinking the waistband of his trousers.                    *Ibid.*

—A person who drops a quarter in the collection plate and expects a five-dollar sermon.            *Banking*

—A man who thinks he can build a $12,000 house for $12,000.                               *Frances Rodman*

—Someone who thinks that love is a game of chance.
                                                *Cy N. Peace*

—The fellow who first called it free love.   *Cy N. Peace*

—A ninety-year old newlywed who moves near a school.
                                                *Anon.*

—A person who puts his shoes back on when the speaker says, "And now, in conclusion—"            *Anon.*

—A man who looks forward to marriage.

PESSIMIST   A married optimist.                    *Playboy*

—A man who sees a light that is not there.

PESSIMIST   The guy who tries to blow it out.      *Anon.*

—A guy who looks at an oyster and expects a pearl.

PESSIMIST   A guy who looks at an oyster and expects ptomaine poisoning.              *Eugene P. Bertin*

—A man who greets the day with "Good morning, God."

PESSIMIST One who says, "Good God—morning!"

**optometrist** A contact man for contact lenses.

OPTOMETRIST'S SHOP A site for sore eyes.

**orange juice** To an Englishman, a kind of mouthwash.
*Clifton Fadiman*

**orangutan** These members of the order Primates contemplate you, when you meet them, with melancholy eyes, as if they had just read Darwin's *Origin of Species* and were painfully aware of being your poor relations who have not done so well in life. *Malcolm MacDonald*

**orator** A talker whose only speech difficulty is knowing when to stop.

ORATOR (HOLIDAY) A kind of interruption between the hotdogs; a fly in the lemonade. *Adlai Stevenson*

ORATORY A form of acting.

—A conspiracy between speech and action to cheat the understanding. *Ambrose Bierce*

**organized demonstration** Trained zeal. *H. E. Martz*

**organizing** A favorite prescription Americans use to cure society's ills.
*Donald Wood, National Commission on Safety Education*

**orgy** Group therapy. *Playboy*

ORGIES Mad rites of Bacchus; frantick revels.
*Dr. Sam'l Johnson*

UNBRIDLED ORGY A wild horse. *Anon., Jr.*

**originality** Only an unaccustomed method of tickling the world. *Bernard Shaw*

**orphan** A living person whom death has deprived of the power of filial ingratitude. *Ambrose Bierce*

**orthography** The science of spelling by the eye instead of the ear. Advocated with more heat than light by the outmates of every asylum for the insane.

> A spelling reformer indicted
> For fudge was before the court cited.
> The judge said: "Enough—
> His candle we'll snough,
> And his sepulchre shall not be whicted."

*Ambrose Bierce*

**Oscar** To inquire of a female, as: "Oscar if she's free tonight." Sometimes pronounced "Esther." *New Yorkese*

**otherwise** No better. *Ambrose Bierce*

**otter** The animal that gives us otter of roses. *Anon., Jr.**

**out**  A place that makes home seem attractive.

**outdo**  To make an enemy.                         *Ambrose Bierce*

**outer space**  When you're twenty feet away from the bar.
                                                     *Joe E. Lewis*

**outlandish**  Not native; foreign.        *Dr. Sam'l Johnson*

**overkill**  The capacity to kill more people than there are.
                                                     *Pentagonese*

**overpass**  A bridge across a sea of autos.

**overtime**  Salary with a fringe on top.

—Making slavery pay.

**overweight**  The only problem that's worse after it's settled.
                                                     *A. David Griffith*

**ower**  Above or too much, as in: "ower-head." *New Yorkese*

**owl**  The monster of the night.                         *Pliny*

# P

**P**  Among other things, P is a Roman numeral for 400
(G is, too); in genetics, it is a symbol for parental generation; in chemistry, for phosphorus; in mechanics, for power
or pressure. To mind one's p's and q's is to be careful of
one's words and actions. *Webster's New World Dictionary*

**pack**  A public place of beauty; e.g., "Our children are en-
titled to more packs and playgrounds."          *Bostonese*

**pailmail**  (This is commonly written pellmell; nor do I know
which of the two is right.) Violent; boisterous.
                                                *Dr. Sam'l Johnson*

**painting**  The art of protecting flat surfaces from the weather
and exposing them to the critic.            *Ambrose Bierce*

—A bridge connecting the painter's mind with the viewers.
                                                     *Delacroix*

—An art that attains its result by laying on.           *Anon.*

**palace**  A fine and costly residence, particularly that of a
great official. The residence of a high dignitary of the
Christian Church is called a palace; that of the Founder
of his religion was known as a field, or wayside. There is
progress.                                    *Ambrose Bierce*

**Palamides**  According to Sophocles, the inventor of dice.

**Palm Beach** A city where customers pay their bills with money which came from their parents.

    MIAMI BEACH Here the customers pay their bills with money which came from their children. *Sylvia Lyons*

**Palm Springs** The dessert of the desert.

**palpitate** To beat as the heart; to flutter; to go *pit a pat.*
*Dr. Sam'l Johnson*

**panic** A word based on the ancient belief that startling noises at night, otherwise unaccounted for, were made by Pan.

**pantomine** A play in which the story is told without violence to the language. *Ambrose Bierce*

**pants** Short for pantaloon, originally trousers and stockings in one piece, named for the Venetian saint, San Pantaleone.

**papoose** A consolation prize for a chance on an Indian blanket. *Playboy*

**par** Craving indulgence. "Par me, but did you drop this hanky?" *New Yorkese*

**paradox** What grownups tell. When kids do it, it's called a big lie. *Anon., Jr.*

**paramour** A lover or wooer. A mistress. It is obsolete in both senses, though not inelegant or unmusical.
*Dr. Sam'l Johnson*

**parapsychological phenomena** Anything you can't explain to your wife.

**parasite** A poor person invited to a meal.
*Original Greek meaning*

—On ships they call them barnacles; in radio they attach themselves to desks, and are called vice presidents.
*Fred Allen*

—One who goes through the revolving door of life on somebody else's push.

    HUSTLER One who goes in a revolving door after you and comes out ahead.

**paratrooper** A soldier who falls down on the job.

**pardon** To forgive one who has done you a favor. *Anon.*

**parents** People who lie awake wondering if daughter's dreamboat is one of those ships that make a pass in the night. *Imogene Fey*

—People who bear infants, bore teen-agers and board newly-weds. *Paul V. Hale*

—Things that are so simple that even a child can operate them. *Changing Times*

—We get our parents when they are so old it is hard to change their habits.                    *Anon., Jr.*

—The sum of the squares on both sides of the family.
                                        *Anon. teenager*

—What children wear out faster than shoes. *Changing Times*

—People with problems not all of them unpleasant.

PARENTHOOD  A process whereby a pediatrician gets the money that formerly went to florists.

—Along with citizenship, the most difficult careers, and they're entrusted to amateurs.
                    St. John's (Newfoundland) *Herald*

—The only job that requires infinite experience to perform and none whatsoever to achieve.

—To give yourself heirs.

Paris  The original playboy.

—Where the good food from the north of France meets the good cooks from the south.
                    *Col. Newnham Davis and Algernon Bastard*

—What would be a wonderful city—if it weren't for the French.                    *Anon. Frenchman*

—The place where good Americans go when they are dead but don't know it.

—A pedant-ridden failure in everything it pretends to lead.
                                        *Bernard Shaw*

PARISIAN  A Gallic conservative anarchist.        *Anon.*

park  A haven where some of the trees and some of the animals are protected against some of the people.

PARKS  The lungs of London.            *Lord Chatham*

Parker, Dorothy  An odd blend of Little Nell and Lady Macbeth.                    *Alexander Woollcott*

parking  Parking spaces,
          Every time
          Never head
          The same way I'm.                *Lois F. Pasley*

PARKING FEE  The tax they take for not taking a taxi.

PARKING LOT  An enterprise whereby a land pirate leases out space at exhorbitant rates.

PARKING METER  A device that enables you to do two hours' shopping in one.            *Changing Times*

PARKING SPACE  A place where you leave your car to have the wheelbase shortened and the back trunk caved in.
                                        *Anon.*

parole  A cell out.                        *Anon.*

**part**  To die a little.                    *Edmond Haraucourt*

**party leftover**  One who doesn't know when to leave.

**passengers**  A name for the shock absorbers on buses.

**passion**  A rage to love.

—Love in action.

—The twin sister of blindness.              *Arabic proverb*

**past**  The future of the present.              *Anon.*

—Valuable as a guidepost but dangerous if used as a hitching post.              *Indiana Parent-Teacher*

—The only paradise from which one cannot be driven. *Anon.*

—Prologue.              Shakespeare, *The Tempest*

  PAST TENSE  A phase meaning I used to be nervous.

                    *Anon., Jr.*

**patience**  A minor form of despair, disguised as a virtue.

                    *Ambrose Bierce*

—Inability to make a decision.              *Anon.*

**patient**  A large body of pain surrounded by cures.

                    *Frank Scully*

—A haystack bristling with needles.

**patio**  A Spanish word meaning $500 more.

                    *Mrs. James W. Muller*

**patio, private**  Real-estatese for a six-foot by three-foot yard with two trash cans.              *William V. Shannon*

**patrimony**  The reason for much matrimony. *Ogden Nash*

**patriotism**  Combustible rubbish ready to the torch of any one ambitious to illuminate his name.      *Ambrose Bierce*

—A lovely sense of collective responsibility.

  NATIONALISM  A silly cock crowing on its own dunghill

                    *Richard Aldington*

**patron**  One who countenances, supports or protects. Commonly a wretch who supports with insolence, and is paid with flattery.              *Dr. Sam'l Johnson*

**patterson**  Fanatically devoted to a faction; e.g., "I will not play patterson pawlitics with national defense."

                    *Bostonese*

**Paul**  Contraction meaning "Father will."      *New Yorkese*

**pauper**  A father; e.g., "The Candys' pauper was ambassador to the Cawt of St. James'."              *Bostonese*

**pawn shop**  The place where you trade your ten-carat turnip for five berries.              *Fibber McGee*

**payola**  The only aspect of "payola" that is solely American is the word "payola" itself. In Rome, the under-the-counter payment is identical, but the word is "busterella." In Hong

Kong it's "hai yo." And in Mexico it's "mordida"—translated, "the bite." *McGraw-Hill*

**pea** A vegetable pill. *Anon.*

**peace** The entr'acte in the theatre of war.

—Like a beautiful woman, it's wonderful, but has been known to bear watching. *Will Rogers*

—In international affairs, a period of cheating between two periods of fighting.

> O, what's the loud uproar assailing
>  Mine ears without cease?
> 'Tis the voice of the hopeful, all-hailing
>  The horrors of peace.

> Ah, Peace Universal; they woo it—
>  Would marry it, too.
> If only they knew how to do it
>  'Twere easy to do.

> They're working by night and by day
>  On their problem, like moles.
> Have mercy, O Heaven, I pray,
>  On their meddlesome souls! *Ambrose Bierce*

—A breathing spell.

—Where they make a desert, they call it peace.
*Tacitus, quoting an ancient Briton's
reference to the Romans*

—The luxury you enjoy between the children's bedtime and your own. *Lester D. Klimek*

**peacock** A Technicolor turkey.

—Chicken in bloom. *Steve Richards*

—A living color. *Anon., Jr.*

**peasant** A European pedestrian.

**peat** A little fondling; a darling; a dear play thing. It is now commonly called *pet*. *Dr. Sam'l Johnson*

**peddle** To be busy about trifles. Ainsworth. It is commonly written *piddle*; as, what *piddling* work is here.
*Dr. Sam'l Johnson*

**pedestrian** A man who didn't believe his wife when she told him the family needed two cars. *Earl Wilson*

—A driver who assumes there are several gallons left in the tank when the gauge says "Empty."

—A man who counted on his wife to put some gas in the car.
*Anon.*

—In Texas it is somebody who walks in his sleep.

**pedigree** The known part of the route from an arboreal ancestor with a swim bladder to an urban descendant with a cigarette. *Ambrose Bierce*

—A teacher in college. *Anon., Jr.*

**Peeping Tom** A window-shopping wolf.

—An art lover.

**penicillin** A medicine which, if you are full of and sneeze, you can cure somebody.

**penny** A fractional coin really not worth saving any more.
*Anon., Jr.*

**pense** To save, hold. *Newords*

**pension** Pie in the pocket.

PENSIONER A kept patriot. *H. L. Mencken*

**Pentagon** A log going down the river with 25,000 ants on it, each thinking he's steering.
*Henry Rowan, Assistant Secretary of Defense*

—Disneyland East. *Jerry Kluttz*

—An eight-sided general. *Anon., Jr.*

**pentameter** A lion with five feet. *Anon., Jr.*

**people** That part of the state which does not know what it wants. *Georg W. F. Hegel*

—Each of us is either a part of any problem that may be concerning us as people, or a part of the answer.
*Bankers Monthly*

CIVILIZED PEOPLE Those who laugh at savages who take a tribal pride in the size of their totem poles, but judge the status of our fellows by the length of the cars in their driveways. *Sydney J. Harris*

**perennial** A flower that continues to live after it dies.
*Anon., Jr. (Art Linkletter Dept.)*

**perfection** Something to be achieved by anyone who follows the advice he gives others. *Anon.*

—Something you read about in ads.

PERFECTIONISM A thing perfectionists think is the same as perfection—but it isn't. *Harry Ruby*

**period** A mark you put after a true statement. After a lie, put an exclamation point. *Anon., Jr.*

—Commas are used when you need to take a breath and periods when you have to stop and think. *Anon., Jr.*

**perjury** Four-fifths of it is expended on tombstones, women and competitors. *Thomas R. Dewar*

**Perrault, Charles (1628–1703)** The father of Mother Goose.

**perse** To gather, attract; e.g., "The auctioneer persed the crowd." *Newords*

**perseverance** A lowly virtue whereby mediocrity achieves an inglorious success. *Ambrose Bierce*

**persiflage** A green vegetable belonging to the spinach family. *Anon., Jr.*

**personality** Glitter and glib and oomphiness and itness . . . all very shabby, very fraudulent—and now it is becoming very tiresome. *A. Powell Davies*

—Merely a persistent error. *Max Jacob*

**personnel** Twice as many people are engaged in clerical work as in 1940. Maybe we are no more mixed up than ever, but we are getting it all down on paper. *Journal of the American Medical Association*

PERSONNEL MANAGER A guy who would describe Delilah as "a lady barber."

**pessimism** A philosophy forced upon the convictions of the observer by the disheartening prevalence of the optimist with his scarecrow hope and his unsightly smile. *Ambrose Bierce*

PESSIMIST One who believes today that only the sky is the limit. *Changing Times*

—One who builds slums in the air.

—One with a difficulty for every solution.

—One who expects nothing on a silver platter except tarnish. *Franklin P. Jones*

—One who has been intimately acquainted with an optimist. *Elbert Hubbard*

—A man who financed an optimist. *Anon.*

—A person who keeps an optimist from becoming satisfied with himself. *Herbert V. Prochnow*

—Someone who likes to listen to the patter of little defeats. *Edith Ogutsch*

—One who goes through life wearing morose-colored glasses.

—A person who, when smelling flowers, looks around for the funeral. *Oral Hygiene*

—A woman who thinks she can't get her car into the only available parking space.

OPTIMIST A man who thinks she won't try. *Changing Times*

—One who sees only the dark side of the clouds and mopes.

PHILOSOPHER One who sees both sides and shrugs.

OPTIMIST   One who doesn't see the clouds at all—he's walking on them.                                    *D. O. Flynn*

**pest**   A guy with a cocktail glass in one hand and your lapel in the other.

**pet shop**   A Chock Full O' Mutts emporium.   *Louis Sobol*

**phaeton**   An open carriage named after the son of the sun god.

**pharmacy**   A department store with a prescription counter.
                                              *Changing Times*

**Ph.D.**   In the feminine, stands for "Petticoat Hangs Down."
                                                        *Anon.*

**philanderer**   One who's always ready to give up a passing fancy for something fancier.                   *Anon.*

**philanthropist**   One who steals privately and gives publicly.

—A person who spends most of his time persuading others to contribute to charity.                           *Anon.*

—A rich old gentleman who has trained himself to grin while his conscience is picking his pocket.   *Ambrose Bierce*

PHILANTHROPY   Leaving your money where it may be appreciated instead of to your relatives.
                                              *Changing Times*

—Vanity conquering greed.

**philately**   The worship of bad workmanship in printing stamps.                                      *Patrick Ryan*

**philistines**   Islands in the Pacific.

                                   *Anon., Jr. (British Division)*

**philosopher**   A person who knows how to take anything that doesn't happen to him.

—There was never yet a philosopher that could endure the toothache patiently.                        *Shakespeare*

—One who wishes to be a wise man.             *Anon., Jr.*

PHILOSOPHY   Something rich people use to convince the rest of us that it's no disgrace to be poor.
                                              *Changing Times*

—Misery dissolved in thought.                      *Anon.*

—Reason as religion.

—Common sense in a dress suit.            *Oliver Braston*

—A route of many roads leading from nowhere to nothing.
                                              *Ambrose Bierce*

**philters**   Magic things put on cigarettes a thousand years ago. Of course there were no cigarettes that long ago, which is what made the philters magic.          *Anon., Jr.*

**Phoebus**   An ancient Greek mode of transportation.

                          *Anon., Jr. (Art Linkletter Dept.)*

**phony** A guy who listens to the radio while eating a TV
dinner.                              *Arthur Murray's press agents*

**photograph** A picture painted by the sun without instruction in art. It is a little better than the work of an Apache,
but not quite so good as that of a Cheyenne.

*Ambrose Bierce*

PHOTOGRAPHER A person who collects shadows.

**physician** A man who still has his tonsils and appendix at
the age of thirty.

—A doctor who treats what you have.

SPECIALIST A doctor who thinks you have what he treats.
*Changing Times*

**piano** A parlor utensil for subduing the impenitent visitor.
It is operated by depressing the keys of the machine and
the spirits of the audience.           *Ambrose Bierce*

—A peculiar instrument. Its habitual relation to the rest of
the instrumental family may be described as motherly.

*G. E. F. Dickinson*

**pickleherring** A jack-pudding; a merry-andrew; a zany; a
buffoon.                              *Dr. Sam'l Johnson*

**picnic** An outdoor eating event where you enjoy with gusto
food you wouldn't touch at home.

**pie** An advance agent of Indigestion.

"Cold pie was highly esteemed by the remains."—the Rev.
Dr. Mucker, in a funeral sermon over a British nobleman

"Cold pie is a detestable
American comestible.
That's why I'm done—or undone—
So far from that dear London."—From the headstone
of a British Nobleman, in Kalamazoo.

*Ambrose Bierce*

**piety** Reverence for the Supreme Being, based upon His
supposed resemblance to man.          *Ambrose Bierce*

**pig** An animal (Porcus omnivorus) closely allied to the
human race by the splendor and vivacity of its appetite,
which, however, is inferior in scope, for it sticks at pig.

*Ambrose Bierce*

—To select, as: "toot-pig," a tool used to select your teeth.
*New Yorkese*

**pigeon** A rat with feathers (carrying filthy diseases).
*Arthur J. Benline, Commissioner of New York City,
Department of Pollution Control*

—A wormy bird that gets up early.

**pigsney** A word of endearment to a girl. It is used by Butler for the eye of a woman. I believe, improperly.
*Dr. Sam'l Johnson*

**pillow** An upright support or supporter, such as: "He's a pillow of the church." *New Yorkese*

**pimp** A bawdy guard.

**pioneer** A person whose annual property tax exceeds what he paid for the place to begin with. *Changing Times*

> PIONEERS The men who found their way across the trackless wilderness of this vast continent have great-grandsons who get lost in a supermarket. *Senator Soaper*

**Pirandello, Luigi** The agitator of the question mark. *Fodor*

**pirate** Any robber; particularly a bookseller who seizes the copies of other men. *Dr. Sam'l Johnson*

> PIRATE FAN A guy who hates his wife so much he will use any excuse to get out of the house. *Jimmy Cannon*

**pish** A contemptuous exclamation. This is sometimes spoken and written *pshaw*. I know not their etymology, and imagine them formed by chance. *Dr. Sam'l Johnson*

**pitch** A fruit what goes wit crim. *New Yorkese*

**pitiful** The state of an enemy or opponent after an imaginary encounter with oneself. *Ambrose Bierce*

**plagiarism** The basis of all literature except the first one, which is, however, unknown. *Giraudoux*

> PLAGIARIST From *plagiarius,* one who abducts the child or slave of another.

**planet** A body of earth surrounded by sky.

**plastic surgeon** A nasal architect. *Anon.*

> PLASTIC SURGERY An operation that can do anything with the human nose except keep it out of the other guy's business. *Austin Butcher*

**platitude** An epigram with a steady job. *College Humor*
—An old saw that has lost its teeth. *Anon.*
—Civil drivel.

**Plato** A scholar who succeeded in becoming well educated without knowing any Shakespeare.

> PLATONIC FRIENDSHIP The interval between the introduction and the first kiss. *Sophie Irene Loeb*

**plausible** Something someone will swallow.

**playboy** A cagy guy
Who has lots of fun
He samples every pretty wench
And never Mrs. one.
*Playboy*

**playwriting** One of the lesser arts, like woodcarving and dancing. *W. Somerset Maugham*

—Like begging in India, an honorable but humbling profession. *Moss Hart*

**pleasure** The absence of physical pain and of mental and spiritual distress. *Epicurus*

—The object, the duty, and the goal of all rational creatures. *Voltaire*

**plenipotentiary** Having full power. A Minister Plenipotentiary is a diplomatist possessing absolute authority on condition that he never exert it. *Ambrose Bierce*

**plethora** An intellectual glut.

**plight** A difficult or unpleasant position, such as a promise, especially to marry.

**plop** A sound characteristic of the pouring of liquid tomato which is predominantly pulp rather than the more expensive juice.

**plot** The curse of serious drama, and indeed of serious literature of any kind. *Bernard Shaw*

**plum** Raisin; grape dried in the sun. (In the cant of the city.) The sum of one hundred thousands pounds. *Dr. Sam'l Johnson*

—A kind of play, called how many *plums* for a penny. *Ainsworth*

**pocket** The small bag inserted into cloaths. *Dr. Sam'l Johnson*

POCKETBOOK The only thing that is opened by mistake more frequently than the mouth. *Changing Times*

**poet** A man who can see faces in the glowing coals of the fire. *Anon.*

—A thief of fire. *Rimbaud*

—In history is divine, but a poet in the next room is a joke. *Max Eastman*

—A poet can survive anything but a misprint. *Oscar Wilde*

—Publishing a volume of verse is like dropping a rose petal down the Grand Canyon and waiting for the echo. *Don Marquis*

POETS Writers who talk to themselves out loud; and the world overhears them. But it is horribly lonely not to hear someone else talk sometimes.

Marchbanks in *Candida*, by Bernard Shaw

POETASTER A vile petty poet. *Dr. Sam'l Johnson*

POETRY  A sort of truancy, a dream within the dream of life, a wild flower planted among our wheat.

*Michael Oakeshott*

—Imaginary gardens with real toads in them.

*Marianne Moore*

—Truth in its Sunday clothes.  *Joseph Roux*

—Nothing but healthy speech.  Thoreau's *Journals*

—Writing where every line begins with a capital letter.

*Anon., Jr.*

—A thing you make prose of.  *Anon., Jr.*

poise  The difference between flipping your lid and raising your eyebrow.  *Paul and Helen Martin Denis*

—The ability to continue talking while the other fellow picks up the check.  *Changing Times*

poison  Any substance that in relatively small quantities can cause death or illness in living organisms by chemical action. The qualification "by chemical action," is necessary because it rules out such . . . effects as those produced by a small quantity of lead entering the body at high velocity.  *Scientific American*

Poles  People who say "Thank God for that big buffer state between us and Red China."  *Victor Zorza*

politeness  The most acceptable hypocrisy.  *Ambrose Bierce*

—Benevolence in small things.  *Thomas Macaulay*

political campaign  The interval between elections.

*Changing Times*

POLITICAL CAMPAIGNING  The art of listening to the nation's pulse with your mouth open.  *Phil H. Tuseth*

political oratory  Strong lungs coupled with weak minds.

political reformer  A politician who is out of work.  *Anon.*

political science  The science by which civilization must live or die . . . busy explaining the past whilst we have to grapple with the present; it leaves the ground before our feet in black darkness whilst it lights up every corner of the landscape behind us.  *Bernard Shaw*

politicaster  A petty ignorant pretender to politicks.

*Dr. Sam'l Johnson*

—There are quacks of all sorts; as bullies, pedants, hypocrites, empiricks, law-jobbers and *politicasters*.  *L'Estrange*

politician  A man who runs for office and then runs for cover.

*Anon.*

—A man who makes his bunk and has to lie out of it.

*Henry Youngman*

—A man of artifice; one of deep contrivance.
*Dr. Sam'l Johnson*

—A guy who remains consistently perpendicular with equal
pressure from all sides.          *Sen. Clair Engle*

—An acrobat who keeps his balance by saying the opposite
of what he does.          *Maurice Barrès*

—A man who is sharply aware of men's disposition to docility
and who exploits it systematically for the attainment of
ends which he regards as good.     *Bertrand De Jouvenel*

HONEST POLITICIAN   One whose campaign manager doesn't
tell him how he won the election.          *Jerry Robinson*

TEXAS POLITICIAN   One who can straddle anything but a
horse.          *Tex O'Rourke*

CHEAP POLITICIAN   A member of the other party.   *Anon.*

SUCCESSFUL POLITICIAN   He who says what everybody is
thinking most often and in the loudest voice.
*Theodore Roosevelt*

—One who can get in the public eye without irritating it.
*Vesta M. Kelly*

**politics**   The conduct of public affairs for private advantage.
*Ambrose Bierce*

—The paradise of voluble windbags.          *Bernard Shaw*

—A constant choice between two evils.          *John Morley*

—Still the only profession in which a man can make a living
solely by bragging.          *Ben Hecht*

—That which makes strange postmasters.
*Frank McKinney Hubbard*

—A balancing act between people who want to get into it
and people who don't want to get out of it.
*Jacques De Bourbon-Busset*

—A three-ring circus made up of the two-party system—
Northern and Southern Democrats and Liberal and Old
Guard Republicans.

—The path of glory leading to the gravy.

—Our local congressman admits his opponent resembles
Abraham Lincoln, "If you can imagine a short, fat, dishonest Abraham Lincoln."          *Bill Vaughan*

—The trouble with political jokes is that sometimes they get
elected.          Kokomo *Tribune*

—A lot of politicians make the mistake of forgetting that
they've been appointed, instead of anointed. *Atlas News*

—That which has ruined more good men than women, liquor
and horses put together.     *Reported by Harry Golden*

—Many a man goes into politics with a fine future and comes out with a terrible past.          *York Trade Compositor*

—The art of the possible.

THEATRE   The art of the impossible.          *Jed Harris*

PRACTICAL POLITICS   Ignoring facts.          *Henry Adams*

**Pollyanna**   When a woman has many husbands.   *Anon., Jr*

**polo**   Hockey on horseback.

WATER POLO   A rumble in tights.          *Jimmy Cannon*

**polycarp**   A very rare many-sided fish.          *Anon., Jr*

**polygon**   A man with several wives.

*Anon., Jr. (British Division)*

**pomegranate**   A lap dog.          *Anon., Jr*

**poor old . . .**   Ha-ha, not like me.          *Stephen Potter*

**popularity**   Fame in the form of small change.   *Victor Hugo*

—Knowing a lot of uninteresting people.          *Anon*

**population explosion**   The pleasure of playing with dynamite

—When people take leave of their census. *Malcolm K. Jeffrey*

—The thunder of little feet.

—The day will come when people will have to obtain a license to have children.

**porcupine**   A perambulating pincushion.

**pornography**   The copulation of clichés. *Vladimir Nabokov*

—Writing about prostitutes.          *Original Greek meaning*

**Porter, Sylvia**   A girl who is well-stocked.

*Sen. Kenneth Keating*

**positive**   You raise your voice when you should reinforce your argument.          *Dr. Sam'l Johnson*

**posse**   An armed power; from *posse comitatus*, the power of the shires. A low word.          *Dr. Sam'l Johnson*

**possession**   Nothing makes you doubt that possession is nine points of the law so much as having a tiger by the tail

*Franklin P. Jones*

**postage stamp**   A parking place for a portrait of a past president.

**posterity**   What you write for after being turned down by publishers.          *George Ade*

—The patriotic name for grandchildren.

*Anon., Jr. (Art Linkletter Dept.)*

**postulate**   To stand up straight while giving the answer.

*Anon., Jr*

**pot**   Portion; e.g., "The pot I like is the drumstick."

*New Yorker*

**potato**   (I suppose an American word.) An esculent root.
*Dr. Sam'l Johnson*

POTATOE   A goutlike ailment of the toe resulting from continued overuse of potables.   *Fred Beck*

**potty**   A group of people combined for political or social action.   *New Yorkese*

MITT-INK   A potty where no food is served. *New Yorkese*

**potvaliant**   Heated with courage by strong drink.
*Dr. Sam'l Johnson*

**poulterer**   A fancier chicken fancier.

**poverty**   A sin that the rich cannot forgive. *Russian proverb*
—The condition we try to conceal at the time and then brag about in our memoirs.   *F. G. Kernan*

**praise**   Only a debt.

FLATTERY   A present.   *Dr. Sam'l Johnson*

**Pravda**   A Russian newspaper that is running a contest for the best political joke. The first prize is twenty years.
*Irving R. Levine*

**pray**   To ask that the laws of the universe be annulled in behalf of a single petitioner confessedly unworthy.
*Ambrose Bierce*

—A man was arrested by a London policeman for praying in Westminster Abbey. When the magistrate asked the policeman what was wrong with praying in Westminster Abbey, the reply was: "Your Honor, if this sort of thing got started, we might have people praying all over the place!"
*Howard Hanson*

PRAYING   What on earth you are doing for heaven's sake.
—Yessin' deity.

**preacher**   Have Bible—Will Babble.   *Teen-Ager*

PREACHING   Personal counseling on a group scale.
*Rev. Harry Emerson Fosdick*

**precision**   The writer's varnish.   *Marquis de Vauvenaigues*

**precocious**   Ripened beforehand.   *Original Latin meaning*

**pregnancy**   The shape of things to come.   *Anon.*

PREGNANT   Full of consequence.   *Dr. Sam'l Johnson*
—Heir conditioned.   *Robert Levinson**
—The past tense of virgin.

**prehistoric**   Antedating the art and practice of perpetuating falsehood.   *Ambrose Bierce*

**prejudice**   A vagrant opinion without visible means of support.   *Ambrose Bierce*
—The reason of fools.   *Voltaire*

—A great time-saver. You can form opinions without having to get the facts. *Wisconsin Journal of Education*

—The difference between a prejudice and a conviction is that you can explain a conviction without getting mad.
*York Trade Compositor*

PREJUDICED Not believing in the same things we do.
*Anon., Jr.*

PREJUDICES What fools use for reason. *Voltaire*

premature A baby born before its parents are married.
*Anon., Jr.*

premeditation What you do before the doctor comes.
*Anon., Jr. (Art Linkletter Dept.)*

pre-owned A used car that is a Rolls-Royce.
*Gordon Gammack*

preposition A word you shouldn't end a sentence with, as: "Mother, why did you choose this book for us to be read to out of for?" *Judith Beach**

prescription A physician's guess at what will best prolong the situation with least harm to the patient.
*Ambrose Bierce*

present The ever moving shadow that divides yesterday from tomorrow. *Frank Lloyd Wright*

—An indivisible point which cuts in two the length of an infinite line. *Diderot*

—That part of eternity dividing the domain of disappointment from the realm of hope. *Ambrose Bierce*

PRESENTS A good gift to have, like presents of mind.
*Anon., Jr.*

preside To guide the action of a deliberate body to a desirable result. In Journalese, to perform upon a musical instrument; as, "He presided at the piccolo." *Ambrose Bierce*

president The best reason for not being President is you have to shave twice a day.

PRESIDENCY The greased pig in the field game of American politics. *Ambrose Bierce*

—An office that converts vanity to prayer. *Adlai Stevenson*

PRESIDENTIAL ELECTION That great quatro-annual drama in which the nation selects the leader who is for the next four years to become the target of their abuse and criticism.

Presley, Elvis After listening to his "Hound Dog," I've decided that his bark is worse than his beat.
*Robert Sylvester*

**press**  The greatest curse of civilization.  *Randolph Churchill*

**prestork age**  In the beginning—before people were born.

*Anon., Jr.*

**pretender**  One who was born with a silver spoon in his mouth with someone else's initials.

**pretzel**  A cracker with convulsions.

PRETZELS  The only reason a lot of guys aren't on a liquid diet.

**prices**  The cause of high wages.

WAGES  The cause of high prices.  *Changing Times*

**priest**  A man who goes to church because it's good for business.

**primitive country**  One that has no taxes to handle juvenile delinquency, in case they get civilized enough to achieve it.  *Pat Kraft*

**printing press**  Either the greatest blessing or the greatest curse of modern times, one sometimes forgets which.

*James M. Barrie*

—The mother of errors.  *Anon.*

**prisons**  Artificial hells.

—The first prison I ever saw had inscribed on it 'Cease to do evil: learn to do well'; but as the inscription was on the outside, the prisoners could not read it.  *Bernard Shaw*

**pro**  A girl who is always pushed for money.

**procrastination**  A fault that most people put off trying to correct.  *Indianapolis News*

PROCRASTINATOR  One who puts off until tomorrow the things he's already put off until today.  *Griff Niblack*

—A person who can't put away the garden tools until the snow thaws.  *Bruce Lefler*

**prodigy**  A young man who runs away from home and spends all his money.  *Anon., Jr.*

—Nobody has yet calculated how many lazy ancestors it takes to produce an indefatigable prodigy.  *Bernard Shaw*

**producer**  An executive who wears a worried look on his assistant's face. A producer does not write; he does not direct; he does not photograph; he does not even dress the sets or do the leading lady's hair. He may, at best, possibly advise, console, try to help and guide. He may be a father confessor. He may be a sympathetic and even intelligent organizer and editor. But he certainly does not produce.

—The guy who gives the public what they want—and then hopes they want it!  *Hal Roach*

**professional** A man who can do his job when he doesn't feel like it.

AMATEUR A man who can't do his job when he does feel like it. *James Agate*

PROFESSIONAL COURTESY A lawyer swimming through shark-infested waters. *Anon.*

**professor** Not smarter than other people, he has his ignorance better organized. *Edgar Dale*

**profit** A social institution that provides one of the foundation stones of liberty. . . . In a competitive society, it is the reward for social service which the community, of its own free will, bestows on the enterpriser. *Dr. Claude Robinson*

PROFITS Money that has not been wasted. *A. V. Burdine*

**profusion** The charm of hospitality. Have plenty, if it be only beer. *William Makepeace Thackeray*

**profusively** The way Toots Shor bleeds.

**progress** Imposing on children nobler beliefs and better institutions than those at present inculcated and established. *Bernard Shaw*

—Merely the substitution of a complicated nuisance for a simple nuisance. *Sydney J. Harris*

—Advancing the Christmas shopping period to the point where Santa Claus tosses out the first ball at the opening of the baseball season.

—If we could have made as much progress these last fifty years with people as we have with things, what a world this would now be. *Wheeler McMillen*

—The courage of our confusions. *Ashley Montagu*

—Going around in the same circles—but faster.

**prolefeed** Entertainment and news.
*George Orwell's "Newspeak," 1984*

**promise** The thing which is easier said than done.

LARGE PROMISE The soul of an advertisement.
*Dr. Sam'l Johnson*

**promoter** A man who shakes your hand to pump money out of your pocket.

**proofreader** A malefactor who atones for making your writing read like nonsense by permitting the compositor to make it unintelligible. *Ambrose Bierce*

—A type-righter. *Anon.*

**propaganda** All great Art and Literature. *Bernard Shaw*

**property** Theft. *Pierre-Joseph Proudhon*

—A bleach to take stains out of character *Anon.*

**proposal** A proposition that lost its nerve. *Playboy*

—A girl listening faster than a man can talk.

*Lester V. Berrey*

—A declaration of dependence.

**proposition** A preface to a questionable work.

—Something that sounds nicer in French.

*Robin degli Espinosa\**

**proselyte** A woman of the streets. *Vassar senior*

**prosperity** Having the smallest car and the biggest lawn mower in the neighborhood.

—When the two-car garage is replaced by the two-garage car.

—Making ends overlap. *Thomas Usk*

—It currently results in part from the production of arms that we do not expect to use, and in part from our new way of getting rich, which is to buy things from one another that we do not want at prices we cannot pay, on terms we cannot meet because of advertising we do not believe. *Robert Maynard Hutchins*

—The feeling you get when you make the last car payment. It is the same feeling that makes you go right out and buy another. *Changing Times*

—Bigger cars on longer credit terms.

—When conversation switches from car pools to swimming pools. *Lew Parker*

—When most people make more money than they earn and spend more than they make. *Puck*

—Not being quite as broke this month as you were last month. *Al Cooper*

—When people buy things they can't afford.

RECESSION When they stop doing it. *H. E. Martz*

**prosperous** To be so wealthy that after paying your income tax you are penniless. *Mannie Manheim*

—Being able to get a haircut the day before payday.

**pross** A girl who hates poverty worse than sin.

**prostitute** A woman of undubious character.

—A girl who may be good for nothing, but never bad for nothing.

—A woman who has been tried and found wanton. *Anon.*

**protagonist** First actor. *Original Greek meaning*

**protectorate** An arrangement by which a strong country agrees to protect a weak country from all tyranny. Except from the strong country itself.

*Anon., Jr. (Art Linkletter Dept.)*

**Protestant** A woman who gets her living through an immortal life.                                        *Anon., Jr.*

**proverb** A short sentence based on long experience.
                                                    *Cervantes*

**providence** The Christian name for Chance.
                                                    *Alphonse Karr*

**providential** Unexpectedly and conspicuously beneficial to
the person so describing it.                        *Ambrose Bierce*

**provinces** Where rain is a diversion. *The Goncourt brothers*

**provocative** Any thing which revives a decayed or cloyed
appetite.                                           *Dr. Sam'l Johnson*

**provost** The president makes speeches. The student's job is
to think. The provost's job is to see that the students don't
make speeches and the president doesn't think.
       *Shannon McCune, provost, University of Massachusetts*

**prune** A plum that didn't take care of itself.   *Anon., Jr.*

**pseudonym** The state or condition a poet gets into just before
writing.                                            *Anon., Jr.*

**psychiatric examination** A check-up from the neck up.
                                                    *Richard Wheeler*

**psychiatric treatment** A treatment that enables us to correct
our faults by confessing our parents' shortcomings.
                                                    *Changing Times*

**psychiatrist** A mental Peeping Tom. *She Wouldn't Say Yes*
—A motive prophet.
—An ambivalence chaser.                             *Cary Grant*
—A man who, when a pretty girl enters a crowded room,
looks at everybody else.                            *The Carpenter*
—A doctor who guarantees a cure or you get your mania back
                                                    *Changing Times*
—A fellow who convinces you that your parents were failures
because you turned out to be a louse.               *Jack Herbert*
**PSYCHIATRY** The art of analyzing ouches on couches.
                                                    *S. Omar Barker*
—The art of teaching people how to stand on their own
feet while reclining on couches.                    *Shannon Fife*

**psychoanalysis** Spending forty dollars an hour just to squeal
on your mother.                                     *Mike Connolly*
—Panned parenthood.                                 *Harold Coffin*
**PSYCHOANALYST** A smashing bloke who finds you cracked
and leaves you broke.                               *Keith Preston*
—A man who makes a living out of running a complaint
department.

**psychologist** A man you pay to ask you questions your wife asks for nothing. *Changing Times*
—A person who pulls habits out of rats. *Dr. Douglas Bush*
**psychotic** One who thinks two plus two is five.
> NEUROTIC One who knows that two plus two is four—but hates it. *Gordon Gammack*
**pub** The layman's monastery. *Arland Ussher*
**puberty** The time when kids stop asking questions and begin to question answers. *Anon.*
—The time of life in which the two sexes begin first to be acquainted. *Dr. Sam'l Johnson*
—The cause of changing the voice at the years of *puberty* seemeth to be, for that when much of the moisture of the body, which did before irrigate the parts, is drawn down to the spermatical vessels, it leaveth the body more hot than it was, whence cometh the dilatation of the pipes.
> *Francis Bacon*
**public opinion poll** The nonsensus of opinion.
**public relations** Very much like those indulged in on the street by a couple of dogs.
**public schools** Where the teachers are afraid of the principals, the principals are afraid of the board, the board members are afraid of the parents, the parents are afraid of the children, and the children are afraid of nobody.
> *Anon. schoolteacher*
**public speaking** Intensified conversation. *C. W. Wright*
—Forensics which would be easier to listen to if it were based on more private thinking.
**public utilitarianism** The ethical doctrine that if you rope in enough stockholders and keep them reasonably happy with a 3½ per cent annual return, they are on your side in your efforts to screw the public. *Newords*
**public works** Government activity that never ends because we cannot finish one job without creating ten fresh ones.
> *Bernard Shaw*
**publicity** Concealed advertising.
—He thinks he is deaf because he no longer hears himself talked about. *Talleyrand*
> PUBLICITY (HOLLYWOOD) A story about some well-known person doing something he didn't somewhere he wasn't.
> *Jimmy Starr*
**publish** In literary affairs, to become the fundamental element in a cone of critics. *Ambrose Bierce*

**puddle** A tadpole's ocean.

**puisne** (*Puis nè*, French. It is commonly spoken and written *puny*.) Young; younger; later in time. Petty; inconsiderable; small. *Dr. Sam'l Johnson*

**pullet surprise** An egghead award list supervised by Columbia University. *New Yorkese*

**pun** The lowest form of wit, because so much humor is based on it. *Ira Gershwin*

—Did you hear about the glass blower who inhaled one day? Now he has a pane in his stomach.
*Louisville Courier-Journal Magazine*

**punctual** Getting there ten seconds before the other fellow.
*Bernard Simon*

PUNCTUALITY The only meeting that ever started on time was held up for an hour while things were explained to people who came in late and didn't know what was going on. *Doug Larson*

**punster** A quibbler; a low wit who endeavours at reputation by double meaning. *Dr. Sam'l Johnson*

**pups** On Wall Street, low-priced, inactive stocks, too cheap to be called dogs.

**purgatory** The most fantastic ceremonies, conjurations and ordeals to have our scarlet souls made whiter than snow.
*Bernard Shaw*

—The laundromat of the Lord.

—A place where those go who are too good to go to heaven and too bad to go to hell. *Anon., Jr.*

**Puritan** A man who is sincerely repentant for other people's sins. *Anon.*

—A person who pours righteous indignation into the wrong things. *G. K. Chesterton*

**purse-snatching** The gift of grab.

**push** One of the two things mainly conducive to success, especially in politics. The other is Pull. *Ambrose Bierce*

**pushover** A girl who bends over backwards to please.

PREGNANT A girl who bent over backwards to please.

**pute** To have no quarrel. *Newords*

# Q

**quack** To cry like a duck. This word is often written *quaake*, to represent the sound better. *Dr. Sam'l Johnson*
—A false doctor who kills you. A real physician lets you die.
*La Bruyère*

QUACK DOCTORS The kind for curing lame ducks.
*Anon., Jr.*

**quadrilingual** Able to make yourself misunderstood in three other tongues in addition to your native language.

**qualm** The feeling of having wasted his life that comes over a bandit when he puts his car in a big city parking lot.

**quarantine** A four-masted ship. *Anon., Jr.*

**quarrel** What a bad workman does with his tools.
*Herbert, 1640*

—Those who in quarrels interpose
Must often wipe a bloody nose. *John Gay*

**quart** The shortest distance between two pints. *Anon.*
—A place where a George presides. *New Yorkese*

**quartet** A singing group in which all four think the other three can't sing. *Doris Maloney*

**questions** Something that makes animals such agreeable friends because they don't ask any. *From George Eliot*

**quibble** A low conceit depending on the sound of words; a pun. *Dr. Sam'l Johnson*

**quiet** The opposite of female.

**quill** An implement of torture yielded by a goose and commonly wielded by an ass. This use of the quill is now obsolete, but its modern equivalent, the steel pen,[1] is wielded by the same everlasting Presence. *Ambrose Bierce*

**quintuplets** Products of a woman who belabored the issue.
*Maxwell Shane\**

**quixotic** Absurdly chivalric, like Don Quixote. An insight into the beauty and excellence of this incomparable adjective is unhappily denied to him who has the misfortune to know that the gentleman's name is pronounced Ke-ho-tay.
*Ambrose Bierce*

**quizmaster** A lie-detector with a jackpot. *Ralph Edwards*

[1] Before the ball-point.

**quorum** Enough people to start the quorrel.
> *Anon., Jr. (Art Linkletter Dept.)*

**quotation** The act of repeating erroneously the words of another. The words erroneously repeated. *Ambrose Bierce*

**quoter** Next to the originator of a good sentence is the first quoter. *Ralph Waldo Emerson*

—Some for renown, on scraps of learning dote,
And think they grow immortal as they quote.
> *Edward Young*

# R

**R** Medieval Roman numeral for eighty; in chemistry, it is the symbol for radical, especially organic radical; in electricity, for resistance; in mathematics, for radius or ratio; in physics and chemistry, for gas constant. The three R's are regarded as the fundamentals of an education.
> *Webster's New World Dictionary*

**rabid fan** A drunk in a ball park. *Jimmy Cannon*

**race horse** An animal that can take several thousand people for a ride at the same time. *Playboy*

HORSE RACING It is easy to pick plenty of winners at the track. Just don't take any money with you.

**racket** A permanent register of evidence. "Strictly off the racket." *New Yorkese*

**rackoon** The *rackoon* is a New England animal, like a badger, having a tail like a fox, being cloathed with a thick and deep furr; it sleeps in the day time in a hollow tree, and goes out a-nights, when the moon shines, to feed on the sea side, where it is hunted by dogs.
> *Nathaniel Bailey in Johnson's Dictionary*

**raconteur** A French bore.

**radicalism** The conservatism of tomorrow injected into the affairs of today. *Ambrose Bierce*

**radio** An entertainment medium that has never yet been accused of showing an old movie. *Lester D. Klimek*

—And nobody ever got sore eyes from listening to it.
> *Walt Streightiff*

—The liar box.

RADIO ADVERTISING  An invisible message on a transparent screen.                                         *Anon.*

RADIO COMMENTATOR  A man with opinions on subjects he never heard of.

FM RADIO  Radio ecstatic.

**radioactive fallout**  Those damned transistors they play wherever you go.

**Raft, George**  An actor, who, when he gets all dressed up, looks like a stolen car.                  *Orson Bean*

**ragamuffin**  (From *rag* and I know not what else.)
                                  *Dr. Sam'l Johnson*

**railroad**  The chief of many mechanical devices enabling us to get away from where we are to where we are no better off.                         *Ambrose Bierce, 1900*

**rain**  Huddled and snuggled vapor.
                      *Anon., Jr. (Art Linkletter Dept.)*

—What raineth on the just
And also on the unjust fella;
But chiefly on the just, because
The unjust steals the just's umbrella.   *Charles Bowen*

**"Rake's Progress"**  A book about a garden cultivator.
                                              *Anon., Jr.*

**rant**  High-sounding language unsupported by dignity of thought.                        *Dr. Sam'l Johnson*

**rapacity**  Providence without industry.   *Ambrose Bierce*

**rapist**  A neurotic who takes things into his own hands.

**rare judgment**  Judgment that turns out to be right.

**rascal**  A fool considered under another aspect.
                                          *Ambrose Bierce*

**rattlesnake**  Our prostrate brother.      *Ambrose Bierce*

**"The Raven"**  Poe's trauma.

**raving beauty**  A girl who finished second in a beauty contest.                                      *Salada Tea*

**raw bit**  First name of New York's junior senator. *Bostonese*

**ray**  next to a roar steak is one that's ray.   *New Yorkese*

**reading**  A pleasant way of avoiding thinking.

—What made Don Quixote a gentleman; believing what he read made him mad.                      *Bernard Shaw*

—A dangerous amusement.                     *Bernard Shaw*

—The beginning of education.                 *Bernard Shaw*

—The end of it.                              *Bernard Shaw*

**readjustment**  When your neighbor loses his job.

RECESSION  When you lose your job.

DEPRESSION   When your wife loses her job.
*Changing Times*

**realism**   The art of depicting nature as it is seen by toads.
*Ambrose Bierce*

**really**   Apparently.                    *Ambrose Bierce*

**realtor**   One who makes mountains out of molehills for a living.
—A salesman with lots on his mind.

**rear**   In American military matters, that exposed part of the army that is nearest to Congress.          *Ambrose Bierce*

REAR ADMIRAL   A naval back-seat driver.   *Anon. sailor*

**recession**   When you have to move in with your in-laws.

DEPRESSION   When they move in with you. *Harold Coffin*
—Man next to you loses his job.

DEPRESSION   You lose your job.

PANIC   Wife loses her job.   *Anon. professor of economics*

**recollect**   To recall with additions something not previously known.                          *Ambrose Bierce*

**recompense**   Too many people cast a crust of bread upon the waters and expect a seven-course dinner in return.
*York Trade Compositor*

**reconciliation**   An armed truce for the purpose of digging up the dead.                    *Ambrose Bierce*

**recount**   In American politics, another throw of the dice, accorded to the player against whom they are loaded.
*Ambrose Bierce*

**recreation**   Relief after toil or pain; amusement in sorrow or distress.                    *Dr. Sam'l Johnson*
—What you do when nobody tells you what you must do.
*Joseph Prendergast*
—Getting all tired out on your own time. *Changing Times*

**reducing**   A method of shrinking your birthday suit.

**redundancy**   The art of teaching a dolphin to swim.

**references**   What you need these days if you try to pay with cash.

**reform**   Organized suspicion.

REFORMER   A member of the meddle class.          *Anon.*
—A person who wants his conscience to be your guide.
*Changing Times*
—One who sets forth cheerfully toward sure defeat.
*Richard S. Childs*

**refugees**   People who vote with their feet.
*Berliner Illustrierte*

**rehearsal**   Acting under orders.

**Rehoboam**  Solomon's successor and only named son, who had eighteen wives, sixty concubines, twenty-eight sons and sixty daughters. Also a measure of champagne equal to sixteen to twenty-four quarts.

**relations**  Claqueurs given by nature.                    *Berlioz*

**relax**  To imitate a piece of liver.

RELAXATION  Oh, Lord, teach me when to let go.
*W. G. Carleton*

**religion**  Man's search for some assurance that he won't be dead when he will be.

—A system which keeps hitting you over the head with the idea of God.

—A subject you talk about in what is assumed to be a God-like voice.

—A kind of insurance against hell.    *The Country Parson*

—The future tense of fear.                    *Blackmore*

—This withered thing.                    *Bernard Shaw*

SCIENCE  This dry thing.                    *Bernard Shaw*

OLD RELIGIONS  Antique monuments to ignorance, superstition and savagery.

MODERN RELIGIONS  Merely ancient follies rejuvenated.
*Baron d'Holbach*

**reluctant**  Persuadable.

**reminiscent**  Driving ahead with both eyes on the rear-view mirror.                    *Richard L. Evans*

**Reno**  Sue City.                                *Anon.*

—The land of the free and the grave of the home.    *Anon.*

—City of Anotherly Love.                    *Mary C. Dorsey*

**renown**  A degree of distinction between notoriety and fame —a little more supportable than the one and a little more intolerable than the other.            *Ambrose Bierce*

**reparations**  A ten-dollar word for ruin.    *Merrill Blosser*

**repartee**  What a person thinks of after he becomes a departee.    *Journal of the American Medical Association*

—What you wish you'd said.                    *Heywood Broun*

**repentant**  Sorry enough to quit.            *C. H. Kilmer*

**replica**  A reproduction of a work of art, by the artist that made the original. It is so called to distinguish it from a "copy," which is made by another artist. When the two are made with equal skill, the replica is the more valuable, for it is supposed to be more beautiful than it looks.
*Ambrose Bierce*

**reporter**  Something between a whore and a bartender.
*Wallace Smith*

**Republican** One who thinks a commonwealth without monarchy the best government. *Dr. Sam'l Johnson*

—A man who, when he makes you a highball, takes the jigger and measures out the whisky. A Democrat just pours. *Eric F. Goldman*

**research** Much of what passes for it today is the alignment of data in orderly piles, hallowed by sacred hymns and sung to the goddess Objectivity in the shrine of Statistics. *William B. Bean*

—Looking for the guy who moved the file. *Governmentalese*

—Something that tells you a jackass has two ears. *Albert D. Lasker*

—The principal function of an advanced design department nowadays is to keep up with the public relations department. *Peter Masefield, British Aircraft managing director*

BASIC RESEARCH What I am doing when I don't know what I am doing. *Wernher Von Braun*

**resentment** The most precious flower of poverty. *Judith Beach\**

**reservation, Indian** A tract of land entirely occupied by Indians and entirely surrounded by white thieves. *Gen. William Tecumseh Sherman*

**resign** To renounce an honor for an advantage. To renounce an advantage for a greater advantage. *Ambrose Bierce*

**resipiscence** Wisdom after the fact. *Dr. Sam'l Johnson*

**resolute** Obstinate in a course that we approve. *Ambrose Bierce*

PIGHEADED Obstinate in a course we oppose.

**resorts, pleasure** Places where irritable and overworked professional entertainers hypnotize credulous Britons into believing that they are enjoying themselves when they are only paying through the nose for being worried and pillaged. *Bernard Shaw*

**responsibility** A detachable burden easily shifted to the shoulders of God, Fate, Fortune, Luck or one's neighbor. In the days of astrology it was customary to unload it upon a star. *Ambrose Bierce*

**rest** A monarchial idea. There is no rest for free people. *Georges Clemenceau*

**restaurant, swank** A place where you are sentenced to bread and water for thirty minutes. *Changing Times*

**restrict** To limit; to confine. A word scarce English. *Dr. Sam'l Johnson*

**etail**  To divide into small parcels.          *Dr. Sam'l Johnson*
—To sell in small quantities.                     *Dr. Sam'l Johnson*
—To sell at second hand.                          *Dr. Sam'l Johnson*

**etainer**  What you pay a lawyer before he does any work for you, like putting a quarter in the gas meter before you get any gas.                                    *Anon., Jr.*

**etaliate**  What you do to somebody who gives you a present or dinner.                                         *Anon., Jr.*

**etrospect**  If God wanted us to look backward, he would have put our eyes in the rear of our heads.

**eveille**  A signal to sleeping soldiers to dream of battlefields no more, but get up and have their noses counted.
                                                  *Ambrose Bierce*

**Revere, Paul**  A man who rode through the villages warning them that the red coach was coming.          *Anon., Jr.*
—That fellah who had to ride for help.      *Texas definition*

**evolution**  A form of government abroad.          *Anon., Jr.*

**REVOLUTIONS**  Movements that attract those who are not good enough for established institutions as well as those who are too good for them.                  *Bernard Shaw*

**hinoceros**  A vast beast in the East Indies armed with a horn in his front.                               *Dr. Sam'l Johnson*

**hubarb**  A plant that angries people.              *Anon., Jr.*

**ich**  What to be if you want to enjoy the simple things in life.                                              *Gene Barry*
—The poor, with money.                                 *Anon.*
—Having the time to do what you want to.

**RICHEST**  Who is satisfied with the portion allotted to him.
                                                  *Arabic proverb*

**ighteous**  One who takes his life in his hand whenever he utters the truth.                              *Bernard Shaw*

**igor mentis**  The inability to change in the face of change, to modify primitive, selfish desires when they conflict with the welfare or happiness of others, to accept new ideas when they are good ideas.                    *Walter Pitkin*

**iot**  A popular entertainment given to the military by innocent bystanders.                              *Ambrose Bierce*

**oad hog**  Formerly a motorist who drove too fast; now one who drives too slow.                           *E. S. Turner*

**obin**  A sparrow dipped in catsup.               *Milton Berle*
—The first harbinger of fall—in the deep South.

**obot**  From the Slav *robotnick*, workman.

**Rockefeller, Nelson** The best child actor since Jac
Coogan.                              *Alice Roosevelt Longwor*

**rockets** What you develop when you don't get enou
Vitamin D.                                        *Anon.,*

**rock 'n' roll** A modern St. Vitus Dance that relieves tensio
by sending its addicts into fits of primitive ecstasy. Beco
a follower of rock 'n' roll and a thousand years of civili
tion fall away in a single moment. *Dr. Joost A. M. Mee*

—A fate worse than deaf.                        *Dick Wh*

—The kind of music we used to play when the lights we
out.                                            *Bob Cros*

—Migrain music.                                *Carter Harm*

ROCK 'N' ROLL DANCING Catch-as-catch-cancan.
*Changing Tim*

ROCK 'N' ROLL LYRICS A combination of noises resulti
from gastric stress occurring while stamping the feet a
plucking on a gee-tar.                        *Robert Fonta*

**romance** A military fable of the middle ages; a tale of w
adventure in war and love.                *Dr. Sam'l Johns*

—A lie; a fiction. In common speech.        *Dr. Sam'l Johns*

—The offspring of fiction and love.          *Benjamin Disra*

ROMANCE LANGUAGES Having nothing to do with roma
but springing from the speech of Roman or Latin trad
and soldiers. They are Italian, French, Spanish, P
tuguese, Provencal, Roumanian, Corsican, Sardinian, a
the Swiss Romansch.

**Rome**—Rumor is the old name of the Tiber.

**Romeo and Juliet** A pair who got married, spent one nig
together and the next day he committed suicide. Then s
committed suicide. That's a hell of a way to start a marria
*Alan K*

**ront** An animal stinted in the growth.    *Dr. Sam'l Johns*

**room divider** Something between you and where you wa
to go.                                       *Carolyn Gree*

**rostrum** The beak of a bird.               *Dr. Sam'l Johns*

—The beak of a ship.                         *Dr. Sam'l Johns*

—The scaffold whence orators harangue.       *Dr. Sam'l Johns*

—In Latin, the beak of a bird or the prow of a ship.
American, a place from which a candidate for office en
getically expounds the wisdom, virtue and power of t
rabble.                                       *Ambrose Bie*

**Rotarian** A person who is sober when he sings at lunche
*An*

**rotgut** Bad beer.                              *Dr. Sam'l Johnson*

**rotisserie** A Ferris wheel for chickens.      *Robert Orben*

**roué** "One who has been wheeled" or has gone through the mill.

—The guy who makes out with a girl who has ignored you.
                                                        *Anon.*

  OLD ROUÉ A man who chases women, but only if it's downhill.

**roundup** Doing it the herd way.

**routes** How trees get their moisture.        *Anon., Jr.*

**rule the roast** To govern; to manage; to preside. It was perhaps originally *roist* which signified a tumult, to direct the populace.                                  *Dr. Sam'l Johnson*

**rules** Rules are for when brains run out. *George Papashvily*

**rum** Generically, fiery liquors that produce madness in total abstainers.                              *Ambrose Bierce*

—The real spirit of 1776.

**rummage sale** A charitable bazaar which enables your wife to get rid of the suit you just bought without consulting her.

**rumor** A rumor is about as hard to unspread as butter. *Grit*

**runagate** A fugitive; rebel; apostate.       *Dr. Sam'l Johnson*

**rural** The opposite of senile.               *Anon., Jr.*

  RURAL LIVING To live happily in the country one must have the soul of a poet, the mind of a philosopher, the simple tastes of a hermit—and a good station wagon.
                                        *Automotive Service Digest*

**ruse** Cunning; artifice; little stratagem; trick; wile; fraud; deceit. A French word neither elegant nor necessary.
                                                *Dr. Sam'l Johnson*

**rush hour** The sixty minutes when traffic comes to a standstill.                                        *Anon.*

**Russell, Jane** A can of tomatoes with a fancy label.
                                                        *Jane Russell*

**Russia** A helpful country. If we didn't have them how would we know whether we were ahead or behind?
                                                *Changing Times*

—A country where they have push-up breaks instead of coffee breaks.

  RUSSIAN One, a professor; two, a chess game; three, a revolution.                              *Jerome Lawrence**

—A language that presents notable difficulties.
                                                *Calvin Coolidge*

RUSSIAN ATHEIST   A guy who doesn't believe in Lenin.

*Grace Dow*

RUSSIAN POLICY   To halve and to hold.     *M. C. Dorse*

rustler   The shepherd's crook.

rut   A grave with no end to it.

ruth   Mercy; pity; tenderness; sorrow for the misery of a
other.                                    *Dr. Sam'l Johnso*

# S

sack dress   A costume that makes a girl look like a kangard
with everybody home.                                *Anoı*

sacrifice   Nowadays means doing without things our paren
never had.                                          *Puc*

sadie   To exhort to speak, as in: "Dull-ink, Sadie mag
void!"                                       *New Yorkeı*

sadism   The most effective weapon of the sinful many again
the virtuous few.                         *Bernard Sha*

SADIST   One who has never revealed his deafness to h
barber.

safety belt   The best way to keep from leaving the scene ı
the accident.                              *Changing Tim*

—When a girl slaps an eager beaver.                 *Ano*

saint   A dead sinner revised and edited.   *Ambrose Bieı*

SAINT BERNARD   A dog with a liquor license.        *Ano*

—A big dog that is half saloon.

—A rum hound.

ST. DUNSTAN   An Irishman by nationality and a saint l
profession.                                       *Voltaı*

ST. FRANCIS   A super-tramp.                  *Bernard Sha*

ST. VITUS   In view of our nervous high-strung emotion:
ism, the ideal patron saint of the United States.

*Norman Vincent Pea*

ST. VITUS DANCE   Medically, chorea. Named after tl
young Roman saint because after twelve or thirteen ce
turies young people, especially in Germany, danc
around his statue on June 15 to insure good health ı
the following twelve months. The dancing frequent
reached a frenzy that resembled the nervous afflicti

given the same name. The saint's aid is also invoked against hydrophobia.

**salad** The same all the way through as: "This is a twenty-four carat salad goal rink." *New Yorkese*

SALAD DAYS When a man can raise enough lettuce to mix with the tomatoes. *S. S. Biddle*

**salary** An amount of money that no matter how large it is some people spend more than. *Banking*

—A sum of money approximately equal to half of what you're worth. *Changing Times*

**sales talk** A trade wind. *George T. Zalud*

**salesman** One who sells cloaths ready made.
*Dr. Sam'l Johnson*

TOP SALESMAN A live wire with good connections.

**salesmanship** The difference between rape and rapture.
*Playboy*

**saloon arthritis** Stiff in every joint.

**salt** The most ice-free season. *Anon., Jr.*

**San Francisco** The wonderful thing about this city is when you get tired climbing the streets you can always lean against them.

**San Marino** A small mountainous Coney Island.
*David Dodge*

**sandman** A guy who sells sleeping pills without a prescription.

**sang-wish** Two pieces of bread held apart by any other solid food. *New Yorkese*

**Santa Claus** Someone who comes down the chimney December twenty-fourth and goes through the roof on the first of the month. *Harold Coffin*

SANTA CLAUSTROPHOBIA Fear on the part of parents of being with their children in a showroom full of toys.
*Changing Times*

**sardine** A stunted smelt.

—A whale that has gone through all phases of socialization.
*Anon. Yugoslav*

**"Sartor Resartus"** Simply unreadable. For me that always sort of spoils a book. *Will Cuppy*

**satire** A poem in which wickedness or folly is censured. Proper satire is distinguished, by the generality of the reflections, from a lampoon which is aimed against a particular person; but they are too frequently confounded.
*Dr. Sam'l Johnson*

—A sort of glass wherein beholders do generally discove everybody's face but their own. *Jonathan Swif*

SATIRIST A writer with an advanced sensitivity to decay

**satisfaction** A state of mind produced while witnessing an other person's discomfort. *Anon*

**Saturday** Never cash a check for anybody on a Saturday That leaves you two days to worry. *Florian Zabac*

**Saturnalia** A hot time when no license was needed for th wildest license.

**saucebox** An impertinent or petulant fellow.
*Dr. Sam'l Johnso*

**saucers** Origin or place where something comes from: "Th police have their own saucers of information."
*New Yorke*

**sausage** A ground hog. *Anon., Jr*

**savage nation** One that doesn't wear oncomf'rtable clothes *Mr. Doole*

**savoir-faire** The ability to lie without previous notice.
*Changing Time*

**saying** An epigram that became a proverb.

**scalawag** A dog that acts friendly for his own purposes.
*Anon., Jr*

**scandal** Gossip made tedious by morality. *Oscar Wild*

—When nobody does nothing and everybody goes aroun telling of it everywhere. *Anon., Jr*

SCANDALMONGER One who is always pouring social sewer age into people's ears.

—The knife of the party.

—A person who puts who and who together and get whew! *Anon*

**scate** A kind of wooden shoe, with a steel plate underneath on which they slide over the ice. *Dr. Sam'l Johnso*

**scath** Waste; damage; mischief; depopulation. *Scath* in Scot land denotes spoil or damage; as, he bears the *scath* and th scorn. A proverb. *Dr. Sam'l Johnso*

**scatterling** A vagabond; one that has no home or settle habitation. *Dr. Sam'l Johnso*

**scavenger** A petty magistrate, whose province is to keep th streets clean. *Dr. Sam'l Johnso*

**scene** The act of viewing; e.g., "Slung, I'll be scene you.
*New Yorke*

SCENE STEALER A guy who puts up billboards.
*Francis O. Wals*

**schedule** A small scroll. *Dr. Sam'l Johnson*

—That wonderful little gimmick which enables a housewife to do approximately one half of the things she had planned. *Lester D. Klimek*

**schizoid** A person with insight and double vision.

SCHIZOPHRENIA A state in which two can live as cheaply as one. *Robert Williams*

SCHIZOPHRENIC One who lives his private life in public. *V. S. Pritchett*

**schlemiel** A clumsy waiter who spills the soup. *Sid Solow\**

**schlemazel** The poor schnook the soup gets spilled on. *Sid Solow\**

**school** A Child's Garden of Virus. *Anon. father*

—A part-time orphan asylum.

SCHOOLING Simply dragging a child's soul through the dirt. *Bernard Shaw*

SCHOOL BOARDS What God made, after he practiced by making idiots. *Mark Twain*

SCHOOL BUS DRIVER A man who thought he liked children. *Harold Coffin*

**Schweitzer, Albert** A premature saint.

**science** The topography of ignorance. *Oliver Wendell Holmes*

—The cemetery of dead ideas.

—Organized knowledge. *Herbert Spencer*

—Organized superstition.

—A force that made gods of us before we had earned the right to be people. *Jean Rostand*

—In less than two generations science has become untranslatable and its speculations about the world come to us more and more faintly, like the dwindling shouts of a search party that have disappeared into an enormous maze. The news they succeeded in sending back to us (with the press as messenger) often seems contradictory of earlier bulletins; the gift of it comes across as a progressive disillusionment with accepted facts and an immense widening and deepening of the unknowable. But this is depressing and therefore unacceptable. . . . So the press continues to hail scientific "discoveries" (the substitution of a new theory for an abandoned one) as if they were real news, big news and good news. *T. S. Matthews*

—Always wrong: it never solves a problem without creating ten more. *Bernard Shaw*

—Finding a substitute for plastics.

APPLIED SCIENCE   A conjurer whose bottomless hat yields impartially the softest of Angora rabbits and the most petrifying of Medusas.   *Aldous Huxley*

MEDICAL SCIENCE   A department of witchcraft.

*Bernard Shaw*

TRUE SCIENCE   Teaches above all, to doubt and to be ignorant.   *Miguel Unamuno*

SCIENCE FICTION   Comic books—without pictures.

*Adapted from Kurt Vonnegut, Jr.*

GREAT SCIENTIST   Anyone who will sign an endorsement.

*Ballyhoo*

SCIENTIST   A man who makes sciens.   *Anon., Jr.*

**scoom**   A buffoon. A word out of use, and unworthy of revival.   *Dr. Sam'l Johnson*

**scrabble**   To paw with the hands.   *Dr. Sam'l Johnson*

**scrape**   Difficulty; perplexity; distress. This is a low word.

*Dr. Sam'l Johnson*

**scratch**   Getting it up is the writer's itch.

SCRATCHING   The rent you pay on the skin you occupy.

—A rash action.

**scrimmage**   Football's attempt to make both ends meet.

**scruze**   (Perhaps from *screw*. This word, though now disused by writers, is still preserved, at least in its corruption to *scrouge,* in the London jargon.) To squeeze; to compress.

*Dr. Sam'l Johnson*

**scuddle**   To run with a kind of affected haste or precipitation. A low word.   *Dr. Sam'l Johnson*

**sculler**   A gentleman who gets ahead by going backward.

**scuttle**   (From *scud* or *scuddle*.) To run with affected precipitation.   *Dr. Sam'l Johnson*

**scythe**   A tool used to cut against the grain.

**seal**   A fish with a one-trick mind.

**seasickness**   Crossing the ocean by rail. *Hudson Newsletter*

**seaweeds**   What you don't want the people next door to do when they look at your garden.   *Anon., Jr*

**second rater**   One who suffers from an affliction for which medicine has found no cure—the delusion of adequacy.

*James Wadsworth*

**second sight**   The cure for love at first sight.   *Anon*

**second Stanley Ketchel**   A middleweight who generally finishes second.   *Jimmy Cannon*

**secret**   Something you tell one person at a time. *The Buzzer*

—What you tell someone else not to tell because you can't keep it to yourself. *Arthur Orloff*

SECRETS  Things we give to others to keep for us.

*Elbert Hubbard*

**secretary**  A stenographer who doesn't mind working overtime if it's a good show.

PERFECT SECRETARY  One who types fast and runs slow.

SECRETARY OF DEFENSE  An umpire between the admirals, generals, airmen and other brass.

**seduction**  Double talk by a single-tracked mind.

**seed catalog**  A prelude to a backache.

**self-control**  Mind over madder. *P. K. Thomajan*

**self-esteem**  An erroneous appraisement. *Ambrose Bierce*

**selfishness**  That detestable vice which no one will forgive in others and no one is without in himself.

*Henry Ward Beecher*

**self-made**  If many a self-made man had it all to do over, he'd call for help. *Cy N. Peace*

**self-satisfaction**  An endemic disease of the movie business.

*Anthony Carthew*

—Of any business.

**selling**  Something like hog-calling; it isn't the noise you make, it's the appeal in your voice. *Weekly Animator*

**seminary**  The ground where any thing is sown to be afterwards transplanted. *Dr. Sam'l Johnson*

—Breeding place; place of education, from whence scholars are transplanted into life. *Dr. Sam'l Johnson*

**senator**  Half horse and half man. *Anon., Jr.*

—I've discovered the best way to entertain a senator—sit down and listen!

SENATOR TAFT  The greatest living authority on which General Eisenhower thinks.

*Adlai Stevenson, October 5, 1952*

**senior citizen**  A guy who keeps saying "I remember when" instead of "What's new?"

—A man that gets tired just wrestling with temptation.

**sense of humor**  What makes you laugh at something which would make you mad if it happened to you. *Anon.*

**sentence finisher**  One who listens too fast.

**sentiment**  Feeling sorry for everyone you know.

*Judith Beach**

**sentimentality**  Feeling sorry for people you don't know.

*Judith Beach**

**September** The month when home gardeners put off until October the chores they should have started in August. *Changing Times*

—A lovely month—too late to put up the screens and too early to put up the storm windows. *Ibid.*

—Now comes the inevitable season
When kids, with disconsolate looks,
Go back to the little red schoolhouse,
And back to the little-read books. *Stephen Schlitzer*

**serenade** To press one's suit. *Anon.*

**serfisticated** A woman with green eyelids and a dress without any straps that stays up all night.

*Anon., Jr. (British Division)*

**sermon, good** One that goes over your head and hits a neighbor. *Changing Times*

**servants** Unavoidable enemies. *Spanish proverb*

**sex** This farmyard world. *Granville Barker*

—The thing that takes up the least amount of time and causes the most amount of trouble. *John Barrymore*

—The sleepless struggle. *Lucius Apuleius, c. A.D. 125*

—A more intimate form of dancing.

—The difference between right and wrong. *Morton Thompson*

—The lowest common dominator. *Maxwell Shane**

—A driving force that frequently runs out of gas.

—The most fun you can have without laughing. *Anon.*

—The most fun you can have.

—An activity that may be so popular because it is so centrally located. *Playboy*

—The enjoyment is quite temporary. The cost is exorbitant and the position is simply ridiculous. *Lord Chesterfield*

—The scream of life. *Dr. Lao*

—If men in youth knew what they find out when older,
Their attitude toward women would be one hellava lot bolder.

—Something you can't manufacture with nudity. *Sophia Loren*

—Breathes there a man with hide so tough
Who says two sexes aren't enough? *Samuel Hoffenstein*

—The old mathematics: $1 + 1 = 3$. *Robert Levinson**

—A woman thinks differently from a man and she talks differently. . . . Most men think of *knives and forks,* but a woman thinks of *silver.* Men think of *glasses,* but a woman thinks of *crystal.* A woman may make a *lovely casserole.* He complains about the *leftovers.* She serves *potatoes lyonnaise;* he eats *spuds with onions.* Different words conjure

up different images. To a man range may mean scope,
ranch, firing range or home on the, if he's musical; to a
woman it's a beautiful new built-in oven. Base to him
means air base or first base, a bag somebody slid into; to a
woman it is a new makeup.                    *Bernice E. Connor,*
  *Director of Editorial Promotion, Ladies' Home Journal*

SEXES   There are two: the feminine and the muscular.
                                             *Anon., Jr.*

—There are three: men, women and clergymen.
                                             *French proverb*

—A woman worries about the future until she has a husband, but a man never worries about the future until
  he has a wife.                            *Liselotte Pulver*

SEX APPEAL   An American expression meaning charm.
                                             *French dictionary*

SEX SYMBOL   An actress whose public relations are so bad
  because her private relations are so public.

**shabby**   (A word that has crept into conversation and low
  writing; but ought not to be admitted into the language.)
  Mean; paltry.                            *Dr. Sam'l Johnson*

—The dean was so *shabby,* and look'd like a ninny,
  That the captain suppos'd he was curate to Jenny.
                                             *Jonathan Swift*

**Shakespeare**   The Babe Ruth of literature.
—A dramatist of note
  Who lived by writing things to quote.
                                             *Henry Cuyler Bunner*

—A man who wrote plays in which the main characters are
  trying to do what they can't possibly do. *Mark van Doren**
—The greatest public relations man England ever had.
                                             *Clifton Fadiman*

**sham**   To trick; to cheat; to fool with a fraud; to delude
  with false pretences. A low word.        *Dr. Sam'l Johnson*

**shapesmith**   One who undertakes to improve the form of the
  body. A burlesque word.                  *Dr. Sam'l Johnson*

**shaving**   The difference between man and monkey.   *Anon.*

**Shaw, Bernard**   A ghost of the future.   *Stephen Winston*
—A centipede with a foot in every cause.   *Stephen Winston*
—A man with a perfect passion for representing himself as a
  scoundrel.                               *Annie Besant*
—The writing machine.                      *Bernard Shaw*
—A bearable companion on bicycle rides.    *Bernard Shaw*
—An excellent man; he has not an enemy in the world, and
  none of his friends like him.            *Oscar Wilde*

—A writer who discovered himself and gave ungrudgingly of his discovery to the world. *Hector Hugh Munro (Saki)*

—A natural-born mountebank. *Bernard Shaw*

"My specialty is being right when other people are wrong. If you agreed with me, I should be no use here."

—All I had to do was to open my normal eyes and with my utmost literary skill put the case exactly as it struck me, or describe the thing exactly as I saw it, to be applauded as the most humorously extravagant paradoxer in London. The only reproach with which I became familiar was the everlasting "Why can you not be serious?" Soon my privileges were enormous and my wealth immense. *Bernard Shaw*

—A man of genius. *Bernard Shaw*

—When I was first in company with Anatole France he asked who I was. Answering for myself I said, "I am, like you, a man of genius." This was, according to his French code, so immodest that it startled him into riposting with "Ah well: a whore has the right to call herself a pleasure merchant." *Bernard Shaw*

—I am myself by profession what is called an original thinker, my business being to question and test all the established creeds and codes to see how far they are still valid and how far worn out or superseded, and even to draft new creeds and codes. But creeds and codes are only two out of the hundreds of useful articles that make for a good life. *Bernard Shaw*

**sheer nonsense**  Calling women the weaker sex. *Carl Jung*

**shepherd**  A bawd to a bellwether. *Shakespeare*

**sheveled**  Every hair in place. *Newords*

**ship**  A large hollow building, made to pass over the sea with sails. *Watts*

**shock absorbers**  Horror-movie fans. *Charles Chick Govin*

**shoplifting**  A private-enterprise attempt to curtail the profit system.

**shopping**  When a woman asks to see something more expensive.

BUYING  When she asks to see something cheaper. *Russell Newbold*

**shotfree**  Clear of the reckoning. *Dr. Sam'l Johnson*

—Though I could 'scape *shotfree* at London, I fear the shot here; here's no scoring but upon the plate. *Shakespeare, Henry IV*

**shotgun wedding**  A matter of wife or death.

**shover**   A professional operator of a private motor vehicle. "Besides being the gamekeeper, he was Lady Chatterley's shover."    *New Yorkese*

**showgirl**   A dame who has cried wolf so many times, she's finally caught one.    *Earl Wilson*

**showoff**   Your TV series has been cancelled. *Irvin S. Atkins**

**shrewmouse**   A mouse of which the bite is generally supposed venomous, and to which vulgar tradition assigns such malignity, that she is said to lame the foot over which she runs. I am informed that all these reports are calumnious, and that her feet and teeth are equally harmless with those of any other little mouse. Our ancestors however looked on her with such terrour, that they are supposed to have given her name to a scolding woman, whom for her venom they call a *shrew*.    *Dr. Sam'l Johnson*

**shunpiker**   A driver who avoids turnpikes and the tolls in cash, patience and human lives thereof.

**shyster**   Legal term for a competitor.

**Sicily**   One of the chief occupations of the Arabs in the fifteenth century.    *Anon., Jr. (Art Linkletter Dept.)*

**sickness**   A good remedy against many a sin. *Russian proverb*

**sidewinder**   A half-asp rattlesnake.    *Fred Beck**

**sign**   Get organized.
       Talk to wife.
       Get reorganized.

**silence**   The music of the spheres.    *Oliver St. J. Gogarty*
—The only place where real truth is to be found.
    *Pablo Picasso*
—A needle passing through water.    *Dylan Thomas*
—One of the hardest arguments to refute.    *Josh Billings*
—The fittest reply to folly.    *Arabic proverb*
—One way of saving face.
—Along with modesty, a great aid to conversation. *Montaigne*
—A good substitute for brains.    *Anon.*
—A way of saying nothing that leaves practically nothing unsaid.
—A tense hush at the movie theatre in which only the crunch of popcorn can be heard.
—A stranger in our world, known only by her absence.
    *Freya Stark*
—A condition a baby born today may not experience for years.
    *Wheeler McMillen*
MAN'S SILENCE   A wonderful thing to listen to.
    *Thomas Hardy*

**silly question**  One a parent can't answer.

**silver lining**  Something that always seems easier to find in someone else's cloud.     *Changing Times*

**simple**  A single ingredient in a medicine; a drug. It is popularly used for an *herb*.     *Dr. Sam'l Johnson*

**sin**  Something that used to be called a sin; now it's called a complex.     *Eva Bartok*

—The way of the transgressor may be hard—but it ain't lonely.

—What writes history. Goodness is silent.     *Goethe*

—Whatever obscures the soul.     *André Gide*

—A priest's business.

SINNER  A person with halos under his eyes.

**sinecure**  A disease without a cure.     *Anon., Jr.*

**Sioux-cilian**  Half Italian and half Indian.     *Dick Capri*

**sipate**  To walk the straight and narrow path.     *Newords*

**sit**  Our language is full of suggestions that it is a privilege to work sitting down. We respect our chairman; we honor the throne; we speak of a professor's chair, a seat in parliament. The lawyer looks to the judge's bench; and the Turks speak of their divan, and the Hebrews of the sanhedrin, all in the same sense. Even the word "president" means the man in the best seat. All this betokens a habit of mind, respecting the man who does his work sitting down.     *Prof. David L. Thompson*

**sixty**  When it takes longer to rest than to get tired.

**skeptic**  A person who can read an article about some new disease without feeling any of the symptoms described.     *Changing Times*

—One who does not believe Siamese Twins are related. *Anon.*

—One who won't take know for an answer.     *The English Digest*

**skiing**  A sport that is best when you have lots of white snow and plenty of Blue Cross.     *Al Cooper's press agents*

SKI INSTRUCTOR  A rich widow's second husband.     *Jimmy Cannon*

EXPERT SKIER  One who knows what's good for frostbite on top of chilblains over a broken ankle.     *Dan Bennett*

**skim**  A plot or plan, frequently underhanded. "It was a nit skim, but it din work."     *New Yorkese*

**skimbleskamble**  (A cant word formed by reduplication from *scamble*.) Wandering; wild.     *Dr. Sam'l Johnson*

**skin diving**  A spectacular means of demonstrating that a man is fully as intelligent as a fish.     *Gordon E. Thatcher*

**skittles**  Bowling at the brewery.

**skull**  A deadhead.

**sky**  A wall-to-wall ceiling.        *Anon., Jr.*

**sleazy scandal**  The kind *Life* magazine doesn't publish.

**sleep**  Something that always assumes much more importance the morning after than it did the night before.
         *Lester D. Klimek*

—The poor man's wealth.        *Ledney*

    SLEEPING PARTNER  A man who goes to sleep playing bridge.      *Anon., Jr. (British Division)*

**sleet**  Rain or snow that cannot make up its mind which.
         *Anon., Jr.*

**slim**  (A cant word as it seems, and therefore not to be used.) Slender; thin of shape.      *Dr. Sam'l Johnson*

—I was jogg'd on the elbow by a *slim* young girl of seventeen.
         *Joseph Addison*

**slip**  To relax by the temporary suspension of consciousness. "Let's slip on it."      *New Yorkese*

**slipslop**  Bad liquor. A low word formed by reduplication of *slop*.      *Dr. Sam'l Johnson*

**slogan**  The good old American substitute for the facts.
         *Jacob M. Braude*

**slot machine**  A type of steel trap for catching dumb animals.
         Grand Island *Independent*

**sluggard**  A person whose hobby is letting birds watch him.

—A man who wants a prematurity of Social Security.

**slum clearance**  Legal bulldozing to permit the erection of the slums of twenty years from now.

**slurbs**  Sloppy, sleazy, slovenly, slipshod semi-cities.
       *Harold F. Wise, planning consultant,*
       *University of Pennsylvania*

**slush**  Snow with all the fun melted out.     *Art Linkletter*

**small town**  One where you can chat for a while on the phone even if you get a wrong number.     *Bob Hawk*

—A place where a person with a private-line phone is considered anti-social.     *Herb Shriner*

—A place where people buy a newspaper just to verify what they heard earlier over the phone.
       *Earl Wilson wished he'd said it*

—A locality where there are no rich policemen.
       *Changing Times*

—A place where you wear your own clothes to formal parties.

—A place where you pinch a girl and everybody squeals.

*Franklin P. Jones*

**Smith, Kate**  Only a bulge in a girdled cage.

**Smithsonian Institution**  Where they keep Dinah Shore's bones.  *Anon., Jr., reported by Les Carpenter*

**smoking**  If the cigarette industry ever succeeds in making man think for himself, the government will be looking for a new source of revenue.  *Agnes Guilfoyle*

**smuggler**  A businessman who has no respect for a country's customs.  *Anon.*

**snake**  A tail wagging without any dog.  *Anon., Jr.*

**sneb**  (Properly to *snib*. See *sneap*.) To check; to chide; to reprimand.  *Dr. Sam'l Johnson*

**sneeze**  An orgasm of the nose.  *Dr. Marion Hilliard*

—To emit wind audibly by the nose.  *Dr. Sam'l Johnson*

**snob**  A person who wants to know only the people who don't want to know him.  *Paul and Helen Martin Denis\**

**snobs**  People who talk as if they had begotten their own ancestors.  *Herbert Agar*

**soap opera**  A kind of sandwich. Between thick slices of advertising, spread twelve minutes of dialogue, add predicament, villainy and female suffering in equal measure, throw in a dash of nobility, sprinkle with tears, season with organ music, cover with a rich announcer sauce and serve five times a week.  *James Thurber*

**soap maker**  One man whose success can be attributed to clean living.

**soaper**  A late evening meal; e.g., "We gave the senator soaper."  *New Yorkese*

**S.O.B.**  Son of the Boss.  *Hensleigh Wedgwood\**

**social leader**  A dignitary who opens the season by throwing the first brawl.

**Socialism, Creeping**  An antidote for Galloping Reaction.

**socialist**  One who should be reminded that there's always free cheese in a mousetrap.

*KVP Philosopher (Kalamazoo Vegetable Parchment Co.)*

**SAVAGE SOCIALISTS**  Housebroken Communists.

*Prof. E. Merrill Root*

**socialite**  An Emily Post-graduate.

**society**  Composed of two great classes: those who have more dinners than appetite, and those who have more appetite than dinners.  *Nicholas Chamfort*

**sociologists**  The spies of life.

**sodden** Hasty. Like: "We had a sodden rain." *New Yorkese*

**sofa** (I believe an eastern word.) A splendid seat covered with carpets. *Dr. Sam'l Johnson*

**soil** Helpful dirt. *Anon., Jr.*

**sol** Brooklynese contraction for "It is all."

**soldiering** The coward's art of attacking mercilessly when you are strong and keeping out of harm's way when you are weak. That is the whole secret of successful fighting. Get your enemy at a disadvantage; and never, on any account, fight him on equal terms.

Sergius in *Arms and the Man,* by Bernard Shaw

SOLDIERS Men especially trained not to think for themselves. *Bernard Shaw*

**solemnity** The fool's shield. *Baron de Montesquieu*

**Solid South** A region as thick as its description.

**solitude** Shutting oneself up in the wide open spaces.

**soloist** A musician of note who dispenses with them in public.

**song** The licensed medium for bawling in public things too silly or sacred to be uttered in ordinary speech.
*Oliver Herford*

—Something you shouldn't buy anything for until you know what the pitch is. *Instrumentalist*

—The act of stitching; e.g., "They have a new song machine." *New Yorkese*

POPULAR SONG One that makes us all think we can sing.
*Arnold H. Glasow*

**sonic boom** Pane killer. *Edith Ogutsch*

**sophisticate** A person who acts as if his first long distance call was his hundreth.

SOPHISTICATION Adulteration; not genuineness.
*Dr. Sam'l Johnson*

—Owning a sports car which entitles its driver to look down on other people from below. Toronto *Daily Star*

—The art of recognizing a new joke and then acting as if it's an old one. *Ken Kraft*

—Being tough—politely. *Anon. collegiate*

—Dying in instalments. *Walter Winchell*

—Knowing enough to keep your feet out of the crack of the theatre seat in front of you. *Don Herold*

**S.O.S.** A musical term meaning same only softer. *Anon., Jr.*

**soul** That part of the brain that attempts to control ethical behavior.

**sound** A rapid series of osculations. *Anon., Jr.*

SOUND BARRIER What you should have between th
rumpus room and the rest of the house.
*Francis O. Wals*

**South Pole** Great God! This is an awful place.
*Robert F. Sco*

**Soviet Union** A political system built on English histor
written in London by Karl Marx. *Bernard Sha*

**space travel** There is nothing about space travel which ma
can't stand—except perhaps the expense. *L. A. DuBridg*

—When space travel becomes common there will still b
those of us who can afford a vacation only on the dark sid
of the moon. Door County (Wisc.) *Advocat*

**sparrow-grass** A tall, thin green vegetable. *New Yorke*

**Spartacus' uprising** The most legitimate war ever fought.
*Montesquie*

**special ale (British)** Two or three pints of which will blo
a soft hat through a concrete ceiling. *Drew Middleto*

**specialist** A doctor consulted at the last minute to share th
blame. *Ano*

—One step above a man who gets paid overtime. *Ano*

**speck** To anticipate. "I don't speck him for an hour yet."
*New Yorke*

**speculator** One who builds a pyramid to take a tobogga
ride.

**speech** Something you make every time you open yo
mouth with a purpose. *David C. Philli*

—A talent given to man in order that he may disguise b
thoughts. *Molière/Voltaire/Talleyra*n

—"The hardest part of a lecture," insists an experience
speaker, "is waking up the audience after the man wh
introduces me has concluded his remarks." *Baptist Observ*

—The deepest gulf that separates class from class and so
from soul. Higgins in *Pygmalion*, by *Bernard Sha*

**speed** An action frequently confused in the U.S. wit
progress.

**spendthrift** A neighbor who makes more money than you d
*Pep Meali*

**spick and span** (This word I should not have expected
have found authorised by a polite writer. *Span-new* is us
by Chaucer, and is supposed to come from *spannan*,
stretch, Sax. *expandere*, Lat. whence *span*. *Span-new*
therefore originally used of cloath new extended or dress
at the clothiers, and *spick and span* is newly extended

the *spikes* or tenters; it is however a low word.) Quite
new; now first used.                      *Dr. Sam'l Johnson*

**spinster**   A girl who lives alone and looks it.
—A gal who never learned how to tie a beau.   *Pat Suzuki*
—An unlusted number.                           *Playboy*

**split-level house**   Where the occupant owns one half and the
banks own the other.                         *Roger Price*

**split second**   The interval between reading the freeway sign
and realizing you've missed the off-ramp.

**sponsor**   A man who commits television.
SPONSORS   People who make television programs possible
and impossible at the same time.           *Dan Bennett*

**spoon**   The most fattening thing you can put into a banana
split.                                   *Franklin P. Jones*

**sport of kings**   The guy who thinks it is horse racing is off
his track and the fellow who thinks it is golf has holes in his
head. The Sport of Kings is Queens.

**spring**   An experience in immortality. *Henry David Thoreau*
—One touch of nature.
—The time when you turn on the heat that yesterday you
thought you'd turned off for the year.   *Changing Times*
—That glorious time of the year when your neighbor comes
by with an invitation for golf just as you have your hands
full of storm windows.                   *Lester D. Klimek*
—The season when husbands wander out into the yard, feel
the stir of things growing, breathe deep of the fresh air and
have an irresistible urge to get inside and watch the baseball game on TV.                         *Changing Times*

**spy**   A licensed delinquent who is above the law. *Eric Ambler*
—A person with a code in the head.
SPYING   Today's hot front in the cold war.
                               *U.S. News and World Report*
—The art of perfidy.                      *Dr. R. Lewinsohn*

**square**   A circle with four corners.          *Anon., Jr.*
—A person who, when there is nothing more to be said, starts
talking.                                      *Bobby Van*
—Someone else.                                *Rod Reed*

**squeal**   To cry with a shrill sharp voice; to cry with pain.
*Squeak* seems a short sudden cry; and *squeal* a cry continued.                                   *Dr. Sam'l Johnson*

**stage**   A place where Shakespeare murdered Hamlet and a
great many Hamlets have since murdered Shakespeare.
                                          *Robert Morse*

**stain** The act of remaining. "You go. I'm stain." *New Yorke*

**stalemate** A spouse who has begun to pall. *Peter DeVri*

**stand did** What the candidates bear; e.g., "Candy is o stand did bearer." *Bostone*

**starlet** Any girl under thirty in Hollywood who is not reg larly employed in a brothel. *Ben Hec*

**State Department** A hydra-headed monster, with two co mittees springing up whenever one is lopped off, its offici latter-day Laocoöns entwined in miles of red tape.
*Henry Serrano Villa*

**statesman** One who sheers the sheep. A politician ski them. *Austen O'Mall*

—A man who meets every problem with an open mouth.
*Adlai Stevens*

**stateswoman** A woman who meddles with publick affai In contempt. *Dr. Sam'l Johns*

**statistics** Figures used as arguments.

—He uses statistics as a drunken man uses lampposts—f support rather than illumination. *Andrew La*

**steak** The first refuge of the gastronomic coward.
*Clifton Fadim*

**Steele, Richard** A rake among scholars, and a scholar amo rakes. *Thomas Babington Macaul*

**steganography** The art of secret writing by characters cyphers, intelligible only to the persons who correspond o with another. *Nathaniel Bai*

**Stein, Gertrude** The mamma of Dada. *Clifton Fadim*

**Steinway** A family that was instrumental in developing t piano business.

**stereo** An unceasing stream of sound passing from t stereophonic speakers into each of a listener's ears. One impaled upon an electronic barb and dare not move head lest he miss a ruddy grace note. *Anon. Englishm*

**stethoscope** A magnifying glass for looking into peopl chest with the ears. *Anon.,*

**Stevenson, Adlai** I feel very much like a corn-fed Illin lawyer who has gotten into the big time unintentional *Adlai Stevens*

**stewardess** A cute young waitress preparing to trip dow more important aisle.

**stockfish** Dried cod, so called from its hardness.
*Dr. Sam'l Johns*

**stockjobber**  A low wretch who gets money by buying and selling shares in the funds.            *Dr. Sam'l Johnson*

**stomach**  The best clock.            *Russian proverb*

FULL STOMACH  The kind that likes to preach about fasting.            *Russian proverb*

**stool-pigeon**  A jailbird with a lamentable lack of group-loyalty.

**stowaway**  The man with the biggest appetite on the boat.            *Anon., Jr.*

**Stravinsky, Igor**  "I don't create. I just sniff about and discover musical truffles."

**street**  A road that has a very good class of people in it.            *Anon., Jr. (British Division)*

**stretch socks**  The trouble with them is you rarely know when you are putting on your own or your ten-year-old son's.

**strident**  Beefing it up.

**strip poker**  One game in which the more you lose, the more you have to show for it.            *Playboy*

**strip-teaser**  A skin diva.            *Russell Newbold*

**stuck-ins**  Long hose (ladies', not fire).            *New Yorkese*

**stuffing**  Suffering from lack of food; e.g., "I'm stuffing to debt."            *New Yorkese*

**stupid**  Educated beyond the capacity to think.            *American Mercury*

**stutterer**  A man who breaks his word while giving it.

**subconscious retention**  An elegant phrase meaning that you have copied something from somebody else but you weren't conscious of it at the time, and it is one of those phrases that holds society together and makes it possible for authors to associate with each other without mayhem.            *Morton Thompson**

**submarine**  A ship that sinks on purpose.            *Anon., Jr.*

**suburb, exclusive**  A place where a man owes more on his house than he does on his car.            *Changing Times*

**suburban husband**  A gardener who sleeps in.            *Alvin M. Josephy, Jr.*

**suburbanite**  One who thinks "dining out" means having charcoal-burned hot dogs in the back yard.            *Dan Kidney*

—A big-city dropout.            *Anon.*

—A yardbird with sex privileges.            *Samuel Stark**

SUBURBIA  Where the houses are farther apart and the payments are closer together.            *Maurice Seitter*

SUBURBS  Where you have to drive out to so you can par
and take a bus in to work.

—The region where each year there are more statio
wagons and fewer stations.  *Bill Vaugha*

—Where the people have more interesting gossip to te
about their appliances than they have about their neig
bors.  *Burton Hill*

success  The brief interval between a stroke of luck and
stroke of apoplexy.  *Ano*

—The ability to get along with some people and ahead
others.  *Dunning*

—The successful people are the ones who can think up thing
for the rest of the world to keep busy at.  *Don Marqu*

—The one unpardonable sin against one's fellows.
*Ambrose Bier*

—When a man stops keeping track of the money and star
counting calories.

—One of the biggest troubles with success these days is th
its recipe is about the same as that for a nervous brea
down.  *Ano*

—Making more money to meet the obligations you wouldn
have if you didn't make so much money.  *Ano*

—One of the great advantages of success lies in the fact th
you don't have to listen to good advice any more.
*Bernard Buff*

—Being in the right place at the right time.  *Andy Griffi*

—Making the greatest profit from the fewest mistakes.
*Highways of Happine*

—The fine art of making mistakes when nobody is lookin
*Phoenix Flan*

—When you make enough money to hire management eng
neers to tell you why you didn't make more.
*Changing Tim*

—An achievement that covers a multitude of blunders.
*Bernard Sha*

—To have succeeded is to have finished one's business
earth, like the male spider, who is killed by the female t
moment he has succeeded in his courtship. *Bernard Sha*

—A toy balloon among children armed with sharp pins.
*Gene Fowl*

—There is only one—to be able to spend your life in yo
own way.  *Christopher Morl*

SUCCESSFUL  Behind every successful man you'll find
woman who has nothing to wear.  *Harold Cof*

**suicide**  Resigning from the human race.
—Cheating the doctors out of a job.              *Josh Billings*
—The sincerest form of self-criticism.
—One who is allergic to himself.

**summer**  The topsy-turvy season when the goldfish have to
be boarded out while the family goes on a fishing trip.
                                    Cincinnati *Enquirer*
—The time of year when mothers need a teacher's patience.
                                                    *Nuggets*
—The time of year when you could use the money you were
going to save for a vacation.          *Changing Times*
—That most pleasant season when there's not much on the
radio, the TV or the girls at the beach.          *Ibid.*
—The time of year when you ride bumper to bumper to get
to a beach where you sit the same way.
              *Journal of the American Medical Association*
—The season when children slam the doors they left open all
winter.                                              *Anon.*
  ST. MARTIN'S SUMMER  Indian Summer before America and
  its Indians were discovered.
  SUMMER RAIN  Rather like catsup out of a bottle: you're
  becoming exasperated because you don't get any, then
  suddenly you get too much.              *Brock Bell*
  SUMMERTIME  When you take a vacation from friends
  you've been seeing all year. You travel to a remote spot
  where the big event of the day is waiting for the mail
  to arrive with letters from those same friends.
                                              *Harold Coffin*

**sun**  It is all sunshine that makes a desert. *Arabian proverb*
—A very slow-burning hydrogen bomb. *Dr. Herbert Friedman*

**sunday**  According to many people, a sponge to wipe out
all the sins of the week.          *Henry Ward Beecher*
—The day to stay home, turn on the radio and listen to the
traffic reports.                          *Rusty Draper*
  SUNDAY DRIVER  One who doesn't drive any better during
  the week.          *Illinois Educational Press Bulletin*
—The weak end of the weekend.
  SUNDAY PAPER  What gives us our weekend exercise.

**suntan**  A poor substitute for the authentic glow of fever or
alcoholic flush.                          *Bill Manville*

**superhighway**  An automobile road which frequently makes
bad manners fatal.
—A kind of prison in motion.              *Clifton Fadiman*

**supercilious**  With raised eyebrows. *Original Latin meaning*

**superfluous** A very necessary thing. *Voltai*

**supermarket** A place where you travel farther than you money. *Lavonne Mathiso*

—A shopping block.

—The factor that keeps most would-be investors out of th stockmarket. *The Headlin*

—A place where you can find anything you want except th kids when you're ready to leave. *F. G. Kerna*

**supermen** A few accidental superior beings who must live precariously as lion tamers do, taking the humor of the situation, and the dignity of their superiority, as a set-o to the horror of the one and the loneliness of the othe *Bernard Sha*

**Supreme Court Justice** An official without the authority perform marriages.

—I guess it is because marriage is not considered a feder offence. *Justice Felix Frankfurt*

**The Supremes** A girl singing group who have recorded son of the Beatle material but remain "Les belles dames sa Mersey." *Music lover quoted by Richard D. Free*

**sure bet** The one you didn't make.

**survival** The only Jewish art form. *Ano*

**suspense** What makes dramatic writing good and marit relationships really permanent. *William Feath*

**suspicion** The poison of friendship. *French prove*

—An emotion that often creates what it suspects. *C. S. Leu*

SUSPICIOUS A trout in the milk.

**swain** Casanova coming through the rye.

**Swansea** The womb with a view. *Dylan Thom*

**swash** To make a great clatter or noise; whence *swas. buckler. Dr. Sam'l Johnsc*

**sweater** A garment worn by a girl to pull men's eyes ov the wool. *Ano*

**Swede** Saccharine to the taste. "Have some swede potatoe: *New Yorke*

**sweetheart** A bottle of wine.

WIFE A wine bottle. *Baudela*

**sweets** Two minutes on the tongue, two hours in the tumn and the rest of your life on your torso.

**swelled head** Nature's effort to fill a vacuum.

**Swetty** Name for a spray-on for men who don't smell ma nish.

**swim pool** A splashy status symbol. *Robert Levinso*

**swimming instructor**  A hold-up man.  *Arnold H. Glasow*

**Swinburne**  A poet who got everything from books and nothing from nature. Read his poems about the sea and they will convince you that he never was near the sea in his life and had only read a lot about it; and yet the truth is that the fellow was never out of the sea: he was always swimming about.  *William Morris*

**swine**  Creatures which by now should be the best judges of pearls.

**swing**  Jazz with a college education.  *Anon.*

**swingebuckler**  A bully; a man who pretends to feats of arms.  *Dr. Sam'l Johnson*

**syb**  Related by blood. The Scottish dialect still retains it.  *Dr. Sam'l Johnson*

**sycophant**  A person who shows figs. *Original Greek meaning*

**sympathy**  Your pain in my breast.  *Halford E. Luccock*

**—A** musical confession of the soul.  *Tchaikovsky*

**syndrome**  A big brothel.  *Leslie Pearl\**

**synonymania**  A compulsion to distract, and, if possible, puzzle the reader by calling a spade successively a garden implement and an earth-turning tool.  *Theodore M. Bernstein*

# T

**T**  The twentieth letter of the English alphabet, was by the Greeks absurdly called tau. In the alphabet whence ours comes it had the form of the rude corkscrew of the period, and when it stood alone signified Tallegal, translated "tanglefoot."  *Ambrose Bierce*

**tabloid**  A scream-lined newspaper.  *Anon.*

**tact**  The ability to hammer home a point without hitting the other fellow on the head.  *Changing Times*

**—Giving** someone a shot in the arm without letting him feel the needle.  *Anon.*

**—Knowing** how far we may go too far.  *Jean Cocteau*

**—The** ability to close one's mouth before someone else decides to.  *Beverly Tracton*

—Tongue in check. *Sue Dyrtri*

—A quality that fails the moment it is noticed.

*Edward Longstreth*

**tail** A happy ending. *Anon., Jr.*

**take** To acquire, frequently by force but preferably by stealth. *Ambrose Bierce*

**tale** A narrative; a story. Commonly a slight or petty account of some trifling or fabulous incident; as, *a tale of a tub.* *Dr. Sam'l Johnson*

**talent** A gratuitous grace, completely unconnected with saving grace or even with ordinary virtue or sanity. This has been true of such disparate talents as Carlo Gesualdo and Dylan Thomas.

TALENT AGENT A man of business who heeds the call to be of service much as a bull does.

**talisman** A man who calls every week for the furniture money. *Anon., Jr. (British Division)*

**Talleyrand** If that man is not a scoundrel, God does not write a legible hand. *Gilbert Stuart*

**tangerine** A loose-leaf orange. *Des Moines Register*

**Tanglewood** An outdoor musical gathering celebrated for Brahms bursting in air. *Peter DeVries*

**tarantula** An insect whose bite is only cured by musick. *Dr. Sam'l Johnson*

**tariff** One form of government interference business doesn't resent. *Leo C. Rosten*

**Tarkington, Booth** An author who, if he were writing *Seventeen* today, would call it "Twelve."

*Connecticut high school teacher*

**tart** A merry magdalene.

**taught** An idea or mental entity. *New Yorkese*

TAUGHT HERRING Falling over; e.g., "The Republic is taught herring." *Bostonese*

**tawdry** Meanly shewy; splendid without cost; fine without grace; shewy without elegance. It is used both of things and of persons wearing them. *Dr. Sam'l Johnson*

**tax reform** When you take the taxes off things that have been taxed in the past and put taxes on things that haven't been taxed before. *Art Buchwald*

**taxation** Consists in so plucking the goose as to obtain the largest amount of feathers with the least amount of hissing.

*Jean Baptiste Colbert, Louis XIV's finance minister*

**taxes** The price the place puts on the right to live in it.

—The chief business of a conqueror of the world.

                   *Caesar in* Caesar and Cleopatra, *by Bernard Shaw*

—Count that day won when, turning on its axis, this earth
    imposes no additional taxes.         *Franklin P. Adams*

—In seventeen hundred and seventy-six.
    A group of American mavericks
Renounced the yoke of tyranny—
    The tax on stamps, the tax on tea.
Our fathers felt that we were fit
    To tax ourselves and you'll admit
We have been very good at it.         *Howard Dietz*

—Something for people who are not smart enough to start
    their own country.

    *Leicester Heminway, President, Republic of New Atlantis*

—Things what people won't pay. They are used to keep the
    roads nice.              *Anon., Jr. (British Division)*

TAX RETURN   An annual work of fiction whose authorship
    is not confined to writers.

taxicab   A word coined and copyrighted by Harry N. Allen
    of New York City in 1907, who explained: "The 'cab' part
    was a natural.[1] The 'taxi' came from a French company that
    made meters for horse cabs, called 'taximetres.' That means
    a meter that arranges for the tax. I merely combined the
    two."

TAXI WRECK   A hackcident.

taxidermist   A hare restorer.

—A kind of thick fog.                 *Anon., Jr.*

tea   A Chinese plant, of which the unfusion has lately been
    much drunk in Europe.         *Dr. Sam'l Johnson*

TEA BAG   A dame hung up on marijuana.

                        *Broadway version*

TEA WAGON   A pushcart that's made it in Society.   *Anon.*

teacher   A scapegoat in the home, a necessary nuisance to
    the board of education and a footstool in national politics.

                            *Leo A. Lerner*

—Somebody who likes somebody else's children—and has
    strength left to go to the PTA meeting.

                     *Georgia Education Journal*

—The only kind of woman who can ask a question and then
    keep her mouth shut long enough to hear the answer.

                              *Anon.*

ELEMENTARY TEACHER   An unmarried den mother.

                         Chicago *Sun-Times*

---

[1] Short for "cabriolet."

TEACHERS  The ones who are underwriting education in this country today.  Ashley Montagu, *Indiana Teacher*

TEACHER'S PET  A school-pigeon.

**tears**  The hydraulic force through which masculine will power is defeated by feminine water power.

East Dubuque (Ill.) *Reporter*

—Glum drops.  *Anon.*

**technology**  The knack of so arranging the world that we don't have to experience it.  *Max Frisch*

—While adding daily to our physical ease, throws daily another loop of fine wire around our souls. *Adlai Stevenson*

**tee-hee**  The house where Minehaha lived.  *Anon., Jr.**

**teem**  To pour. A low word, imagined by Skinner to come from *tommen*, Danish, *to draw out; to pour*. The Scots retain it; as, teem *that water out;* hence Swift took this word.  *Dr. Sam'l Johnson*

—*Teem* out the remainder of the ale into the tankard, and fill the glass with small beer.

Jonathan Swift, *Directions to the Butler*

**teen**  Sorrow; grief.  *Dr. Sam'l Johnson*

TEEN-AGER  One who has reached the age of dissent.

*Harold D. Leslie*

—Huck Finn remodeled by Charles Addams.

*Clifton Fadiman*

TEEN-AGERS  Nonconformists who prove their differences by dressing exactly alike.

—Girls who have not yet realized that their weaknesses are their strengths.  *Brigitte Bardot*

—The "Get Lost" generation.

LATE TEENS  That painful time when a boy is tall enough to drive the family car but usually too short to buy the gas.  *Pep Mealiffe*

**teetotaler**  Just another kind of toper.  *Walt Whitman*

**teh-he**  (A cant word made from the sound.) To laugh with a loud and more insolent kind of cachinnation; to titter.

*Dr. Sam'l Johnson*

**telekinesis**  Transmission of muscular energy and its mechanical power over both animate and inanimate objects at a distance.

—A twitch by a witch.

**telepathy**  Perception of some other person's psychic experiences without their transmission by means of speech or other sense organ. Radio without a set.

**telephone**  A communication instrument that begins to ring as soon as you begin to take a bath.                    *Anon.*

—An instrument used to meet strangers (see Wrong Number).                                          *Robert Levinson**

—There never was truer word spoken,
Though not scientifically known:
A connection that cannot be broken
Is a teen-ager's grip on the phone!            *Anita Raskin*

—There is something about saying "O.K." and hanging up the receiver with a bang that kids a man into feeling that he had just pulled off a big deal, even if he has only called up to find out the correct time.            *Robert Benchley*

—An inconvenient convenience.

TELEPHONE POLE  A tall, upright object that never strikes a car unless a woman is driving.

**temper**  What gets us into trouble.

PRIDE  What keeps us there.            *Arnold H. Glasow*

**temperament**  A disease that afflicts amateurs.
                                          *G. K. Chesterton*

**tenement**  Any thing held by a tenant.   *Dr. Sam'l Johnson*

**ten-gallon hats**  The perfect topper for those who think big.
                                          *Quote*

**tenner**  Easily masticated. "What's tenner today?"
                                          *New Yorkese*

**tension**  The American people are so tense that it is impossible even to put them to sleep with a sermon.
                                          *Norman Vincent Peale*

TENSION HEADACHE  What you get from looking at television commercials about tension headaches. *Alan King*

**tenter**  A hook on which things are stretched.
                                          *Dr. Sam'l Johnson*

**tête-à-tête**  A double-header.            *Jeanette L. Lowry*

**Texas**  A state where everything either sticks, stinks or stings.
                                          *Anon. visitor*

—A state where you can see farther—and less—than any other place in the U.S.A.

—Second largest state in the Union—where Alaskans should spend the winter.   *Slogan reported by Les Carpenter*

TEXAS RIVER  One a mile wide and an inch deep.   *Time*

**Thanksgiving**  A holiday that was founded by the Puritans to give thanks fr bein' presarved fr'm th' Indyans, an' we keep it to give thanks we are presarved fr'm th' Puritans.
                                          *Mr. Dooley*

—A day on which we express gratitude for the past months when nobody reminded us there were only so many days left until Christmas. *Changing Times*

—The day when Americans are thankful they've got a bellyfull.

**thawed** The past tense of think. *Anon., Jr.*

**theatre** A place where long-bodied people sit in front of us, talkative ones behind us and the nomadic type on either side. *Dave Flynn*

—Holding a mirror up to a keyhole. *Anon.*

—Literature for the general public who have no time to read. *Sainte-Beuve*

—A place for miracles. *Robert Anderson*

—Polite voyeurism, sex, people running away from their Mums, escaping from Life. *Joan Littlewood*

—The exhibition of examples of personal conduct made intelligible and moving to crowds of unobservant unreflecting people to whom real life means nothing. *Bernard Shaw*

—My battering ram as much as the platform or the press. *Bernard Shaw*

—Continually occupied with sex appeal. It has to deal with sex appeal exactly as a costermonger has to deal in turnips. *Bernard Shaw*

—A great equalizer; it's the only place where the poor can look down on the rich. *Will Rogers*

**thence** Like Ten, only much longer ago. *Anon., Jr.*

**theology** The effort to explain the unknowable in terms of the not worth knowing. *H. L. Mencken*

**theory** A green fact. *Anon., Jr.*

**thew** In Shakespeare it seems to signify brawn, or bulk, from the Saxon *theow,* the *thigh,* or some such meaning. *Dr. Sam'l Johnson*

—Will you tell me, master Shallow, how to chuse a man? Care I for the limbs, the *thewes,* the stature, bulk and big semblance of a man? give me the spirit, master Shallow. *Shakespeare, Henry IV*

**Thibault, Jacques** A wise French novelist and essayist who deemed it best to write under the frivolous name of Anatole France.

—"If fifty million people say a foolish thing, it is still a foolish thing." *Anatole France*

**thick skin** A gift from God. *Konrad Adenauer*

**THICKSKIN** A coarse gross man; a numskul. *Dr. Sam'l Johnson*

**thinking** When your mouth stays shut and your head keeps talking to itself. *Anon., Jr.*

**third degree** Professor Quiz with a rubber hose. *Anon.*

**thirty-five** A very attractive age; London society is full of women who have of their own free choice remained thirty-five for years. *Oscar Wilde*

**Thomas, Dylan** A poet who lacked the strength of character to support his genius. *Stanley Kunitz*

**thoughts** What a man has about women after he reaches thirty-five. Feelings are what he has before. *Austin O'Malley*

**Three Graces** Eat, drink and be married. *Anon., Jr.*

**thrift** Wanting less than you can afford. *Changing Times*
—No longer a virtue, but a threat to the economy.
*Burton Hillis*
—Today it seems to mean saving trading stamps.

**throne** Sit we upon the highest in the world, yet sit we on our own tail. *Montaigne*

**throng** The act of hurling; e.g., "Boys, stop throng stones!" *New Yorkese*

**thruway** A toll road that is obsolete the day the ribbon is cut.

**thumb** The thick finger. *Anon.*

**thunder** The noise that air makes when lightning jumps through it. So would anybody.
—Thunder does all the barking but it's lightning that bites.
*Anon., Jr.*

**Thursday** Thunderday. *Original meaning*

**tides** There are two, Eb and Flo. *Anon., Jr.*\*

**tidewaiter** An officer who watches the landing of goods at the customhouse. *Dr. Sam'l Johnson*

**tiff** (A low word, I suppose without etymology.) (1) Liquor; drink. (2) A fit of peevishness or sullenness; a pet.
*Dr. Sam'l Johnson*

**tiger** A 300-pound pansy that eats you. *Anon.*

**time** A cosmic stuff that glues together the otherwise unrelated happenings of this world. *Bill Manville*
—A dog that only bites the poor. *Leon Bloy*
—The not-so-very subtle thief of youth.
—The greatest of all tyrants. *Russian proverb*
—The price of eternity. *Louis Bourdalone*
—The moving image of immobile Eternity.
*Jean-Baptiste Rousseau*
—A dressmaker, specializing in alterations. *Faith Baldwin*

—I would I could stand on a busy street corner, hat in hand, and beg people to throw me all their wasted hours.
*Bernard Berenson*

—Money, and many people pay their debts with it.
*Josh Billings*

"**TIME**" A weekly newsmagazine in the nick of which a stitch of saves. *Fred Beck**

**tis of thee** The name of my country. *Anon., Jr.*

**toad** An animal resembling a frog; but the frog leaps, the toad crawls; the toad is accounted venomous, I believe truly. *Dr. Sam'l Johnson*

—In the great plague there were seen, in divers ditches about London, many *toads* that had tails three inches long, whereas *toads* usually have no tails.
*Francis Bacon, Natural History*

—A dry frog.

**toastmaster** The cement between the bricks, sometimes to keep the speakers together, sometimes apart.
*Harry Hershfield*

—A pill that you have to take after dinner.

**tobacco** The Indians' revenge.

**toboggan** To haggle or make deals; e.g., "I'm not going toboggan with the opposition patty." *Bostonese*

—The act of whittling down the price. For example: "I hate toboggan, but that's too much." *New Yorkese*

**tock** A female tick. *Anon., Jr. (Art Linkletter Dept.)*

**today** Yesterday shaking hands with tomorrow.
*Alfred Stieglitz*

—A hardy, beautiful virgin. *Mallarmé*

—Not only the era of the ghost writer—but of the ghost thinker. *Sydney J. Harris*

—An age proud of machines that think and suspicious of men who try to. *Mumford Jones*

**TODAY'S MODELS** Tomorrow's junk. *Joseph J. Seldin*

**togetherness** The ability to agree on which TV channel to switch to next. *Changing Times*

**Tokyo** A city containing all the charm of downtown Jersey City, only bigger. *Caskie Stinnett**

**tolerance** Seeing certain things with your heart instead of your eyes. *Desk Notes*

—The only real test of civilization. *Arthur Helps*

—The patience shown by a wise man when he listens to an ignoramus. *Anon.*

—The ability to keep your shirt on when you're hot under
the collar.                                    *Cy N. Peace*

—The virtue of the man without convictions.

*G. K. Chesterton*

—The uncomfortable suspicion that the other fellow may be
right after all.                              *Traffic Safety*

**toll** Not smoll.                             *New Yorkese*

**tomb** Lodging for the night.

TOMBSTONE About the only thing that can stand upright
and lie on its face at the same time. *Mary Wilson Little*

**tomcat** The original cat's paw.

**tomorrow** Time enough for revenge.         *Russian proverb*

—Now be ready for the last great countdown!

*Evangelist in Central Park*

**tongue** A misguided muscle.

—Remember that your tongue is in a wet place and likely to
slip.                             *Margaret Blair Johnstone*

**toothache** A pain that drives you to extraction.

*The English Digest*

**top** To perform eminently: as, *he tops his part.* This word,
in this sense, is seldom used but on light or ludicrous occa-
sions.                                       *Dr. Sam'l Johnson*

—A spot where there's plenty of room—but no place to sit
down.                                          *Laurence Harvey*

**torch** When your sugar becomes a lump in your throat.

*Walter Winchell's column*

**tornado** A cloud with a quicksilver lining.

**torpedo** A fish which while alive, if touched even with a
long stick, benumbs the hand that so touches it, but when
dead is eaten safely.                       *Dr. Sam'l Johnson*

**torture rack** A marvelous invention for destroying an innocent man of weak constitution and for saving a strong
guilty one.                              *La Bruyère (1645–95)*

**touchy** Peevish; irritable; irascible; apt to take fire. A low
word.                                       *Dr. Sam'l Johnson*

**tourist** A rich vagabond.                    *David Dodge*

—A rich hobo.                                    *Paul Richard*

—A person with a heavy tan on his right forearm.

*Changing Times*

—A man who sublets a mirage and writes home glowing
letters describing the scenery.            *Morton Thompson\**

—A delegate without a convention.                *Hi-court*

TOURIST RESORT A place where no one knows how unimportant you are at home.

**tournament** What you tie around a person's neck to stop the blood when they cut their head. *Anon., Jr.* *

**tout** A man who has nothing to sell and sells it. *Alvin Davis*
—A free-lance handicapper. *Jimmy Cannon*

**tower** A high head-dress. *Dr. Sam'l Johnson*

**town crier** The early version of the TV commentator but one who had the good sense to keep his mouth shut when he didn't have anything to say.

**town, ideal** It will have one garage, one drugstore, one grocery store that thinks it's a supermarket, and a postmistress who knows everything about everyone because she steams open the envelopes. *Thornton Wilder*

**trade unionism** The Capitalism of the Proletariat. *Bernard Shaw*

**trade winds** What sailors took along to bargain with the natives. *Anon., Jr.*

**tradition** Something you make up as you go along. *Columbia Jester*

**traffic** The mother-in-law of the otherwise perfect marriage between the American motorist and his car. *Henry A. Barnes*
—The two greatest highway menaces are drivers under twenty-five going sixty-five and drivers over sixty-five going twenty-five.

TRAFFIC JAM Proof that haste makes waits. *Changing Times*
—A thick vehicular congestion where you sit in your car and watch the pedestrians whizz by.

**training** Learning the rules.
EXPERIENCE Learning the exceptions. *Office Economist*
—One of the hardest things to teach a child is that the truth is more important than the consequences. *O. A. Battista*

**traipse** (A low word, I believe, without any etymology.) *Dr. Sam'l Johnson*

**travel** To labour; to toil. This should be rather *travail*. *Dr. Sam'l Johnson*
—I've watch'd and *travell'd* hard;
Some time I shall sleep out; the rest I'll whistle. *Shakespeare*
—In America there are two classes—first class and with children. *Robert Benchley*
—It is amazing how nice people are to you when they know you are going away. *Michael Arlen*

—Every year it takes less time to fly across the Atlantic and more time to drive to the office.                    *American Mercury*

—I dislike feeling at home when I am abroad.

　　　Englishman in *Widowers' Houses,* by Bernard Shaw

TRAVEL BUREAU   An organization for lousing up foreign trips from afar.

TRAVEL EXPERT   Anyone who has been fifty miles away from home.

**travesty**   An idea in actual operation.

**travill**   Returning from a foreign trip looking like your passport picture.                                    *Newords*

**treason**   The coup that fails.

PATRIOTISM   Successful treason.                    *Joseph Barry*

**tree**   A tall vegetable.                    *Ambrose Bierce*

—A large vegetable rising, with one weedy stem, to a considerable height.                    *Dr. Sam'l Johnson*

—A curious natural printing press that produces identical pieces of green typography we call leaves.

　　　　　　　*Adapted from Jonathan Miller*

TREE SURGEON   A doctor who wears a safety belt to keep from falling out of patients.

**tricksy**   Pretty. This is a word of endearment.

　　　　　　　*Dr. Sam'l Johnson*

—All this service have I done since I went.

My *tricksy* spirit.                    Shakespeare, *The Tempest*

**tricycle**   A tot rod.

**triumph**   Just "umph" added to "try."                    *Salada Tea*

**trivial**   Vile; worthless; vulgar; such as may be picked up in the highway. Light; trifling; unimportant; inconsiderable. This use is more frequent, though less just.

　　　　　　　*Dr. Sam'l Johnson*

**Trojan War**   The only war I ever approved of. It was fought over a woman and the men knew what they were fighting for.                    *William Lyon Phelps*

**trolleynomenclatumania**   A desire to name streetcars.

　　　　　　　*Newords*

**trouble**   A sieve through which we sift our acquaintances. Those too big to pass through are our friends.

　　　　　　　*Arlene Francis*

TROUBLE-MAKER   Person au gratin.                    *Paul H. Oehser**

**truce**   When shouting replaces shooting.

**truck**   A swear word used by railroad men. *Changing Times*

TRUCK DRIVERS   There are 7,350,000 of them in the U.S.,

making them the largest single occupational hazard in the country.

**true** In one side and out the other; e.g., "True dick and din."
*New Yorkese*

**trunk** A container in which valuables are kept.

   HUMAN TRUNKS Containers for holding such valuables as stomachs, hearts, etc. *Anon., Jr. (Art Linkletter Dept.)*

**truth** A thorn on life's rose. *Bill Manville*

—The opinion that survives. *Anon.*

—A torch that is seen through the fog without burning it away. *Helvétius*

—It is more from carelessness about truth than from intentional lying that there is so much falsehood in the world.
*Dr. Sam'l Johnson*

—He who cannot lie doesn't know what truth is. *Nietzsche*

—It is hard to believe that a man is telling the truth when you know that you would lie if you were in his place.
*H. L. Mencken*

—The club that knocks down and kills everybody.
*French proverb*

—What most contradicts itself in time. *Lawrence Durrell*

—Correspondence of beliefs to facts. *Bernard Shaw*

—The one thing nobody will believe. *Bernard Shaw*

—The funniest joke in the world. *Bernard Shaw*

—A commodity so precious some people use it sparingly.
*Arnold H. Glasow*

—Not a diet but a condiment. *Christopher Morley*

—And an extremely expensive condiment, at that.

   HALF-TRUTH Beware of a half-truth. It may be the wrong half. *Burton Hillis*

   TRUTHFUL Dumb and illiterate. *Ambrose Bierce*

**tube steaks** Cylindrical sirloins, hot dogs.
*Honest John of Las Vegas*

**tucker** A small piece of linen that shades the breast of women. *Dr. Sam'l Johnson*

**tumbler** A glass that can't bounce or a person who can.

**tundra** A vast treeless forest. *Anon., Jr.*

**tup** To but like a ram. *Dr. Sam'l Johnson*

**turbine** A big woman's hat worn by an Oriental man.
*Anon., Jr.*

**turkois** A blue stone numbered among the meaner precious stones, now discovered to be a bone impregnated with cupreous particles. *Dr. Sam'l Johnson*

**turnip** A vegetable with only one virtue—no bones.

**tutonic** People with white skin and black hair. *Anon., Jr.*

**TV** An instrument of intense pressure that convinces the immature mind that violence is an accepted way of life. It is a subtle form of American brainwashing. The fatal consequences will be best known by posterity. Hour after hour, simply by the flick of a switch, a child can see a swiftly flowing panorama of human misery, despair, homicide and thievery. Exposing children to such violence can be compared with taking children to public tortures and hangings in medieval times.                    *Judge Frank J. Kronenberg*

—One of the oldest forms of advertising. It was common in the patent-medicine shows. The medicine man put a couple of minstrels on the let-down tailgate of his wagon and set them to playing the banjo, singing and dancing. When this had attracted a crowd, the old Doc came out and sold the Snake Medicine. TV has only extended the tailgate.
                                                    *James Webb Young*

—An electronic device which permits you to be entertained in your own living room by characters you would never entertain in your own living room.          *Imogene Fey*

—Radio with eyestrain.                                      *Anon.*

—Eyestrain with knobs.                                      *Anon.*

—A mechanical invention which has changed a whole generation of kids from an irresistible force to immovable objects.                                      *Changing Times*

—An entertainment that keeps growing, getting curiouser and spuriouser, as well as honkier and tonkier.
                                                    *Harriet Van Horne*

—Two guys seeing which is faster on the draw. Then the news comes on and everything changes. A couple of other guys are seeing which one can be last to take his finger off the trigger.                                      *Changing Times*

—A medium of entertainment which permits millions of people to listen to the same joke at the same time and yet remain lonesome.                                      *T. S. Eliot*

—On days when it is cold or wet
The children watch the TV set
In just the way the darlings do
When it is warm and skies are blue.          *Tom Pease*

—Just think of all the commercials, old movies, westerns, politicians, comedians, quiz shows, soap operas and other intrusions we can keep out of our homes just by turning off one little knob. *Fred Randall*

—At least when you can't afford to have the TV fixed, you don't see a lot of plays about people who are bored because they have money. *Terry McCormick*

—Where you see the movies you've been avoiding for years. *Grace Downs*

—Television is education. If it weren't for the old movies, today's kids might not know that there was a time when the Russians were the good guys and the Germans were the bad guys. *Bill Vaughan*

—A wonderful invention. It lets a person in New York see someone in Los Angeles suffering from acid indigestion. *Jack Cassidy*

—Like your wife—it's home and it's free. How can you beat it? *Alexander Ince*

—A medium, so called because so little of it is either rare or well done. *Mrs. Deane Binder*

—A thimbleful of imagination, with buckets of commercials thrown on top. *Ross D. Siragusa, president, Admiral Corp.*

—The greatest aid to sleep since darkness. *Changing Times*

—The triumph of Lawrence Welk as a musician and Leonard Bernstein as a teacher.

TV AUDIENCE A group characterized by the fickleness the medium deserves.

TV BOTTOM Either a muscular affliction of addicts with poor sitting posture or the body's reaction to the current state of programming.

TV CHANNELS Ruts worn by taking the line of least resistance. *Cincinnati Enquirer*

COLOR TV An invention that eliminates snow on your screen—and substitutes confetti. *Bill Orbin*

—A wonderful invention which permits you to watch a fifteen-year old musical for only $500.

POOR RECEPTION About the only way you can improve some TV programs. *Franklin P. Jones*

TV COMMERCIALS Not so bad, but, oh, so often!

—Something that gives a man a chance to talk to his wife. *Robert Sylvester*

—On western shows there are so many just to give the actors time to reload. *Robert Sylvester*

TV SPONSOR Someone with guts or gall enough to admit responsibility for the program. *Changing Times*

TV WESTERNS Programs where Trigger Mortis sets in.

**twang**  A word making a quick action, accompanied with a sharp sound. Little used, and little deserving to be used.
*Dr. Sam'l Johnson*

**twenty**  No age for prudery.                          *Molière*

**twice**  Once too often.                        *Ambrose Bierce*

**twilight**  The stage manager of night.          *Irving S. Cobb*

**twins**  The same kid twice.                 *Dennis the Menace*

**The Twist**  A sacroiliact.                         *Newsweek*

**twittletwattle**  Tattle; gabble. A vile word.
*Dr. Sam'l Johnson*

**type**  Pestilent bits of metal suspected of destroying civilization and enlightenment, despite their obvious agency in this incomparable dictionary.
*Ambrose Bierce, The Devil's Dictionary*

**tzetze (or tsetse) fly**  An African insect (Glossina morsitans) whose bite is commonly regarded as nature's most efficacious remedy for insomnia, though some patients prefer that of the American novelist (Mendax interminabilis).
*Ambrose Bierce*

# U

**UCLA**  A school more famous for its parking problems than its athletic prowess.                *Art Seidenbaum*

**udder**  A faucet on a cow.                       *Anon., Jr.*

**ugh**  An exclamation of horror or aversion, such as expressed by a small girl when informed that a fourth brother has just been born.

**ugliness**  A point of view: an ulcer is wonderful to a pathologist.                              *Austin O'Malley*

—A gift of the gods to certain women, entailing virtue without humility.                         *Ambrose Bierce*

  UGLY DUCKLING  A repulsive child that everyone hopes will grow out of it.

**Ujiji**  The African town where Stanley presumed to meet Dr. Livingstone.

**ukulele**  A so-called musical instrument which, when listened to, you cannot tell whether one is playing on it or just monkeying with it.                *Will Rogers*

—Flea.                             *Hawaiian literal meaning*

**ultimatum** In diplomacy, a last demand before resorting to concessions. *Ambrose Bierce*

**umbrella** A bit of property which falls into the public domain the moment it looks like rain.

—The only thing most people put away for a rainy day. *Anon.*

—A shelter for one and a showerbath for two. *W. Hitchcock*

**U.N.** The town meeting of the world. *Peter I. B. Lavin*

U.N. DELEGATES It is easy to spot them. They're the ones who keep patting one another on the back while stepping on each other's toes. *Lichty cartoon*

**Un-American** Wicked, intolerable, heathenish. *Ambrose Bierce*

**unattached** A girl who has not been hooked, hitched or had.

**unawares** Lingerie, male as well as female. *New Yorkese*

**unbathed** Not wet. *Dr. Sam'l Johnson*

**unbeliever** One who believes in an opposite direction.

**unbend** To either bend or straighten from a bent position.

**unbidden** The kind of guests that are most welcome when they are gone. *Bedford in Henry V, by Shakespeare*

**unbosom** To take off a tight brass ear. *Anon., Jr.*

**unbreakable toy** The one a child uses to break all of his other toys. *Bates County (Mo.) Democrat*

UNBREAKABLE TOYS The ones that last until December twenty-sixth.

**unbridled** A man just divorced. *Anon., Jr.*

**uncalled-for** A wallflower at a square dance.

**uncanny** Without restrooms.

**uncivilized country** One in which you can safely leave your house unlocked. *Changing Times*

**Uncle Tom's Cabin** A station on the underground railway. *Anon., Jr.*

**unconditional surrender** A condition which will not be complete until everybody is a corpse. *Aldous Huxley*

**uncouth** Odd; strange; unusual. *Dr. Sam'l Johnson*

—Eating with the fingers and talking with the fork.

**uncrowded** In the subway that means having a strap all to yourself.

**unction** Grease applied by the clergy to help you slip into heaven.

**undercover agent** A girl spy. *Playboy*

**underground railroad** A method of transporting slaves, now called "The Subway."

**underjoyed** The feeling you have when your mother-in-law comes to live with you. *Newords*

**underpass** An upside-down bridge.

**underprivileged** An archaic term. Today they are described as "overfinanced."     *Changing Times*

**undersigned** A stiff way of writing "me."

**understand** To confirm a preconceived notion.

**understatement** The British version of a Texas brag.

**undertaker** One who follows the medical profession.

**underweight** A normal condition in underprivileged countries but a luxury in the U.S. achieved by sweat, tears and self-denial.

**underwriter** A lawful bookie.

**uneasy** The lie of the head that wears a crown.

    *Shakespeare, Henry IV*

**unfair** Having a temporary labor dispute.

**unforeseen** What always happens.     *Latin proverb*

**unfrock** To remove a cleric's clothes after a sin.

**ungrateful** Natural.

**unicorn** A beast, whether real or fabulous, that has only one horn.     *Dr. Sam'l Johnson*

—A bird.     *Dr. Sam'l Johnson*

—Of the *unicorn* bird, the principal marks are these: headed and footed like the dunghill cock, tailed like a goose, horned on his forehead, with some likeness, as the unicorn is pictured; spur'd on his wings, bigger than a swan. *Grew*

**unimpeachable source** The one who started the rumor.

    *Changing Times*

**uninvited** Those who come that way sit on the floor.

    *Turkish proverb*

—Nobody can be as agreeable as an uninvited guest.

    *Kin Hubbard*

**Unitarian** One who denies the divinity of a Trinitarian.

    *Ambrose Bierce*

**United States** The biggest slum on earth. The mess that is man-made America is a disgrace of such proportions that only a concerted national effort can hope to return America to the community of civilized nations.

    *British author quoted by Clare Booth Luce*

—The prosperous country that is long on shortages.

    *Max Lerner*

—A country with a one-and-a-half party system.     *Anon.*

—An oligarchy by popularity.     *Sir Pierson Dixon*

    U.S.A. A free country, but the upkeep is pretty costly.

    *D. O. Flynn*

—A land where you can say what you think without thinking. *Arnold H. Glasow*

—A country that occasionally gags on a gnat but also has some talent for swallowing tigers whole. *Adlai Stevenson*

**U.S. SENATE** A legislative body that opens with prayer and closes with an investigation. *Will Rogers*

**universal joint** The U.N. building.
*Construction Engineering News*

**universe** An irrational place not created to conform to human specifications.

—A machine for making gods. *Henri Bergson*

**university** A mental reservation. *Changing Times*

**UNIVERSITIES** Schools full of knowledge; the freshmen bring a little in and the seniors take none away, and knowledge accumulates. *Abbott Lawrence Lowell*

**unkempt** Not combed. Obsolete. *Dr. Sam'l Johnson*

**unloaded** Fatal.

**unmentionables** Those articles of ladies' apparel that are never discussed in public, except in full-page illustrated ads.
*Changing Times*

**unnecessary evil** Most necessary evils.

**unshine** A dulling, nonskid spray for bald heads. *Newords*

**unsophisticated** Not adulterated.
*Dr. Sam'l Johnson* (See "Sophisticated")

**unspeakable** A quality which unloosens a flood of speech.

—Not a feminine word.

**upheaval** It means you shouldn't have ate so much.
*Anon., Jr.*

**upholstered** What a cowboy does with his gun after he shoots somebody. *Anon., Jr.*

**uplift** To raise, socially, morally or mammillarily.

**uppish** Proud; arrogant. A low word. *Dr. Sam'l Johnson*

**uran** Pertaining to the heavens (Greek), hence Uranium, an element likely to send us all there.

**urbanity** The kind of civility that urban observers ascribe to dwellers in all cities but New York. Its commonest expression is heard in the words, "I beg your pardon."
*Ambrose Bierce*

**us** We May-fly mortals. *Clifton Fadiman*

**used car** A vehicle you buy in haste and repaint at leisure.
*Anon.*

**usher** A theatrical leading man.

Utopia  Where a husband with a forty-year-old wife can exchange her for two twenties. *Douglas Jerrold*

—Right now, right here, only we don't know it.

uxorious  Excessively or foolishly fond of one's wife.
*American College Dictionary*

—One's own wife, that is.

## V

vacation  A time when you get away from the people and places you love best so you can put up with them when you get back. *Burton Hillis*

—Two weeks on the sands, and fifty on the rocks.

—The bigger the summer vacation, the harder the Fall.
*Ford Times*

—What the family has to take to recover from the exhaustion of packing for it. *Anon.*

—Whoever said you can't take it with you has never seen the family car packed for a vacation trip. *Lester D. Klimek*

—A holiday from everything except expenses.

—A way to get in the pink by going into the red. *Anon.*

—When you pack seven suitcases, four children, two aunts, a mother-in-law, two dogs and a parakeet and say "It's good to get away from it all." *Red Skelton Show, CBS-TV*

SUCCESSFUL VACATION  The recipe: Take half the clothes you figured on and twice the money. *Changing Times*

VACATIONS  Great social levelers, since people come back from them just as broke as their friends who couldn't afford to go. *Al Bennett*

vaccination  The medical sacrament corresponding to baptism. *Samuel Butler*

vagabond  A man without an address.

LIBERTINE  A man with two addresses. *Bernard Shaw*

vagrant  A vagabond in jail.

valentine  Russia is red,
            Violets are blue,
            No Valentine's Day
            In old Soviet U. *Irving R. Levine*

vallancy  A large wig that shades the face. *Dr. Sam'l Johnson*

**valor** A soldierly compound of vanity, duty and the gam
bler's hope.

—"Why have you halted?" roared the commander of a divi
sion at Chicamauga, who had ordered a charge; "mov
forward, sir, at once."

"General," said the commander of the delinquent bri
gade, "I am persuaded that any further display of valo
by my troops will bring them into collision with the enemy.

*Ambrose Bierc*

**"Variety"** A weekly theatrical journal crouched in the lan
guage of the trade.

**vaticide** A murderer of poets. *Dr. Sam'l Johnso*

**vaudeville** An antique form of amusement kept alive b
Ed Sullivan.

    VAUDEVIL A song common among the vulgar, and sun
    about the streets. *Trevou*

    —A ballad; a trivial strain. *Dr. Sam'l Johnso*

**vegetable** Anything that grows out of or in the ground,
part of which can be sold as food.

—A substance used to ballast a child's plate while it's carrie
to and from the table. *Changing Time*

    VEGETABLE SOUP Looser stew.

**vegetarian** One who won't eat anything that moves.

—One who refuses to believe that if we do not eat the animal
the animals will eat us. *Bernard Shaw*

**vendetta** A Sicilian operetta. *Anon., Jr.*

**vending machine** A mechanical device which can supply u
with practically everything—including bad service.

**venery** The sport of hunting, the chase; archaic, or is it

**Venetian blinds** Drapes of lath. *Helen Pearso*

—A lifesaver; if it weren't for them, it would be curtains fo
all of us. *Ray Carro*

**vengeance** The noblest is to forgive.

*Sixteenth-century prover*

**ventilate** To produce a difference of opinion among th
occupants of a room.

**ventriloquism** The highly acrobatic art of telling jokes with
out moving the lips and blaming them on a nonhuma
dummy.

**Venus de Milo** A statue that would only be half as in
triguing if it had arms.

**verb** A word such as "went," without which a sentenc
don't no place go.

**verdigris** Rust of copper, brass or bronze. Literally, the green of Greece.

**verger** The masculine of virgin.                          *Anon., Jr.*

**vermouth** Wine with bitters, from the German, "Wemuth": wormwood.

**Verse, John Donne's** Like the peace of God: It passeth all understanding.                                    *King James I*

**vertical** The same as horizontal, only just the opposite.
    PERPENDICULAR Like vertical, but even more that way.
                                     *Anon., Jr.*

**very-dells** Little stories told to children too young to understand television commercials.           *New Yorker*

**vestal** Blameless.                               *Alexander Pope*

**vice** Full of knowledge. Example: She had a vice look in her ice.                                        *New Yorkese*
    VICE VERSA Dirty poetry.                     *Anon., Jr.*
    VICE VERSE A poem that makes as much sense backwards.
                                       *Anon., Jr.*

**vichyssoise soup** Attar of old potato.   *Arthur "Bugs" Baer*

**Victoria, Queen** Nothing more than a slightly inconvenient person.                             *Charles Francis Adams,*
        *Lincoln's Ambassador to Queen Victoria*

**Victorian age** When all proper folks thought diamonds were a girl's worst enemy.                       *Changing Times*

**vidiot** One who can't follow the action of a TV western without opening his eyes.                          *Newords*

**village** A town where you can park as long as you want to, but don't want to.

—Nothing makes it easier to resist temptation than living in a small town.

**villain** The most natural man in a play. *Edgar Watson Howe*

**violator** A person who plays the viola.            *Anon., Jr.*

**violin solo** The drawing of the hair of a dead horse across the entrails of a dead cat.          *Bishop Fulton J. Sheen*

**virginal** (More usually *virginals*.) A musical instrument so called, because commonly used by young ladies.
                    *Dr. Sam'l Johnson*

**virtue** Its own reward, although most people are looking for a better offer.                                    *Puck*

—Vice at rest.                                      *Anon.*

—Then there was the good little girl who had been saying "no" so long that she almost loused up her wedding ceremony.                                        *D. O. Flynn*

**virtuoso** A man skilled in antique or natural curiosities; a man studious of painting, statuary, or architecture.

*Dr. Sam'l Johnson*

**visitor** One who thinks that when he stands up, he's gone.

**vituperation** Satire, as understood by dunces.

*Ambrose Bierce*

**vivacious** Long-lived. *Dr. Sam'l Johnson*

**viz** This word is *videlicet*, written with a contraction. To wit; that is. A barbarous form of an unnecessary word.

*Dr. Sam'l Johnson*

**"Vogue"** A powder puff magazine.

**voice** The organ of the soul. *Longfellow*

**volcano** A mountain with a built-in barbecue pit.

—A mountain that acts like a senator.

**Volkswagen** A transistorized Rolls-Royce. *Parade*

**Voltaire** This monkey of genius, whom the devil sent on a mission to mankind. *Victor Hugo*

—Electric volts are named after Voltaire, who invented electricity. *Anon., Jr.*

**volume** A book; so called, because books were antiently rolled upon a staff. *Dr. Sam'l Johnson*

**volunteer** To go for a soldier. A cant word.

*Dr. Sam'l Johnson*

**voluptuous** Having curves in places where other girls don't even have places. *Playboy*

**vomitorium** The annex to a Roman diningroom provided for the use of revelers. Who shall say that we have not advanced in two thousand years?

Oscar Mendelsohn, *Dictionary of Drink and Drinking*

**vote** The instrument and symbol of a freeman's power to make a fool of himself and a wreck of his country.

*Ambrose Bierce*

**vowel** Something two people take before they get married.

*Anon., Jr.*

**vox populi** Vox humbug. *Gen. William Tecumseh Sherman*

**vulgarity** Rugged individualism in society.

—Simply the conduct of others. *Oscar Wilde*

—A necessary part of a complete author's equipment; and the clown is sometimes the best part of the circus.

*Bernard Shaw*

# W

**W (Double U)**  Has, of all the letters in our alphabet the only cumbrous name, the names of the others being monosyllabic. There can be no doubt, however, that by simplifying the name of W (calling it "wow," for example) our civilization could be, if not promoted, at least better endured.  *Ambrose Bierce*

**wabble**  (A low, barbarous word.) To shake, to move from side to side.  *Dr. Sam'l Johnson*

**wade**  Halt, delay, as in "Wade a mint."  *New Yorkese*

**WADING**  What you're doing till the wader brings the beal.  *New Yorkese*

**wages of sin**  The high cost of low living.

**Wagner, Richard**  A composer whose music is better than it sounds.  *Mark Twain*

**wait**  A hard word for the hungry.  *German proverb*

**waiter**  A contact man to make certain that the patron gets a steak done the way the cook likes it.

**waiting**  What a virgin does best.  *A Funny Thing Happened on the Way to the Forum*

**WAITING ROOM**  A place where the doctor hopes you'll catch something from the other patients.  *Changing Times*

**wake**  Seven days in Ireland.  *Harold S. Sharp*
—One less drunk.

**walkie-talkie**  Taking a stroll with your wife. *A. H. Hallock*

**Wall Street**  A symbol of sin for every devil to rebuke. That Wall Street is a den of thieves is a belief that serves every unsuccessful thief in place of a hope in Heaven.  *Ambrose Bierce*

**waltz**  The teen-ager's idea of a square dance. *The Liguorian*

**wampum belts**  Belts worn by many Indians to hold up their wampums.  *Anon., Jr.*

**wantwit**  A fool; an idiot.  *Dr. Sam'l Johnson*

**war**  The trade of kings.  *John Dryden*
—The statesman's game, the priest's delight,
  The lawyer's jest, the hired assassin's trade.  *Shelley*
—A contagion.  *Franklin Delano Roosevelt*

—The worst disease. *Russian proverb*

—Hell. I am tired and sick of war. Its glory is all moonshine. It is only those who have never fired a shot nor heard the shrieks and groans of the wounded who cry aloud for blood, more vengeance, more desolation.

*Gen. William Tecumseh Sherman*

—A million men with guns go out and meet another million men with guns, and they all shoot and try to kill each other.

*Thornton Wilder*

—Everybody's fault.

PEACE Everybody's business. *Samuel M. Lindsay*

—A by-product of the arts of peace. *Ambrose Bierce*

—A primitive blood sport that gratifies human pugnacity.

*Bernard Shaw*

—A compound of hydrogen and oxygen. "Would you like another glass war?" *New Yorkese*

—Man's work.

WOMAN His relaxation. *Nietzsche*

COLD WAR That period in which uneasy coexistence proves better than easy nonexistence. *Judith Beach°*

**warden** The most anxious man in a prison. *Bernard Shaw*

**wardrobe mistress** An inspector of costumes.

**warren** A kind of park for rabbits. *Dr. Sam'l Johnson*

**Washington** A stone quarry that has gone out of business.

*Frank Lloyd Wright*

—A city of southern efficiency and northern charm.

*John F. Kennedy*

—Father Kennedy's boys' town. *W. J. Hooten*

—Where you can buy a bronze reproduction of the Iwo Jima flag-raising that was "Made in Japan." *Quote*

—The last President who was elected the hard way—without telling a lie. *Annel and DeWood*

**wastebasket** Like a garbage can, but it doesn't drip.

*Robert Paul Smith*

**watch repairman** A tick doc. *Changing Times*

**water** A medicine for the cure of thirst. *Ambrose Bierce*

—Just whiskey with all the beneficial ingredients removed.

*Joe E. Lewis*

—100-proof humidity. *Joe E. Lewis*

—A longer abbreviation for the word $H_2O$. *Anon., Jr.*

WATER CONSERVATION Locking the pump after the well is dry.

**Watusi** Loosi Caboosi. *Sarina Martin*

**Waves** Young salts with cute shakers. *W. D. Huntington*

**we** Means "I," but is more Nicechap and far less egotistical.
*Stephen Potter*

**wealth** Any income that is at least $100 more a year than the income of one's wife's sister's husband. *H. L. Mencken*

WEALTHY RELATIVE Frequently one who is at once both distant and close. *Wall Street Journal*

**weary** Extremely: "The weary I dear!" *New Yorkese*

**weather** Today's climate.

CLIMATE Permanent weather.

WEATHER FORECASTER Someone with whom the weather doesn't always agree. *Illinois Educational Press Bulletin*

WEATHERSPY A star-gazer; an astrologer; one that fore-tells the weather. *Dr. Sam'l Johnson*

**wedding** A ceremony at which two persons undertake to become one, one undertakes to become nothing, and nothing undertakes to become supportable.
*Ambrose Bierce*

WEDDING CAKE Altar rations. *Mary H. Waldrip*

WEDDING REHEARSAL Aisle trial. *Wall Street Journal*

WEDDING RING A vicious circle. *Anon. husband*

—A one-man band. *The Re-Saw*

**wedgeable** Food from the ground. *New Yorkese*

**weed** A vegetable with concealed promise.
*George Washington Carver*

**weekend** The time when you slow down to let the strain go by. *Office Economist*

**weighing machine** A device that gives you a girth-certificate for a penny.

**welfare state** One run for the benefit of everyone but the taxpayer. *Imogene Fey*

STATE WELFARE The agency which does half the task. Since everyone takes care of poor people between Christmas and New Year's, State Welfare has the job between New Year's and Christmas.

**Welk, Lawrence** Along with the Red Cross, Disneyland and the sanctity of Motherhood, a subject not to be criticized.
*Gerald Nachman*

—One of the wealthiest mice making Mickey Mouse music.
*Gerald Nachman*

—A bandmaster whose music bears the same relation to champagne as beer does.

—The Pied Piper of the Geritol set.

**well-adjusted** Able to make the same mistake a second time without getting nervous. *Jane Heard*

**well water** The kind that don't make you sick. *Anon., Jr.*

**werewolfs** Wolfs in the past tense.
*Anon., Jr. (Art Linkletter Dept.)*

**West Virginia** A state where a school board decided it would be all right for teachers to whip children who come to school with wild onions on the breath. *Changing Times*

**Western Union** A monopoly to garble text.

    A. T. & T. A monopoly to garble speech.

**wet martini** A cocktail for people who hate gin and love vermouth.

**wetbacks** Rio Grandees.

**wheat** A cereal from which a tolerably good whiskey can with some difficulty be made, and which is used also for bread. The French are said to eat more bread per capita of population than any other people, which is natural, for only they know how to make the stuff palatable.
*Ambrose Bierce*

**Wheaties** The stuff that champions are made of.

**whey** The thin or serous part of milk, from which the oleose or grumous part is separated. *Dr. Sam'l Johnson*

**which** A pronoun except on halloween *Anon., Jr.*

**whiskey** The water of life—and like the milder water, of death, too, if you swallow enough of it.

—By far the most popular of all the many remedies that absolutely won't cure a cold. *Quoted by Earl Wilson*

—About the only enemy man has succeeded in really loving.
*Anon.*

**whist** A game at cards, requiring close attention and silence.
*Dr. Sam'l Johnson*

**whom** An uppity form of "who." *Anon., Jr.*

**whurr** To pronounce the letter *r* with too much force.
*Dr. Sam'l Johnson*

**wicked** To shock the world; to sin in private is not to sin.
*Molière*

**widow** A pathetic figure that the Christian world has agreed to take humorously, although Christ's tenderness towards widows was one of the most marked features of his character. *Ambrose Bierce*

—The expression of an accomplished fact. *Henry James, Jr.*

—A woman who no longer finds fault with her husband.
*Anon.*

RICH WIDOWS   The only secondhand goods that sell at first-class prices.                         *Benjamin Franklin*

WIDOWS' WEEDS   The easiest to kill. You have only to say "Wilt thou?" and they wilt.

wife   A faithful upper-servant.              *Henry Fielding*

—A sleep-in maid.                        *Mary Jo Minutolo**

—A person who can see a blonde hair on her husband's coat ten feet away but can never see a fire plug when she parks.
*Little River News*

—Someone who thinks it is all right to say anything to her husband in public as long as she calls him "Honey."
*Changing Times*

—Never contradict your wife. Listen awhile and she'll contradict herself.                       *Anon. husband*

—A possession which should be chosen by a young man as he would a horse. Look a little at the labour of the teeth, for these correspond with those of the other members of the body and with the operations of the mind. "Quick at meals, quick at work" is a saying as old as the hills. Never mind the pieces of needlework, the tambouring, the maps of the world made by her needle. Get to see her at work upon a mutton-chop or a bit of bread and cheese and if she deal quickly with these, you have a pretty good security for that activity, that stirring industry, without which a wife is a burden instead of a help. And as to love, it cannot live for more than a month or two (in the breast of a man of spirit) towards a lazy woman. Another mark of industry is a quick step and a somewhat heavy tread and if the body lean a little forward, and the eye keep steadily in the same direction while the feet are going, so much the better, for these discover earnestness to arrive at the intended point. I do not like, and I never liked, young sauntering, soft-stepped girls who move as if they were perfectly indifferent to the result.                              *William Cobbett*

—The little woman who'd rather mend your ways than your socks.                                    *Ima Washout*

—A woman who complains that she doesn't have a thing to wear and that there isn't enough closet space for her clothes.                               *Changing Times*

—The passenger in the car who saw the parking space fifty yards back on a one-way street.              *Ibid.*

—A person who sits up with you when you are sick, and puts up with you when you are not.            *Anna Herbert*

—A person who can look in the top drawer and find her husband's socks that aren't there. *Dan Bennett*

—The first is matrimony, the second company, the third heresy. *Italian proverb*

GOOD WIFE  The best household furniture. *German proverb*

IDEAL WIFE  One who remains faithful to you but tries to be just as charming as if she weren't. *Bill Ballance*

PHYSICIAN'S WIFE  The one person who knows what to do until the doctor comes. *Anon.*

SUCCESSFUL WIFE  One who has only married unsuccessful husbands. *Zsa Zsa Gabor*

**wig**  An assumed mane. *The Southern Planter*

—Period of seven days. "It'll be ready in a wig." *New Yorkese*

**Wilde, Oscar**  A man whose soul had swooned in sin and revived vulgar. *Anon., possibly Max Beerbohm*

**will**  A device for splitting heirs.

**will power**  What makes you do what you want to do when you don't want to do it. *Changing Times*

**window dresser**  A girl who doesn't pull down the shades. *Playboy*

**wine**  Fermented grape-juice known to the Women's Christian Union as "liquor," sometimes as "rum." Wine, madame, is God's next best gift to man. *Ambrose Bierce*

—God made Man, frail as a bubble.
God made Love, Love made Trouble.
God made the Vine; was it a sin
That Man made Wine to drown Trouble in? *Oliver Herford*

—Poison for the young and medicine for the old. *Russian proverb*

WINES  By their very nature full of reminiscence, the golden tears and red blood of summers that are gone. *Richard LeGallienne*

**winter**  The time when the days are shortest, and so are we. *Changing Times*

—The one infallible exterminator that kills crabgrass. *Anon.*

—The age of shovelry. *Walter Davenport*

**wisecrack**  A humorous saying that won't stand the test of truth.

**wit**  Instant wisdom. *Time*

—The dandyism of the mind. *Holbrook Jackson*

—The salt with which the American humorist spoils his intellectual cookery by leaving it out. *Ambrose Bierce*

—The salt of conversation, not the food. *William Hazlitt*

WITTICISM  Levity with brevity.

WITCRACKER  A joker; one who breaks a jest.
*Dr. Sam'l Johnson*

witch  (1) an ugly and repulsive old woman, in a wicked league with the devil. (2) a beautiful and attractive young woman, in wickedness a league beyond the devil.
*Ambrose Bierce*

WITCH DOCTOR  A psychoanalyst who does all the talking himself.

without anchor or rejudism  What you should watch a prize-fight with.  *Announcer Harry Balogh*

witness stand  The place you go to perjure yourself. *Anon., Jr.*

woe  The opposite of giddy up.  *Anon., Jr.*

wolf  A man who believes in life, liberty and the happiness of pursuit.  *Helen Sioussat*

—A dry cleaner who works fast and leaves no ring. *Anon.*

—A man of single purpose and double talk.  *Dan Bennett*

—A guy who whistles while he lurks.

—A kind of wild dog that devours sheep. *Dr. Sam'l Johnson*

woman  Something that pays ten cents for a cup of coffee to sit at a lunch counter and blow smoke in men's faces.

—A person who will pay twenty-five dollars for a slip and then be annoyed when it shows.  *Walter Slezak*

—An animal that can cook.

—God's second mistake.  *Nietzsche*

—Unrivaled as a wet nurse.  *Mark Twain*

—The female of the speeches.  *Dan Revello*

—A creature who usually suffers from palpitation of the tongue.

—A dish for the gods.  Shakespeare, *Antony and Cleopatra*

—The so-called tender gender.

—The nuder gender.  *Anon.*

—A destroyer of youth, a pillager of men, the death of the aged, the devourer of inheritances, the destruction of honor, food for Satan, the reinforcement of Hell.
*Enea Silvio di'Piccolomini, later Pope Pius II*

—It is easy to see from the way He has treated us women that God is a man.
*Claudine-Alexandrine Guerin, Marquise de Tencin*

—Or from the way they are constructed.

—Thought to be a member of the human race. Seldom found in natural state. Surface coated with paint. Has low boiling temp and freezing point varies . . . highly explosive. Extremely active when in the vicinity of the opposite sex. Chiefly ornamental. Probably the most powerful seducing agent known. Illegal to own more than one specimen.

*London Technical College students*

—The species which can remember a hat she bought in 1938, but not what's trump. *Senator Soaper*

—After the monkey, the nearest thing to a man. Pourquoi Pas?

*Brussels*

—A creature who always thinks it takes two to keep a secret.

*Anon.*

—A person keeping a swivel tongue in her head.

*Paul and Helen Martin Denis\**

—The best thing, if you want to spend money where it'll show. *Kin Hubbard*

WOMAN DRIVER A person who doesn't let her right hand know what her left hand is doing.

—Someone who gets caught in a traffic jam that wouldn't have happened if she wasn't there. *Jesse Kaplan*

FALLEN WOMAN A mother who neglected to pick up some toys. *Bert Kruse*

INTELLIGENT WOMAN One with whom we can be as stupid as we like. *Valéry*

MODERN WOMAN One who is expected to be a Florence Nightingale on the job, a patient Griselda at home, and a Joan of Arc when the slums need clearing. She must be a shrewd household manager, an accomplished hostess, a connoisseur of the arts and a girl until she is seventy. *Anita Colby*

—One who doesn't need an attic as long as she has a purse.

*Dan Bennett*

WOMAN'S MOVIE One where the wife commits adultery throughout the picture and at the end, her husband begs for forgiveness. *Oscar Levant*

WOMEN'S POCKETBOOK Proof that money isn't everything.

WOMEN Like cows are content as long as you keep feeding them the green stuff. *Mickey Rose*

—Creatures who wrap men either around their little fingers or around their front bumpers. *Dan Bennett*

—Creatures wiser than men because they know less and understand more. *James Stephens*

—Beings with a very positive moral sense; that which they will is right; that which they reject, is wrong.

*Henry Adams*

—The sort of problem men like to wrestle with.
*The Earl of Wilson*

—If women are really so smart, why do they wear blouses that button up the back?

—Creatures meant to be loved, not to be understood.
*Oscar Wilde*

—Creatures who now insist on having all the prerogatives of the oak and all the perquisites of the clinging vine.
*Irvin S. Cobb*

—Brigands demand your money or your life; women require both. *Samuel Butler*

—According to the Bible, woman was the last thing God made. It must have been a Saturday night. Clearly, He was tired. *Alexandre Dumas, fils*

—I think a woman ought to be elected to public office. They have made a mess of things raising so many sorry men. Either they've got to raise better men or take over the government. *Jerry W. Carter,*
*Democratic National Committeeman from Florida*

—A sex by themselves, so to speak, as a pretty girl once said to me. *Max Beerbohm*

—People to blame things on.

—And usually rightly so.

—The American woman's ambitions are too high. In Europe a woman decides early what type she will be—mother, cook or siren. Women here want to be all of these and also run Wall Street. *Alistair Cooke*

—By the time a man understands women, he's no longer interested. *Rex Mobley*

—An entertainment. *Ovid*

WOMEN'S INTUITION   The result of millions of years of not thinking. *Rupert Hughes*

MODERN WOMEN   Supposed to be a cross between a saint and a drayhorse, a diplomat and an automatic washing machine, a psychiatrist and a bulldozer, a sanitary engineer and a mannequin. *Josephine Lowman*

WOMEN POLITICIANS   They remind one of the British tramp steamers decorated for the Queen's birthday.
*H. L. Mencken*

WOMEN WRESTLERS   The only attempt at culture on American TV. *Robert Morley*

woodcock   A husband whose wife has been untrue to him.
*Anon., Jr.*

**wooden horse** The gift the Greeks bore into Troy, giving rise to the Trojan admonition, "Don't take any wooden horses!"

**woodpecker** A knockingbird. *R. B. Keith*

**Worcestershire sauce** Fluid pickles.
*Encyclopaedia Brittanica*

**words** The signs of ideas. *Dr. Sam'l Johnson*

—What have enabled us to rise above the brutes and often sink to the level of the demons. *Aldous Huxley*

—Are like coins (a dozen metaphors show it), and in nothing more so than in this—that the verbal currency we have so ingeniously contrived has out-run our calculations and become an enigma and a matter for endless controversy. We say something; but we can never be quite certain what it is that we have said. *Lytton Strachey*

LAST WORD What a wife has. Anything a husband says after that is the beginning of another argument. *Anon.*

**work** Another way of keeping a diary. *Pablo Picasso*

—The only occupation yet invented which mankind has been able to endure in any but the smallest possible doses.
*C. E. M. Joad*

—Love made visible. *Kalil Gibran*

—Work faithfully eight hours a day, don't worry. Then, in time, you will become the boss and work twelve hours a day and do all the worrying. *Title News*

—Something that when we have it, we wish we didn't; when we don't, we wish we did; and the object of which is to be able to afford not to do any some day. *Changing Times*

—The greatest thing in the world, so we should always save some of it for tomorrow.

**world** A grindstone and life is your nose. *Fred Allen*

—A stage,
And all the men and women merely players:
They have their exits and their entrances;
And one man in his time plays many parts.
*Shakespeare, As You Like It*

—A kind of spiritual kindergarten where millions of bewildered infants are trying to spell "God" with the wrong blocks. *Edward Arlington Robinson*

—This amusement arcade. *Arnold Schoenberg*

—Nothing but a vast attempt to swindle. *Céline*

—A clever swindler, it robs us of our lives while it distracts our attention. *Colin Wilson*

—The world really isn't any worse, it's just that the news coverage is so much better.                    *Changing Times*

—A ghastly drama of will-to-live divided against itself.
                                                    *Albert Schweitzer*

—For many people is divided north and south by lines of lassitude and east and west by lines of loungitude.
                                                    *American Mercury*

—A sane asylum.

—But a small parenthesis in eternity.    *Sir Thomas Browne*

WORLD WAR I    A shock, but not a lesson. *Adlai Stevenson*

WORLD RELATIONS    Perhaps we would be more patient about our hopes for achieving world understanding if we fully grasped the great distances between the way people of different cultures think—and the symbols through which they organize their thoughts. For instance, in India it is a great compliment to tell a woman that she is "graceful as an elephant." And in Iran a common expression of disdain reads: "Stupid as an owl."
                *Property, Merchants National Bank, Topeka, Kansas*

worm    A small harmless serpent that lives in the earth.
                                                    *Dr. Sam'l Johnson*

WORM'S MEAT    The finished product of which we are the raw material.                              *Ambrose Bierce*

worry    An activity as useless as whispering in a boiler factory.                                        *Arnold Glasow*

—If you want to test your memory, try to remember what you were worrying about one year ago today.
                                                    *Leonard Thomas*

worship    To cleanse, as: "I'll be with you in a second. First give me a minute to worship."          *New Yorkese*

Wrigley    The first man to discover that American jaws must wag; so why not give them something to wag against?
                                                    *Will Rogers*

wrinkle-fender    A game drivers play with more abandon in Warsaw than even in Paris.          *James Reston*

wrinkles    Fretwork.                              *Mary C. Dorsey*

wrist watch    Time out of joint.

writer's cramp    An affliction that attacks some novelists between the ears.                      *Arnold H. Glasow*

writer    A man whose enemy is an empty sheet of paper.
                                                    *Wolfe Kaufman**

# X

**X** Is a letter which, though found in Saxon words, begin
no word in the English language.      *Dr. Sam'l Johnso*
—In our alphabet being a needless letter has an added ir
vincibility to the attacks of the spelling reformers, and lik
them, will doubtless last as long as the language. X is th
sacred symbol of ten dollars, and in such words as Xma
Xn, etc., stands for Christ, not, as is popularly suppose
because it represents a cross, but because the correspon
ing letter in the Greek alphabet is the initial of His name—
χρίστος. If it represented a cross, it would stand for S
Andrew, who "testified" upon one of that shape. In th
algebra of psychology x stands for Woman's mind. Word
beginning with X are Grecian and will not be defined i
this standard English dictionary.

> Ambrose Bierce, *The Devil's Dictionar*

# Y

**Y** The letter of Independence—it's the fourth of July.
> *Benjamin Frankl*

**Yankee Pot Roast Southern Style**   Dixie's answer to Souther
Fried Chicken New England Style.

**yarn**   Something spun out to pull the wool over someone
eyes.

**yawd**   The campus of Have Id.            *Bostone*

**yawn**   The thing to do to make a long story short.
> *Grace Dow*

**yelk**   The yellow part of the egg. It is commonly pronounce
and often written *yolk*.            *Dr. Sam'l Johnso*

**Yellow Pages romeo**   The type that lets his fingers do th
walking.

~es　What every young girl ought to know.

*Morton Thompson**

~esterday　When dancing was something a boy and girl did together.　　　　　　　*Leonard Gross*

—The infancy of youth, the youth of manhood, the entire past of age.　　　　　　　*Ambrose Bierce*

~ogi　What happens when you eat too much yogurt.

*Anon., Jr.**

~orick　The topic of the most famous skull session in history.

~ou　Usually the principal thing that's not on your diet.

~oung　A condition it is easy to remain, as long as you sleep enough, work harmoniously, eat sensibly, live relaxedly— and lie about your age.

YOUNGER GENERATION　People who talk about everything, and never talk about anything else. *New England spinster*

~outh　The Period of Possibility, when Archimedes finds a fulcrum, Cassandra has a following and seven cities compete for the honor of endowing a living Homer.

Youth is the true Saturnian Reign, the Golden Age on earth again, when figs are grown on thistles, and pigs betailed with whistles and, wearing silken bristles, live ever in clover, and cows fly over, delivering milk at every door, and Justice never is heard to snore.　　*Ambrose Bierce*

—What will have its fling or swing or sting . . . or something.

—The subtle thief of time.

—The youth of America is their oldest tradition; it has been going on now for three hundred years.　　*Oscar Wilde*

—A whole barrel, condemned for the rottenness of the 2 per cent who are bad apples.

—The denunciation of the young is a necessary part of the hygiene of older people and greatly assists the circulation of their blood.　　　　　　*Logan Pearsall Smith*

—You're only young once. After that you need another excuse.

—That time of life when people are too old to take advice.

*Changing Times*

—Intoxication.

OLD AGE　The morning after.　　　　　　　*F. Dowley*

# Z

**Z** Is found in the Saxon alphabets, set down by grammarians, but is read in no word originally Teutonick; its sound
is uniformly that of a hard *s*.     *Dr. Sam'l Johnson*

**zany** (Probably of *zanei*.) The contraction of Giovanni o
sanna, a scoff, according to Skinner. One employed to raise
laughter by his gestures, actions and speeches; a merry
Andrew; a buffoon.     *Dr. Sam'l Johnson*

—A popular character in old Italian plays, who imitated with
ludicrous incompetence the *buffone,* or clown, and was
therefore the ape of an ape; for the clown himself imitated
the serious characters of the play. The zany was progenitor
to the specialist in humor, as we today have the unhappi
ness to know him. In the zany we see an example of crea
tion; in the humorist of transmission. Another excellent
specimen of the modern zany is the curate, who apes the
rector who apes the bishop, who apes the archbishop, who
apes the devil.     *Ambrose Bierce*

**Zanzibari** An inhabitant of the Sultanate of Zanzibar, off the
eastern coast of Africa. The Zanzibaris, a warlike people
are best known in this country through a threatening diplo
matic incident that occurred a few years ago. The Ameri
can consul at the capital occupied a dwelling that faced
the sea, with a sandy beach between. Greatly to the scanda
of this official's family, and against repeated remonstrance
of the official himself, the people of the city persisted in
using the beach for bathing. One day a woman came down
to the edge of the water and was stooping to remove her
attire (a pair of sandals) when the consul, incensed beyond
restraint, fired a charge of bird-shot into the most conspicu
ous part of her person. Unfortunately for the existing en
tente cordiale between two great nations, she was the
Sultana.     *Ambrose Bierce, 1900*

**zeal** Without knowledge, is only fire without light.   *Fuller*

—What wins out when ability falters.

—A certain nervous disorder afflicting the young and inex
perienced.     *Ambrose Bierce*

**bra**  A white horse with black Venetian blinds. —Chiefly used to illustrate the letter Z.

> *Anon., Jr. (British Division)*

**ZEBRAS**  Horses wearing slipcovers.                *Anon., Jr.*

**d**  The name of the letter z.        *Dr. Sam'l Johnson*

**eno**  Founder of the Stoic school. He was born to a merchant career but losing all in a shipwreck, devoted himself to philosophy.                *Cecil Hunt*

**st**  The peel of an orange squeezed into wine.

> *Dr. Sam'l Johnson*

**eus**  The chief of Grecian gods, adored by the Romans as Jupiter and by the modern Americans as God, Gold, Mob and Dog. Some explorers who have touched upon the shores of America, and one who professes to have penetrated a considerable distance into the interior, have thought that these four names stand for as many distinct deities, but in his monumental work on Surviving Faiths, Frumpp insists that the natives are monotheists, each having no other god than himself, whom he worships under many sacred names.                *Ambrose Bierce*

**ionist**  A New Yorker who pays someone else to live in Israel.                *Leonard Klein\**

**ola, Émile**  This mud-stained Hercules who wallows in the Augean dung and adds his little bit to it.

> *Barbey d'Aurevilly*

**ombie**  Something some men drink and others marry.

> *Playboy*

**ucchini**  A squash masquerading as a cucumber.

**uleika Dobson**  The kind of girl who, on a desert island, would have spent most of her time in looking for a man's footprint.                *Max Beerbohm*


## THE HUMAN RACE

Fellow travelers on a tiny spaceship spinning through infinite space. We can wreck our ship, we can blow the human experiment into nothingness; and by every analogy of practical life, a quarrelsome ship's company and many hands on the steering gear is a good recipe for disaster.

> *Adlai Stevenson, at the United Nations,*
> *New York, January 26, 1965*